To Mary — —
Good luck

The Chronicles of

Boggerthwaite

An Everyday Story of Lakeland Folk

By

David Bean

Copyright © David Bean 1997
Printed and Published by TUPS Books
30, Lime St. Newcastle upon Tyne.
Tel No: 0191 2330990 Fax:0191 2330578
ISBN No.1 901237 03 - 6

To Sue.

1

This being a story set in the English Lake District during the last decade of our century, it must of course start in a council house on the outskirts of Swindon, Wiltshire, some 250 miles away.

This was a perfectly ordinary council house; nothing at all ostentatious about it, as might have been the case if it had been built for some well-placed member of the committee which decreed its building. It was a two-up (three-up if you counted the box-room), two-down structure with a backwards extension which housed kitchen downstairs and bathroom up. Outside its walls were pebble-dashed and its concrete paths cracked. It was inhabited by a middle-aged couple named Gribb, and had been since their marriage in 1976.

Norman Gribb was an electronics engineer. That is to say he worked in one of Swindon's spawn of anonymous-looking factories which produce wonderful music-playing and sound-amplifying equipment rather more expensively than is made in the Far East. His actual function - what he did all day - was of little interest to Gribb himself and would be of none whatever to a non-Gribb. Norman had once played left half-back for one of Swindon Town's nursery teams. Those had been the best years of his life.

His wife, Renie, worked at the same factory as Norman, but in Accounts. She was therefore Staff, while he was Works, and she turned in for work half an hour later each morning than did her spouse. She was a tall woman with a good figure, long legs, hair which she had only recently started to have permed, and no children that anyone knew about. Unlike her husband she was not interested in sport of any kind, and was still awaiting the best years of her life.

One Saturday morning in late winter, the couple were finishing breakfast when their connubial calm was disturbed by a rattling at the front-door letter-box followed by a scuffling and plopping set of sounds as of paper falling to the floor.

"Post, Norman," said Mrs Gribb, not looking up from her copy of Mobile and Holiday Homes.

But Norman did look up from his breakfast reading - a journal apparently devoted to footballs and the men who kick them.

"Oh, is that what it is, my dear?" he said mildly, but making no attempt to investigate. "I'm glad you told me. I was under the obviously mistaken impression that the Archbishop of Canterbury was trying to get through the letter-box in order to effect a religious conversion on us."

Renie Gribb glared over large spectacles which gave her at such moments the look of a barn owl contemplating an undersized vole.

"Sarcasm is the lowest form of wit, Norman," she said.

"If you say so dear."

Mrs Gribb resumed her reading of an article on simple drains for short-stay mobile homes.

"Well?" she resumed after a good half-minute more, "aren't you going to get the mail? Or have you seized up altogether?"

"Not entirely, Renie," said Norman, hoisting himself laboriously from his seat. "Otherwise I wouldn't be able to be sarcastic, would I?"

His wife made no attempt to answer, waiting until she heard him grunt out in the hall in his efforts to pick up the delivery. Then: "Well?"

"Not really, dear," replied Norman. "Three bills, four charity appeals, six promises of free gifts...Oh...now I don't like the look of this one." He re-entered the kitchen peering at a long, brown envelope such as lawyers use.

"What is it?" Mrs Gribb removed her spectacles, immediately

softening her appearance: a rock-dove now, perhaps, rather than an owl.

"Looks official," grunted Norman, slitting the envelope open. "Legal."

"Norman, you haven't been....well, you know..."

Her husband ignored her, read to himself in a quiet monotone, skipping: 'Dear Sir....sad demise....regret....Lord Bogger....Bogger Hall, Cumbria....no direct issue....next in line'.... I don't believe it."

His wife held out a hand. "What are you burbling about, Norman? Give it here."

But her spouse had pulled himself up to his full five feet ten, smoothing out the rumples in his old grey cardigan as he did so.

"In future, madam," he said in a most un-Swindonian tone of voice, "You will address me as 'My Lord', or possibly 'Your Grace': I'll have to check."

"Do what?" Mrs Gribb's accents did not match her husband's.

"Renie my dear, it appears that I am heir to an ancient title through some obscure connection to a family I never even knew existed. I am the latest Lord Bogger, of Bogger Hall, Boggerthwaite, Cumbria."

"It's some joke, Norman. Somebody having us on."

"No joke at all, my dear. It's all signed and sealed, officially."

Mrs Gribb had turned pale. Never florid of complexion, she now looked as if she had swallowed something rather nasty for her breakfast.

"But you're never going to accept, Norman. You know I can't stand the North Country. And I'm a socialist. I do not believe in privilege, and neither do you."

But he did now. On realising that his wife's hatred of both

aristocracy and the rural North was unshakeable, the new Lord Bogger saw his chance, grabbed it, caught the next train up to London, then another for Carlisle, and was never seen by Swindon or Renie Gribb again.

2

"I hope you're keen on fox-hunting," said the lawyer gravely. "Very important thing in the Lake district, fox-hunting."

There was no way that Norman Gribb could decide whether the man was a hunting enthusiast himself, or whether he disapproved. He was not at all as he had expected him to be. The name Peel to start with - and John Peel at that - of the firm Todhunter, Todhunter and Peel, solicitors and notaries public, of Tallyho Chambers, Keswick - seemed to give a misleading impression. On the phone he had sounded hearty enough, and Norman had expected to meet a bluff, brawny, red-faced man dressed at least in a hacking jacket and breeches, if not the full hunting pink. But here was the very stereotype of a lawyer, straight out of Dickens apart from the electronic hearing-aid clamped in his ear. A face with a pallor that reminded him unpleasantly of Renie, a dome almost totally bald, and a pair of pince-nez reading spectacles secured to his lapel by a black shoelace. He had a scattering of dandruff from the little frieze surrounding his tonsure, and he smelt of iodine.

"Of course, you must realise that the Hunt in these parts is not mounted."

"Really?" The new Lord Bogger had only the vaguest idea of what the man was talking about.

"Follow on foot, you know. Terrain's far too rough for nags. Don't know if you're keen - can't stand blood-sports myself. But it'll be expected of you. Your father was MFH for many years."

"Was he now?" If so it was the first Norman Gribb had heard of it.

Mr Peel dropped his chin a fraction, allowing his spectacles to

4

slide to the end of his nose and his large, pale-blue eyes to fix themselves on his client even more intently. "Sorry, correction. Not your father at all. Keep forgetting. Silly of me.

"Your great, great uncle's second cousin's sister's brother-in-law, the last Baron Bogger. We had the most almighty job tracing you. Had to get one of these genealogist chappies. Didn't trust him myself. I mean, what's to stop him reaching for the nearest telephone directory and sticking a pin in. No offence, Mr Gribb er, Your Grace...."

"Say that again," said His Lordship, eyes half-closed, savouring.

"What: 'No offence Mister Gribb' or 'Your Grace'?"

"The latter."

"Your Grace, then," said the old lawyer. "I was saying - very keen on the Chase, the Boggers. Name's Norman French, by the way...."

Gribb blinked. "Sorry? I thought you were called John Peel."

"You misunderstand me, sir," said the lawyer without a smile. "*Your* name. Bogger. Comes from the French spoken in medieval Normandy. Bougre. Some people like to know these things, that's all. Came over with the Conqueror. Or the Bastard, whichever way you look at it. They wouldn't have bothered much with foxes in those days. Hunt peasants, they would. Bloodthirsty lot. Hooligans. Don't hold with privilege myself. Socialist, me. Still, the aristocracy's not your fault, though I suppose you could relinquish the title if you wanted. Give us more work. Where was I?"

The new Lord Bogger frowned. "You were talking yourself into a position where a couple of hundred years ago I'd've had your neck stretched quite unpleasantly."

The little lawyer giggled. "I was just thinking. The idea of sticking a pin in the telephone directory. You might come up with almost anything."

Obviously amused, and clearly not in any great hurry, the man

5

reached across his desk and drew towards him an outdated copy of the British Telecom directory for Cumbria and North Lancashire. Straightening out a paper-clip he flipped through the pages and suddenly stabbed. He peered, then laughed with a kind of dry triumph.

"There you are," he laughed. "Brutes and Bitches."

"Brutes and Bitches?"

"They're some kind of hairdressers. In Morecambe, it says. Modern fashion for out-of-the-way names. Nothing straightforward. No barbers any more. So—Brutes and Bitches Hair Studio might have been the fifteenth Lord Bogger." He peered up at his client to see how he was taking this flight of fancy.

"Can we get on?" said Lord Bogger, who was taking it with a distinct lack of patience.

"This business of fox-hunting. Goes back a heck of a long way. The most celebrated Master was the chap who raised the pack in the first place - 1792, year of the French Republic. The then incumbent of St Ethelbogger's Church, Boggerthwaite, one Reverend Harold Basset, related to the Boggers on the distaff side. Harry the Hound they called him apparently - a hard-riding, red-blooded old boor. You know the type - can't stand 'em myself.

"He died in 1812, year of Napoleon's Retreat from Moscow. Of distemper, I imagine. To be succeeded by the tenth Baron Bogger, a great enthusiast by all accounts. A glorious period followed. In one year, 1826, time of the St Petersburg Protocol for Greek Autonomy, the Bogger Valley Hunt polished off no fewer than 240 foxes, 24 Herdwick ewes, fourteen squirrels, six collie dogs, four farm cats and one slow-worm. That record has never since been equalled."

The little lawyer stretched and grinned, baring beige-coloured teeth. "So you see you've got quite an act to follow."

6

"Or to put a stop to," mused His Lordship (or was it His Grace?)

"You would court unpopularity?" Mr Peel gazed at him as if he was a particularly interesting Bill of Attainder.

"A baron can afford it, I should have thought," said Norman Gribb, as if to the manner born.

The lawyer nodded ruminatively. "The other thing about it, of course - and you'll find this typically Boggerthwaite - is that probably no-one from the village actually follows the Hunt any more. The real enthusiasts are mostly middle-class cretins from the towns - dentists, bankers, even some lawyers, sad to say." He broke off: a sudden digressive thought had hit him. "D'you know what the collective noun for bankers is?"

"A clutch" guessed Lord Bogger. "A grasp?"

Mr Peel shook his head. "A wunch," he said, and laughed a long, dry nasal laugh of the sort that Dickens would have been able to describe to perfection. "A wunch of bankers. Work it out."

"I've never been to Boggerthwaite," said its new Lord. "In fact, I'd never even heard of it."

"Not surprising," said the lawyer. "You might in fact say that Boggerthwaite is not so much a place as a state of mind. Shall you be moving into Bogger Hall?"

"I haven't anywhere else. Though perhaps there's a hotel?" Norman Gribb hoped there would be a hotel; he hadn't got out as much as he would have liked when living with Renie. "Or a pub?:" Better still, a pub - a nice little country inn with log fires, real ale, darts and old oak beams.

"There's a place called the Railway Hotel," said Mr Peel with the sort of distaste with which a Catholic would inform that there was only a Methodist chapel. "At least, it used to be called the Railway Hotel."

"But there's no railway within thirty miles," protested Lord Bogger.

7

"I looked on the map, to see how I could get there."

"You are correct," said the lawyer. "The hotel was built in 1856, a time of great railway optimism as well as the year of the Treaty of Paris, which ended the Crimean War. The planners hadn't noticed that there were a number of large hills in the way. Mountains even. The Railway Hotel is not, I believe, the most salubrious hostelry in Lakeland. But you must judge for yourself."

"I just thought I might put up for a night or two till I see what needs doing to the Hall."

Mr John Peel threatened a recurrence of legalistic laughter. "In that case you might find you'll have to put up there for rather a lengthy time." He looked at his watch - a pocket watch on the end of another bit of black bootlace. "Tempus fugit," he said, rising. "Let me wish you the best of luck, Your Grace." And he held out a pale hand, dry as old parchment.

3

Cumbrian guidebooks are a little, well, reticent is perhaps the best word, when it comes to the subject of Boggerthwaite. Wainwright gives a few lines to Great Mirkin Fell which dominates the village, but must have had an off day when he visited. "Quite the most miserable slog in the Lake District," he writes. "Even the sheep look suicidal."

Lord Bogger had found this reference only after a long search in the local section of Keswick Public Library. The only other thing they had was a translation of part of a work written by one Klaus Springer, a mercenary soldier in General Wade's anti-Jacobite army of 1745. It is entitled *Reise Durch Ein Kaltes Land*, which is to say *Journey Through a Cold Country*, and is an account of Springer's wanderings after the surrender of Carlisle, which took him through most of the least inhabited parts of what we now call the Lake District, until he was sure the fighting was properly over. Boggerthwaite people, he writes, are *"ganz unfreundlich"*, which

8

is translated as 'reserved'. "The natives are given in the month of November to the eating of young owls," he goes on. "Which practice giveth rise to a dreadful colic." That is all. The rest, as they say, is silence.

Lord Bogger decided to press on and discover for himself. He did not at all like the look and feel of Keswick. It was full of shops selling extremely expensive gear for mountain-climbing, and a lot of this gear seemed to have spilled out into the narrow streets on the persons of people who did not look as if they had ever climbed anything higher than a flight of stairs in a rather small house. They clopped around in beautifully burnished boots, gazed at the reflections in shop windows of the smart cagoules they were wearing and the equally splendid rucksacks they were carrying. They opened the doors of teashops with dazzlingly bright ice-axes, and lashed themselves to bar stools and rails with climbing ropes, slings and karabiners. That was the impression Norman got anyway, so he hired himself a car and got out of the place.

He drove roughly eastwards out of Keswick into a rainstorm of such intensity that he could make out virtually no more of the scenery than the sodden grass verges and dry-stone walls which glistened as if just emerging from the depths of a river. The higher his road climbed, the fiercer the rain fell, until, blinded by the spray thrown up by a German caravan towing a vessel which looked as big as a reincarnation of the *Scharnhorst*, which in turn carried half a dozen gaudy mountain bikes clamped to its stern, he pulled into a layby to wait for an improvement.

He waited five minutes, he waited ten; he allowed himself another ten and still the deluge continued. It was also growing dark, although he found it hard to work out which was the natural onset of night and which rain. It fell mostly downwards, but quite a bit fell sideways as well; upwards too when the wind from time to time caught the puddles on the road surface (ponds, more like) and whipped their water back up into the air. Norman switched on the blower, and this making little or no difference, wiped the

9

windscreen with a hank of kitchen tissue. He could still make out nothing.

He tried the car radio. It was, as is usual with hired cars, or indeed with any vehicle which someone else has been alone in for five minutes or more, tuned to Radio One, which was belting out a particularly hideous version of the same number which always comes up on Radio One when you tune in. It was while he was fiddling with the tuning, which he found almost completely incomprehensible (and he had worked in electronics) that he became aware of his side window darkening even more than before, and on peering closer through the misted glass, made out a dark, bulky shape looming beside the car. He squinted. There now was the figure of a man, a very wet-looking man, dressed in a sodden duffel coat of the sort favoured by road-menders and college lecturers in sociology. Beneath the hood a broad face was damply beaming, and its owner seemed to be making thumbing gestures against the glass. Norman opened up.

"Hi," said the apparition, its voice sounding as if bubbling up from some fathoms under a lake. "Any chance of a lift, mate?"

'Mate?' Norman thought. Try 'Your Grace' and you never know your luck. But he kept his thoughts to himself. "Where d'you want?"

"You going anywhere near Boggerthit?" The face was not a vicious one: lumpy, young and not well-shaven, but innocent. "Or Stoatholme? Stoatholme'd do."

Here was perhaps a disguised blessing, for Norman had no longer any clear idea which road he was on, or in which direction it was heading. "D'you know where it is? Boggerthwaite?" He pronounced the 'thwaite' to rhyme with 'bait'.

"Boggerthit I want," said the man with the thumb. "We pronounce it 'thit'. There's hundreds of thits in the Lakes, like. There's Seathit, Rosthit, Braithit, Thornthit...."

"It's OK, I get the general idea," said Norman. "You'd better get in, you'll get soaked."

The man eased himself into the passenger seat with a squelching sound, pushed back his hood, and wiped a damp forehead with the back of a dripping hand. His breath smelt of something rather stronger than rain-water. "Aye, it's a bit damp, like. It means 'clearing' does 'thit'. In the old Norse language. Or 'thwaite' as you say. Boggerthit - a clearing by the Bogger - that's the Bogger Beck."

"Fine," said Norman. "Where is it?"

"Oh, straight on - four miles down here, then left at Thugthit.... there you are, that's another one: Thug*thwaite*, I suppose you'd call it...." He did not seem to have noticed that Gribb's car was still stationary. "Left at Thugthit, as I say, then another four miles, turn left for Stoatholme, then.... But I can show you." And he settled back as if to enjoy an unaccustomed ride. Although the rain had not eased in the slightest, Norman started the engine and moved off into the maelstrom.

"You don't belong round here yourself, though, do you?" Gribb could not have failed to spot the thin, flat, nasal whine of the West Midlands, plaintive as a rusty saw-blade.

"Aye, Boggerthit," said the young man.

"No, I mean originally," coaxed Norman. "A wee bit further South, I'd've said, then over a bit. Birmingham, perhaps?" He could never pronounce the name without doing an imitation of a really thick Brummie.

"Wolver'ampton, actually," said the passenger, with little pride in the statement.

"So what brings you up here? Apart from the M6 of course."

"I'm a poet. I write poetry."

I suppose that figures, thought Norman, but said nothing. "And why Boggerthwaite....er, thit?"

The passenger mopped his brow again and discharged a heavy

spray from his duffel-coat cuff. "Well, it's funny you should mention the M6, but I was hitching up it one day. I thought I was heading for London, but it turned out to be the other direction, and this bloke he gives me a lift as far as Penrith. So I gets out and I sees all these hills - all these blue bumps on the horizon, like, and they kind of freaked me out. They drew me. So I got another lift, and finished up in Boggerthit."

"Like it?"

The poet cocked his head. "Put it this way, mate - have you ever been to Wolver'ampton?"

"Once," admitted Norman. "When they were at home to Swindon Town in the FA Cup Fourth Round. Nineteen fifty-four."

"Fifty-five," said the poet. "You lost three-nowt."

"I was sick on the coach going back. We'd had fish-cakes," recalled Lord Bogger. He paused, smiling faintly at the recollection. He had been as free as the air in those days, wasn't to meet the dreaded Renie for another dozen years. "So," he resumed, "Boggerthwaite, er *thit* - suits you?"

"Listen to this, mate." The poet cleared his throat.

> My heart leaps up when I behold
> The fells around the Bogger.
> They soar in serried ranks so bold....

I've never quite managed the next line. It's what you could call an Unfinished Idyll. But it gives you some idea, doesn't it?"

"It certainly does," said Lord Bogger, but failed to reveal just what that idea might be. "And do you make a living out of this, er, poetry?"

"You've got to be joking, mate." The newly-created peer did wish this sodden young man with his revolting accent wouldn't keep calling him mate. "Did Keats make a living? Did Shelley make a living? Did.... who's that other one? Never mind, my name's Ouskin—Matty Ouskin."

Was he supposed to have heard of him, Lord Bogger wondered. He hadn't, but then he supposed there were a lot of modern poets he had never heard of. You never knew these days: from what he had sometimes seen on the box by mistake, or in a Sunday supplement when he found one discarded on the next bench at work, all sorts of weird and wonderful young people were counted as poets in this age. It didn't do to go by looks. Or, it might seem, by their work.

"Pleased to meet you," said Lord Bogger graciously. Now he was in a bit of a dilemma himself: how to do his own introduction. Strongly tempted as he might be to make the grand pronouncement and reveal his new nobility, to step, as it were, out of the closet of anonymity, he hesitated only slightly before admitting to the name Gribb.

"And what are you heading for Boggerthit for?"

To mind my own business, he felt like saying, or to open up a new branch of Dr Barnado's. That's what he'd have said to Renie if she'd asked. But those days, those attitudes, were over. Then he had a stroke of sheer brilliance: at least, that's how he saw it. "I'm tracing my family back. It's a hobby of mine. Apparently some of them came from Boggerthwaite."

Matty Ouskin looked as if he was trying to concentrate his thoughts, and finding the going pretty tough. "Never heard of no Gribbs in Boggerthit," he said. "Nattrass, there is—Old Billy Nattrass. And Anstruther, Mrs Anstruther, Tot Titmuss the postman. They're about the only originals. The rest's all what they call off-comers."

"Meaning from outside?"

"From the South mainly - particularly at weekends. It's the old

13

M6 again, mate. Lets 'em all in. Like rats up a drainpipe. Mind, there might be some Gribbs at Stoatholme. Stoatholme's different, see? No-one from outside ever seems to want to live in Stoatholme. You'll see why soon." The young poet peered through the drowning windscreen. "We're the next left," he said. "Thugthit."

Lord Bogger was dimly aware through the wall of water of a group of lighted windows and a solitary street lamp looking like some primitive lighthouse. "Not many people go to live in Thugthit either," said Matty Ouskin.

The rain stopped as suddenly as it had started. Now there were hills all round, gradually materialising out of the murk, their tops invisible yet, but wreathed in skeins of cloud like smoke after a battle. Sheep were all over the road and nibbling away at the grass verges, and Lord Bogger marvelled that he had hit none on his way. Down a steep slope, round a bend, and a sign announced 'St-at-ol-e', and the end of it was buckled as if it had got in the way of some passing vehicle. There was a small school, deserted now that early evening was approaching. Two of its lower windows, Lord Bogger noticed, were boarded up, and a sign by the gates which must once have announced the place's identity, was streaked with white, as if someone has scored a direct hit with a sizeable can of paint.

Opposite the school was a little general shop looking very shut, its windows barred with stout rods of iron, and lying back from the road a little way past it, a long, low, rambling building which had once, quite long ago by the look of things, been painted pale blue. 'The Goat and Compasses', it proclaimed, 'No coach parties'. It looked not just shut, but as if it had not been open for some months. An ancient Ford Cortina stood before it, front tyres quite flat and its rear end supported on two beer crates in lieu of wheels. '£55 ONO' was daubed on its rear windscreen in more white paint. Along a little further sprawled an estate of about a hundred council houses, all pebble-dashed, with the damp of wind-driven rain staining the walls. A pack of dogs, of every conceivable shape, size and colour danced their version of a conga through gardens which had long since lost their fences. "Sunny Lea Estate," said Matty Ouskin. "Stoatholme's answer to Grozny."

As if to confirm this two girls of about twelve in extremely short leather skirts each stuck up two fingers and leered as the car passed.

Apart from an old Methodist chapel which looked as if it had been given up as a bad job shortly after being opened by John Wesley himself, that seemed to be Stoatholme. If this was the Lake District, thought Norman Gribb, who had never been near the place before, why did so many people visit it? But then people played golf, went shooting, and took holidays on caravan sites along draughty seaside cliff-tops. Renie liked to go to such places and he had not often been able to avoid being dragged along with her. There was no accounting, it seemed, for taste.

At a road junction at the end of the village a signpost proclaimed 'Boggerthwaite 1 1/2 miles', and the road started to rise again quite steeply. The cloud had not yet completely blown away from the tops, but Gribb guessed that if and when it did little more would be revealed than the prevailing wilderness of grass, bracken, rocks and sheep.

"Who does all this land belong to, Matty?" he asked.

The poet put his head on one side and tried to look like a man who knows a thing or two unknown to the greater part of the human race. "Most of it belongs to Mr Mahmoud. He's a foreign gentleman. From Syria, I think it is. He reckons to be Lord of the Manor now. Since old Lord Bogger passed on."

A thousand years of noble British blood, however diluted, stirred somewhere deep inside the new Lord Bogger. "Oh does he? And what was Lord Bogger like - before he passed on, of course?"

"Couldn't tell you." Matty Ouskin had the expression of someone who rather wouldn't than couldn't, but Norman felt this was being done mostly for effect.

"Bit of a recluse, was he? A lot of these old toffs are, I believe."

15

"Don't know about that," said Matty glumly. "Never saw hide nor hair of him. Spent most of his time in the West Indies."

It was only now that Norman Gribb realised he had found out nothing about the previous Lord Bogger from Mr Peel the solicitor, and that the lawyer had proffered no information except that he, Norman Gribb, had somehow inherited the title, the ancestral home, Bogger Hall, a modest legacy which, after death duties had been settled , and legal fees paid, would leave him little but a few farm rents from properties mainly, for some reason, in East Anglia.

"So, what was the old feller's interest in the West Indies - drug running or watching cricket?"

"Well, I don't know that he was such an old feller, by all accounts," said Matty with as much mystery as he could muster. "Bit of a young tearaway, so I've heard."

It was strange, Norman thought, how easy it was to form an image of someone you had never met. A stereotypical image, of course: Lord Bogger, a country peer from a remote corner of the Lake District, just had to be over sixty, hefty, ruddy-faced, dressed in tweeds, with a voice like a Rugby-educated foghorn and the manners of a well-bred pig. But why? He might just as easily have been young, weedy, pale-faced, slimy, with a squeaky voice, a handy knack with stocks and shares, and the manners of a badly-bred pig. Norman was moved to find out more.

"Did he often come to Boggerthwaite?"

"If he did, mate, then I never saw him. And I've been here over eighteen months now."

"Which makes you one of the oldest inhabitants, from what I've heard?"

Ouskin did not contradict. Instead he craned his neck forward like a pointing dog. "That's Bogger 'All along there," he announced.

Events, and the conversations of the day, had subconsciously prepared Gribb for almost anything, so that a cross between the Taj Mahal and one of the wilder creations of Mad King Ludwig of Bavaria would hardly have surprised him. But first sight of the actual Bogger Hall almost made him gasp. "That?" Matty Ouskin nodded.

"That" was like no ancestral country seat that Gribb had ever experienced, either in reality, on telly, or in his own imagination, which was not extensive. "That" was a three-storey, red-brick house aged abut sixty years, and although it would be an exaggeration to say that it would have fitted well in a seafront row of boarding houses in Eastbourne (because it would have fitted well nowhere), it would have suited the South Coast a lot better than it suited the Lakeland fells. It was quite out of proportion; that is its height was too much for its breadth; and it mocked a whole range of architectural styles. Its windows were mock-Elizabethan and mullioned, its eaves were mock-Tyrolean and badly carved, its gable-ends were brewers' Tudor, and it had two rooftop towers which were mock-Disneyland. Norman Gribb stared hard at the front door with its mock portcullis, as if fully expecting to see the Seven Dwarves issuing out to greet another day of frantic insanity. As it was the place looked shut tight and devoid of life.

Most country houses are set in more or less extensive grounds: if not in a complete deer park, then at least with a broad drive sweeping through thickets of rhododendron and azaleas. Bogger Hall had nothing like either: true to its Eastbourne feel it grew straight up above the roadside, reached by a couple of dozen steep concrete steps flanked by overgrown rockeries with no flowers evident but a small cohort of garden gnomes staggering up the rocks. Some had fishing rods.

"It's a total waste, that place," said Matty Ouskin. "With young people not able to afford a home of their own."

"You mean you? Why don't you squat? There must be a way in round the back."

Matty looked as if he had been accused of some unnatural vice.

17

"Me? Squat in there? Far too big, mate. And it'd cost the earth to heat. No, I'm all right, mate, where I am."

"Who looks after it, then?"

"The old girl I mentioned—Mrs Anstruther. One of the only original natives, and as nasty, a narrow-minded, nosy old bitch as you'd meet anywhere. She's supposed to go in once or twice a week to see it doesn't fall down. If that place was good enough for a squat you can bet your life she'd have let it off on the side herself."

Norman Gribb had been given a key to the Hall by Mr Peel, and was strongly tempted right now to park up and have a closer look. But something - maybe the empty feeling in his stomach which might soon be filled at the pub, or maybe the idiotically hostile look in the eyes of the garden gnomes - told him to wait for another opportunity. "Well, well," he murmured, and put his foot back on the accelerator. As he drove away he failed to see a faint twitch of upstairs curtain and the pale blur of a ghostly face behind.

4

It is a fact not often appreciated that the late Thatcher Government's much-vaunted attempt to liberalise the licensing trade made it in fact more difficult in certain parts of the country to get a drink than had been the case before. In the old days pubs had to keep certain hours, which, if limited, at least allowed the drinker to know where he was. Given freedom, publicans opened when it suited them—sometimes all day, often not at all. Such a hostelry was the Railway Hotel, Boggerthwaite, lately known as the Dehydrated Rambler.

On the afternoon of Norman Gribb's arrival as the new Baron Bogger, the so-called Saddle Bar of the Rambler was open, just about. Three lost tourists had called in at lunchtime in the hope of something to eat, reasonably priced. The first part of their expectation at least had been satisfied, and they had departed with bellies full of pre-packed, micro-waved 'lasagne' and wallets rather emptier of notes than they had imagined possible. Three sodden hikers had arrived in the middle of the deluge, had dripped and sprayed all over the bar stools, drank half a pint of Owd Bogger each and shared two packets of cheese-and-onion crisps between them over a period of two hours, and only reluctantly moved out when the landlord, one Rory McGurk, was quite uncommonly rude to them, even for him, casting public doubts on their parentage and standards of personal hygiene.

Mr Rory McGurk was a native of Ballybogger, in the country of Mayo, in the Republic of Ireland, or so he said. In fact a quick glance at any half-reliable gazeteer would show that there is no such place. There is a village called Ballyboghil some twenty miles north of Dublin, so perhaps McGurk had got himself confused: it is the sort of pointless departure from the truth that the man delights in. If the Bogger Valley Thespians ever wished to stage a show featuring the Seven Deadly Sins, Rory McGurk would be cast perfectly as Covetousness. The man oozes greed from every pore, and being over six feet tall and broad to match, he has plenty of pores. He is a black-haired, oily looking man with the features of a cartoon tom-cat.

Why Mr McGurk chose to establish himself in Boggerthwaite is not known. How is easy enough: the pub, then known as the Railway Hotel, had been ailing for some years, and on the departure of the previous landlord, rather suddenly and leaving no trace, the bank sold it for what it could get swiftly, which was rather little. That rather little came from Mr McGurk, who immediately set about 'improving' what had been a perfectly straightforward if rather dull Victorian pub. Out went the fine old mirrors and the gleaming brass rails, down went walls, and in came acres of cheap carpet, plastic surfaces, and the kind of wallpaper found in city clip-joints. Ceilings were lowered, fruit machines and juke boxes installed, and a pool-table placed in the middle of the public bar so as to get in the way of drinkers coming and going who in turn got in the way of cue arms of the players. There was a large salmon in

19

a glass case which Mr McGurk would tell you was caught in the Bogger Beck by his good self after a two-hour struggle in 1989, but would fail to explain how a fish so obviously made of plastic came to be in the water in the first place.

But the pride of Rory McGurk's establishment was what he called his Carvery, even if this was strictly a misnomer, for it was rare for any joints of beef or ham to be displayed therein for the delectation of hungry customers. In fact it was little more than a slab of zinc on which various warm dishes were from time to time served up through a steam-wreathed hatchway by the licensee's wife, Mrs Pilar McGurk, a lady whose head and shoulders were only rarely seen and whose lower parts never. Mrs McGurk's domain was the kitchen, and her husband saw to it that she kept to that territory. Mr McGurk claimed that his wife was Spanish, daughter of a high-ranking army officer; others said that she hailed from the Philippines and had preferred attaching herself to the devil of McGurk to the deep blue sea of lowly service in a succession of some of the least salubrious hotels in London. Be that as it may, Mrs McGurk said little and had never been known to smile.

"Would you credit it?" McGurk was saying for the umpteenth time that afternoon since he had persuaded the hikers to leave. "Three halves of beer and a couple of lousy packets of crisps. And for that they want to take up half the hotel and drown all the fixtures and fittings."

"It's your own fault for changing the name of the pub," said a skinny old man with a collarless shirt and a cloth cap, the spitting image of old man Steptoe.

"Hotel!" barked McGurk. "And what d'you mean, my fault for changing the name?" If there was one thing the licensee was proud of apart from his 'carvery', it was the new name he had bestowed on the old Railway Hotel. "You don't forget a name like the Dehydrated Rambler."

"You don't forget the prices neither," said the old chap, who was

20

none other than the Old Billy Nattrass who at almost that same moment was being mentioned in Lord Bogger's hired car.

Further argument was temporarily averted by the entry of a strikingly good-looking woman of about thirty, wearing a drenched anorak over a long denim skirt of the sort which used to be favoured by social workers of a certain type. She scowled round the place, removed the anorak, shook out long dark hair, and sat on a stool next to Old Billy. She did not ask for a drink, nor did Mr McGurk inquire what she wanted. Instead he pulled a pint of dark-looking beer and set it before her. "Did you have a nice day, Georgina, my dear?" he purred.

"Geordie to you, you profiteering, fat bog-trotter," said the young lady. "And how is anyone expected to have a nice day trying to control four dozen young assassins and hooligans?" She lifted the pint to a mouth which looked moulded rather for the reception of a delicate nectar, and slurped down four inches of foaming ale.

"Ah yes, the cream of our Stoatholme cousins," said Mr McGurk. He was trying to look deep into the schoolteacher's eyes, but they were shut in appreciation of the ale she was swallowing.

"Did you know that 'hooligan' is in fact an Irish word?" This from a gent seemingly well into his sixties who had been sitting quietly reading an old copy of the Daily Telegraph.

"Thankyou, Mr Otter," returned 'Geordie' D'Arcy the schoolmistress. "One would never have guessed."

"Aye." The old man pushed a pair of reading-glasses up off his nose and regarded Ms D'Arcy from beneath them. "It was the name of a particularly lively Irish family resident in South London in the latter part of the last century - Bermondsey, I believe. The name was actually spelled Houlihan. Then there was of course Kathleen ni Houlihan...."

"Thankyou Mr Otter," said Geordie again. "Then she has a lot to answer for in and around Stoatholme, let me assure you."

21

The old man looked mildly surprised. "Now I don't think there was ever any connection with Stoatholme. Not our Stoatholme anyway."

"We were discussing the name of this pub, Miss D'Arcy," wheezed Old Billy Nattrass, who couldn't bear Jake Otter getting the floor ahead of himself. "What do you think of it?"

"I think it's bloody stupid," said Geordie. "And typical of this shallow age of gimmicks and insensitivity."

"It used to be called the Railway Hotel," resumed Jake Otter. "Which might have been appropriate if there'd ever been a railway...."

"We know," growled Old Billy. "It was called that years afore you turned up. The point I'm making is it was a better bloody name, railway or no bloody railway."

"The present title was designed to attract half-arsed yuppies from the Home Counties who think that rambling the boring set of fells round here is like climbing Annapurna without oxygen," said Geordie D'Arcy.

"Precisely," beamed Mr McGurk. "That is precisely the type I wish to attract. Because they cause no trouble and—another pint, Georgina, dear?—because they have money and they spend it, not knowing any better. Whereas you lot have no money to speak of and begrudge parting with the little you have got."

"It would never have been allowed to have been changed in the old days. Lordy would never have sanctioned it." Old Billy Nattrass glared round the company as if daring contradiction.

"Lordy?" Ms D'Arcy repeated. "Who's 'Lordy' for heaven's sake?"

Old Billy Nattrass began to look important, but Jake Otter was in before him. "I think our friend is referring to Lord Bogger -

22

Barry, the fourteenth Baron Bogger of Bogger Hall, who owned most of the horizons round here. "

Old Billy fairly snarled with triumph. "And that's where you're wrong, clever sod. I was referring to Old Lordy, his father, the thirteenth Baron."

"How terribly feudal," yawned Geordie D'Arcy. "Has Muriel been in?"

"Before my time, I'm afraid," said Jake Otter, ignoring the D'Arcy and slightly on the defensive against Old Billy. "So I'm afraid I didn't have the pleasure."

Old Billy bared a fang or two. "Well you wouldn't of, would you? Only been here five minutes...."

Now it was perfectly true that, although possessed of a near perfect Cumbrian accent, a bit on the pedantic side sometimes perhaps, and sounding like a rural schoolmaster from the old days, Mr Otter had retired to the Bogger Valley only three years or so before, having hailed originally from West Bromwich. But he had shoved roots down quickly, and what he didn't know about local history he made up swiftly, his hobby being to spin out the local lore in the Rambler whenever he could find a likely-looking stranger—likely-looking meaning a possible good touch for a glass of whisky, double preferred. Mr Otter looked like a townie's idea of a Lakeland shepherd, never without a lengthy blackthorn crook with a carved ram's -horn handle and a bad-tempered , wall-eyed little collie bitch stretched out under his stool, teeth ready half-bared.

"I said has anyone seen Muriel?" Geordie D'Arcy hadn't been talking to anyone in particular, so no-one was particularly answering her. "It's all right for her, mucking about with lumps of clay all day."

Jake Otter put his head on one side and looked quizzically at his rival. "You say Old Lordy would never have allowed anyone to change the name of the hotel, but as I understand it his son, the late Lord Bogger, sold off almost anything round here that would fetch money. This pub included. "

"Hotel," growled Rory McGurk.

"That's as mebbes," Billy shuffled uncomfortably. "Fact remains...."

"It hardly sounds like pride in a birthright to me," pressed Mr Otter. "Did you actually know the last Lord Bogger?"

"No-one really knew him," sighed Old Billy. "Leastways no-one round here. But he'll have had his reasons for what he did. Death duties more than likely. Crippling, death duties can be."

"But he sold up the Grange, didn't he? The ancestral home. To that Mr Mahmoud."

"That's right," granted Old Billy. "And a right public benefactor he's been too. Won't have a word said against Mr Mahmoud, for all he's foreign and that."

"Foreign, and very, very rich," put in Geordie D'Arcy. "If I'd been that way inclined I might have made a play for him myself. Are you sure Muriel hasn't been in?"

Mr McGurk shook his head and pulled her another pint. "So go on, Billy," he said, trying to stir the rivalry. "What sort of a chap was Old Lordy?"

Old Billy looked round the bar slowly before speaking. "He was a real gentleman. A thorough toff. He wouldn't have sold this place to a bloody Fenian hinterloper, and then let him change the name to something stupid."

"Well, there's no Lordy now," said Mr McGurk. "So I can call my place what I please."

"There'll be another yet." A strange light had come into Old Billy's eyes, a look as near to the fanatical as any that ever flickered in those old organs used to hours of watching television over the top of the bar. "There'll be a Lordy yet, you mark my words!"

"It doesn't have to be direct descent," said Geordie. "It might be almost anybody. It might be you, Billy, though somehow I rather doubt it. And it wouldn't be you, McGurk, you frightful Hibernian crook."

At which moment the door of the public bar opened and admitted Norman Gribb from Swindon, scion of a noble line. "Two pints of bitter, please," said the latest Lordy.

5

"This stuff," Norman Gribb said a little later out of the corner of his mouth to Matty Ouskin, "Is the filthiest drop of beer I've tasted in 31 years - that being the precise length of time I have been in the habit of taking anything stronger than lemonade."

"Owd Bogger," nodded Matty sleepily. "Aye, it's an acquired taste, mate. Mind, it's worse here than in most pubs. Dearer too."

"I've almost a mind to go over to that boys' lager stuff of yours, Matty. Almost, I said, but it's not quite as bad as that. I shall persevere."

"You mean it's my turn. Fair do's: you gave me the lift." Matty dug down for a purse, opened it cautiously, like someone dealing with a possible parcel bomb. He tried to bring cash to the surface surreptitiously but there were sharp eyes in the Dehydrated Rambler.

"Cashed the old Giro have we?" Geordie D'Arcy wanted to know. "Just try not forget that little matter of the rent, Matty dear. Three weeks it is now." Then she winked at the newcomer. "Matty lives with me. That is, he lodges with me, not cohabits. Muriel does that. Muriel's a potter, or a sculptor, I can't remember which. And she said she'd be here at half past four."

Old Billy was ready to have a go at the poet now. "Did you get yourself a job, then? Or have we got to go on keeping you?"

25

Matt Ouskin silently signalled for drinks for himself and his new friend. "It was a close-run thing, Billy," he began. "You see, I'm signed on as an unemployed sedan-chair carrier. Thought that'd be as safe as anything, because not only aren't there a lot of chairs knocking about these days, but it's a job you need two for—like the front and rear ends of pantomime horses.

"Well, bugger me if they haven't found another one—some creep from over t'other side of Keswick. I had to do some quick thinking. Was this other feller a leading carrier or a follower? You see, they're two entirely different skills. A leader's got to be used to seeing where he's going, and the follower's got to be the trusting sort, going where he's led, not being able to see through the chair. Both require great nerve and many years' experience. Well, I'm a lead man myself, and it turned out this other chap they'd just got on their books is a lead man too. So it's like having two front halves of a panto horse—no use at all, and they haven't got any retraining schemes on the go at the moment, thank God. It gave me a nasty turn, though, Billy. And how about you—I take it you've been busy all day re-distributing government farm subsidies."

"Idle, long haired bugger," said Old Billy Nattrass. "Sedan chair carrier my arse. There's always work for them as wants to work."

"Funny you should mention sedan chairs," put in Jake Otter, and addressing himself not to the poet but to Norman Gribb, whose eye he had been trying to catch ever since he had made his appearance. "It's perhaps not generally known that Boggerthit was once famous for the manufacture of flinches, which was what they called the grips for the handles of sedan chairs." Mr Otter's hand was hovering a few inches above the bar, and suspended from it was a whisky glass, which he had just rather ostentatiously drained. So the glass dangled now, inviting a refill: a courageous move this, for there was no guarantee that a stranger, however pleasantly addressed, would pay for the local knowledge that Jake was about to impart, however rich it might be. Lord Bogger did not oblige.

"Really?" was all he said, plunging his nose into a second pint of Owd Bogger with the look of a rescue worker about to enter a sewer after a trapped casualty.

"Aye, Dabster and Tyson's Flinch Mill. Employed a couple of hundred men at its height. In fact you might say Dabster and Tyson's *was* Boggerthit in the eighteenth century."

"Bloody rubbish," snapped Old Billy Nattrass.

"They made two sorts of flinches," Jake Otter went on, put out neither by Old Billy's interruption nor even apparently by Norman Gribb's lack of interest in buying him a whisky. "There was the Oxford Flinch and the Kilmarnock Flinch. Some customers liked one sort, some t'other. The Scots were apparently very partial to the Oxford Flinch, don't ask me why."

"What were they made out of, Mr Otter?" Mr McGurk was holding out his hand for the savant's empty glass. "The usual?"

Jake Otter looked uncertain. "We'll see about that in a minute. I was just telling this gentleman about our ancient industries. A lot of visitors are very interested in that sort of thing. Anyway, it was tups' horns they made flinches out of - what you'd call rams' horns down south. They used to striggle 'em - which is to say turn 'em - and then they used to flinch them, which gave the grip, like. Aye...." The whisky glass still dangled, empty: the new Lord Bogger seemed to be made of sterner stuff than most visitors.

"Bloody nonsense," said Billy Nattrass mournfully.

"Terrible hard conditions there were. They was always dropping off with what they called sedan lung. Lingering, that was...."

"Fascinating," said Norman Gribb.

Jake Otter looked up with renewed hope in his old eyes. "Well, a lot of people think so. I've had professors, I've had writers. I've had offers to go on television...."

"Lying owd bugger," said Billy Nattrass.

"But I've always said no. I don't want to make money out of what after all is our Heritage. You don't sell your birthright for a mess of pottage. I'll tell anyone who's interested, that's sufficient for me, and if they want to buy me a drink or two, why, that's up to them. Aye." And he put his glass down on the bar top and stared at it.

Norman Gribb let him stare, and inquired about bed and breakfast.

McGurk rubbed pudgy hands together. "We provide the service, sir," he said, "when we can. Which is rarely these days, on account of always being busy, thank God."

"I was just after a single room for a few days," said Gribb. "But if you're full, perhaps...."

"We *were* full," McGurk said. "We were fully booked by a party of scholars from Oxford University. Professors, you might say. A convention to do with geology or some such: we get a lot. Just this morning I got a fax cancelling. They'd gone down with flu, the best part of them, and so the convention's off until the summer. So, you're in luck, sir. You can have your pick. All our apartments are, of course, en suite." And he rubbed his hands with renewed energy. Then he went to the serving hatch and muttered something into the steam beyond. Then returning to Norman: "I'll have our residential staff check everything out sir, in a brace of shakes. Would you be after dining at all?"

And so, a little later, as evening set in, the latest Baron Bogger found himself with his feet under one of the tables in the corner of the bar with a plate of what looked very much like shepherds pie in front of him. The food, McGurk had assured him, was a Speciality of the House - the celebrated Boggerthwaite November Owl Pie. There were other specialities: there were for example Jumbo-Cumbo Sausages, there were Boggerburgers, but sure a hungry traveller like himself might find these a little on the light side for a main meal. But Traditional November Owl Pie....

28

"You don't mean to tell me," Norman had said, "that you put actual owls in your pies?"

McGurk gave him a sly look, as between two men of the world who know what they're talking about. "Not actual owls, sir, you're right. That's not all-*owl*-ed these days." Mr McGurk roared with laughter. "Get it? It's not all-owl-ed. The RSPB, you know. To say nothing of the EC."

"Then how do you get round the Trade Descriptions Act?" persisted Lord Bogger. "It says it up there on the board: November Owl Pie. It's not November; more like March. And now you tell me it's not real owl either."

McGurk drew nearer, whispered with a deep secrecy. "It's owl *flavoured,* sir. With a special Tincture of Owl we make from a very ancient local recipe. And it lasts all the year round these days. In fact you might almost say it's always November in Boggerthwaite."

"You can say that again," interrupted Geordie D'Arcy, who was now starting her fifth pint of Owd Bogger, which increased the volume of her voice without taking away her great schoolteacher's gift of being able to listen to at least four conversations at the same time. Her friend Muriel had still failed to turn up.

So Norman ordered Owl Pie. There was a flurry behind the carvery hatch, a brief glimpse of sad Oriental eyes through a cloudbank of kitchen steam, and up it came, looking, as has already been stated, very much like November shepherd's pie. Norman tackled it and found it had the property of requiring something to wash it down. Which solved his problem of what to do with the rest of his Owd Bogger.

And in the corner of the bar Old Billy Nattrass raised his head and declaimed, in defiance of the whole world: "There'll be a new Lordy yet!"

6

Police Constable Robin de Vere Costive greeted the new morning as a war horse scenting fresh battle in the crisp, bright air. Like the steed in the Book of Job he swallowed the ground with fierceness and rage.... "He saith among the trumpets, Ha ha; and he smelleth the battle afar off, the thunder of the captains, and the shouting." Having done all that he changed his mind, got into bed again, and went back to sleep.

At least, he tried to sleep, but his early morning enthusiasms had woken his wife Bryony, and she in turn had got up, shouted to rouse son Darren (8 1/2), and thumped down to the kitchen singing a medley of songs from *Oklahoma*. She singeth among the pots, pans and dishes, Ha ha, and maketh such a racket that her husband decideth to give up the idea of further sleep as a bad job and get dressed.

He did not expect a particularly busy day. It was still winter, and not a lot happened in winter in the Bogger Valley. Lost dogs there might be to sort out, gun licenses to be checked, car tax discs to be observed, the odd bit of juvenile petty larceny from the Sunny Lea Estate at Stoatholme, a regular trickle of domestic fracas from the same source, and a fairly steady supply of grievous and actual bodily harm from the same area on Friday and Saturday evenings, when the good constable, who did not hold with violence, did his best to be either on a day off or investigating rare cases of speeding on the Thugthwaite road, which was really too narrow and tortuous to enable motorists to do much more than forty even in good daytime visibility.

Today was a Wednesday, though, and apart from the case of three plastic traffic cones which had been reported missing from beside a small hole in the road round Great Mirkin Fell, there seemed to be nothing to stop the officer's enjoyment of at least a morning's fishing in the Bogger Beck. Fishing was a passion with Pc Costive. He was not very good at it, or perhaps it was that there were not very many fish in the local water. However, he found that sitting by the hour beside a flowing stream, or wading in it up to his thighs, relaxed his mind very effectively. His was otherwise an active mind: not deeply intellectual, nor particularly practical, but active. That is, it tended to jump around quite a lot, appalled at one moment by the amount of sin and nastiness in the world, worried the next as to whether he was doing enough to combat this wickedness, and concerned pretty well all of the time as to whether he had done the right thing at all in joining the police force. He had been ambitious once, convinced that his good breeding (his father had been something quite high up at the Bank of England) and his education (six years at a very expensive public school which shall be nameless here except that it was not far from Windsor and began with an E) would combine to waft him gently up to heights where truncheons are carried no more and sore feet are a thing of the past. Unfortunately this had just not happened. Robin de Vere Costive had found himself, after ten years in the force, sole guardian of the law in Boggerthwaite which, however much sought after as a holiday retreat by his social peers from the South, was not the most challenging place for an ambitious policeman. He wondered about it a lot. He thought he had done all the right things. His father had got him into the Masons, he did not consort with low life in the tap-rooms of the district, and he sent the Chief Constable a Christmas card every year.

This morning he sat quietly over a cup of coffee and waited for scrambled eggs, watched his young son come floating into the kitchen wafting his arms about to the music of Tchaikovsky's Swan Lake on the radio. Darren's mother smiled indulgently, but Robin was not happy about the lad. He wanted him to be a rugby player; Darren wanted to be a ballet dancer, and in this unhealthy ambition he was supported by his mother. Sometimes the officer wondered if he had made the right choice of partner. Bryony was a well-

31

bred woman (her father had been a Brigadier) and had gone to a good school (not as good as her husband's perhaps, but still jolly expensive), but she was not really, he suspected, the right material for a policeman's wife. She felt sorry for criminals and had once applied to join the Labour Party and was only after considerable argument persuaded to withdraw. Had word of this somehow got through to the powers that were in the Police Headquarters? Had they read the letters she had from time to time had published in the Bogger Valley Bugle calling for prison reform and a better understanding of delinquents? He had not noticed them himself at the time as he only read (or at least bought) the Daily Telegraph and a number of magazines concerned with angling. Unlike her husband Bryony Costive seemed quite content with her rural lot. She attended meetings of the Women's Institute, cultivated a wondrous flower garden, and baked cakes for the village functions. She would have made a splendid vicar's wife, though not in Boggerthwaite, because the present incumbent seemed not the least bit interested in women, let alone the state of Holy Matrimony.

The vicar of Boggerthwaite was a strange man altogether and Pc Costive worried about him too. He had a Spanish name for all his adherence to the Anglican Church and was reputed to come from somewhere near Valladolid. Actually no-one had seen hide nor hair of the Rev. Miguel Ximenez for some weeks. He had been posted (or whatever the ecclesiastical equivalent is) to St Ethelbogger's after a rather hard time in an inner-city parish on Tyneside, and Pc Costive sometimes allowed himself to wonder whether he too had not been sent to the same place for the good of his mental health rather than from any regard to the number of crimes he might detect. Pc Costive made mental note as his eggs arrived (done as usual to a creamy turn) to have a proper look at the vicarage before he went fishing, if he did go fishing. Missing vicars were a source of worry, if not to their congregation, then at least to the Law. Or so Robin Costive reasoned. He did not like Mr

Ximenez. The man had a thick, black beard like a stage anarchist, and averted his eyes whenever he, Pc Costive, tried to speak to him, which was not often.

So the guardian of the Law finished his scrambled eggs, drank a second cup of coffee, scanned the headlines of the Telegraph with dutiful lack of understanding, and averted his eyes as son Darren minced to the front door, took his satchel from his mother and gave her far too sloppy a kiss for a lad of eight, coming on nine. Darren did not attempt to kiss his father, and it was only after his mother whispered something to him that he made a face and gave an extremely grudging "Bye, Daddy."

Daddy! Why couldn't he call him something less childish? He didn't want 'Sir' or 'Father'; a simple 'Dad' would have done. Pc Robin de Vere Costive wondered what his superiors would think if they knew he had a son who liked ballet dancing and called him 'Daddy'.

"You know I worry about that school sometimes," sighed Mrs Costive as she closed the door after she had waved her son out of sight. "Miss D'Arcy's all right. She has some very progressive ideas. But the other children!"

"Low life," grunted her husband. "Don't worry, I know. Most of my best customers come from Sunny Lea."

"But they don't stand a chance, poor lambs," sighed Mrs Costive. "There's no work for them when they leave school, nowhere for them to play...."

"Nowhere to play?" her husband echoed. "What about all those wide open spaces? People come from all over the country to walk those fells. Pay good money to drive the length of the land to get here. And those little buggers can have 'em within walking distance. They don't bother, though, do they, because you can't set those fells on fire because they're too wet, and there are rarely

33

enough old ladies up there to mug. No, they're no-hopers, the lot of 'em." He paused as he got up to get his tunic. "But at least they don't go in for ballet dancing."

Bryony seemed not to notice the shaft. "Will you be late, Robin?" was all she said.

But Pc Costive knew better than to linger. She would only want him to do some shopping for her down at Stoatholme Co-op. He didn't mind basic foodstuffs, but last time she had wanted a supply of tampons, and that had caused much hilarity among his foes from Sunny Lea.

After the heavy rain of the previous afternoon the day had dawned fair. The sky was blue with strings of cloud streaking quite briskly across it. Costive decided not to take the Land Rover just yet, but to walk (or to proceed on foot, as he would have said in court) to the vicarage.

The visitor will look in vain in any of the popular guidebooks for mention of St Ethelbogger's Church. Pevsner certainly ignores it, and his imitators follow suit, mostly, one suspects, because there is absolutely nothing outstanding or unusual about it, apart perhaps for its patronal name which, if the truth were known, was conjured up by the Mid-Victorian Baron Bogger who had the church built in the first place. This was not because he himself was a man of any great piety, but because it gave his estate workers something to do along the straight and narrow at a time of great unrest among agricultural workers. St Ethelbogger's was a squat, cramped, stone-built edifice with a mock Norman doorway, pseudo Early English window arches, and a phoney Perpendicular nave. It was quite abominably draughty.

And if the church itself was undistinguished, the vicarage which went with it was even less noteworthy. It was—well, it was a country vicarage. That is, it was too large, too costly to heat properly, and subject to dry rot, wet rot, and, for all anyone knew, death-watch beetle as well. It might in its early years have suited a stout English vicar with a large, hardy family and a retinue of servants, but it was absolutely not suitable for a middle-aged bachelor with bad nerves used in earlier years to the ripening sun of the Spanish meseta. No wonder the Rev. Ximenez had made himself scarce, thought Pc Costive as he looked up at the leaky gutters and the damp green patch which extended all down by the side of the front door.

There was, as he had expected, no reply when he tugged at the ancient bell-pull. He imagined he heard a funereal sort of clanging sound echoing inside as he put his ear to the letter-box, but couldn't be sure. Exchanging eye for ear he could just make out in the interior gloom a pile of mail, mostly bills and advertising junk, scattered over cracked, diamond-shaped tiles. There was a damp, musty smell which reminded him of the cold suet pudding of his school-days. The officer put his mouth to the letter-box "Hallo!" he shouted. "Anybody there?" But only faint echoes returned.

A stroll round the side of the vicarage gave the officer the chance of a good look through the kitchen window. Again there were no signs of life. Plates and dishes stood neatly stacked on the draining board, the table was clear apart from a teapot, a salt cellar and a wine bottle with half a candle stuck in its neck and wax which had dripped and congealed down its sides. There was another window round this side of the house, rather too high for the constable to peer through without additional height. Fortunately there was a section of old tree-trunk, obviously once used as some sort of chopping-block, standing by the back door. By placing a large earthenware flower-pot upside down on the top of this, the constable was able to command the height needed for him to try the upper sash, which would not budge, and to peer into the room. It seemed to be some sort of study. It had a book-case, a desk with more books and papers, a swivel chair, an empty parrot cage and a woman's dress.....

"Can I 'elp you?"

The voice was loud, sharp, and above all totally unexpected. With the result that the officer span round, wobbled, dislodged the plant-pot from the chopping-block, stuck one elbow through the window pane, and finished up sitting in the fortunately soft earth of the flower-bed. Staring at his undignified position was the homely dog-like face of Old Billy Nattrass, peering over the garden wall. His look was more accusing than sympathetic.

"Lookin' fer summat?" Old Billy was saying. "Shouldn't you have a warrant for that—breaking and hentering?"

"I am neither breaking nor entering," said the constable, climbing to his feet and looking more than somewhat embarrassed.

"Well, you've broken the window, and your helbow hentered," said the old man unhelpfully.

"I am looking for your vicar," sniffed Pc Costive.

"Well, I don't suppose he can be in," said Old Billy. "Or he'd've heard you mekkin' all that racket. He's gone away, as a matter of fact."

"Suppose you tell me," suggested the constable, dusting down the seat of his trousers and inspecting his tunic for signs of damage.

"Well, if he's not here it stands to reason he's gone somewhere else."

"But gone away, you said. Which means he intends to be away some time."

"Does it?" said Old Billy Nattrass.

"Look, to go means just that. To go away means there is some intent of staying away for some length of time." The constable was growing more exasperated than ever, or he would never have uttered his next phrase: "Look, I don't want to argue semantics...."

"You what?"

"When did you last see the vicar?"

"Can't say exactly." Old Billy cocked his head and examined

the faulty guttering, as if the Rev Ximenez might be discovered sitting above it, legs dangling. "About three weeks since, I should reckon."

"And he didn't make any public pronouncement?" Was it 'pronouncement' or 'announcement', the officer wondered. "Did he tell anyone?"

"Didn't tell me," said Old Billy. "But then I'm only the verger."

The officer said no more, but with a last look at the broken window-pane walked down the garden path and out onto the road again. "Thanks," he said finally. "You've been a great help."

"What are you going to do about that window? Talk about burglary and vandalism. If the poliss is going around breaking and hentering, is it any wonder that the kids today have no respect for property or their helders? What about....?"

But Law and Order had passed on. Law and Order was wondering. Would it have been best to ring the Diocesan offices? Surely they would know if a vicar had gone anywhere in particular. Should he get a search warrant, in case the man was lying upstairs with his throat cut? Vicars could get up to some strange tricks, he reckoned. And there was such a small congregation at St Ethelbogger's these days that probably no-one would particularly notice the incumbent's absence for quite a long while. How did you get a window repaired without getting entry to the premises in order to fit new glass? All these questions perplexed the good officer as he went to get his Land Rover. Solving the mystery of the missing traffic cones might at least give his brain a little time to calm itself.

When he got to the hole at the top of the long, snaking road below Great Mirkin Fell it was to find, sure enough, that the cones were indeed missing. So was any evidence of a labour force which, had it been mending the hole would have been protected from passing traffic by the presence of the cones. They had been reported missing by phone the previous evening by one of the County

37

Council's Highways staff, a cheerful little chap by the name of Larkin who chatted on for a good ten minutes about fishing before and after registering his complaint. If he had spent half as much effort just lifting his eyes over the bit of drystone dyke which skirted the hole in the road he would have seen that his missing cones were nestling there in the grass below. Why they were nestling there, who had put them there, would remain one of the unsolved mysteries in the annals of Bogger Valley crime. Pc Robin de Vere Costive clambered down to retrieve them, rather stiffly because his limbs were objecting to the treatment they had experienced beneath the vicarage window, then he got back in his vehicle and headed for his favourite bit of water on the Bogger Beck just at the foot of the fell.

He had gone only a couple of hundred yards when he made out a shape by the roadside which first of all reminded him of nothing so much as a camel sheltering head down against a desert sandstorm. Not that the constable had ever been to camelly parts of the world, but he had a television set like most people. The figure was lumpish and rounded and turned out to be somehow wrapped round a bicycle. It was in fact, the officer made out as he drew alongside, engaged in trying to pump up a tyre. It was having rather little success.

"Bother, Sylvia?" The officer wound down his window and leaned across.

The camel-shaped figure straightened and metamorphosed into a woman of fairly advanced middle-age, comfortably built as the euphemists would have said, with a thick ex-army great-coat and a woolly hat pulled down firmly over a red-patterned headscarf. All that could be seen of legs was encased in a pair of wellington boots. Give that description to anyone who knows Boggerthwaite and they would tell you straight away that it belonged to none other than Mrs Sylvia Anstruther of Midden Mains, relict of the late Samuel Anstruther, once local roadman, hedger, ditcher, dry-stone waller and grave-digger at St Ethelbogger's. Since his death

38

longer ago than anyone in the village apart from Old Billy Nattrass could remember, Mrs Anstruther had kept considerable body and energetically enquiring soul together by doing a variety of cleaning and caretaking jobs which gave her the entry to most of the weekend and holiday cottages for some miles around. Mrs Anstruther was a fount of knowledge about local goings-on. Pc Costive had always known that it was better to have her on his side than against him. So he smiled helpfully now. "Puncture?"

"Mrs Anstruther glared at him without charity. "Well, it ain't a smashed windscreen, is it?"

The officer smiled, climbed down and felt the flat tyre quite unnecessarily. Mrs Anstruther gave three or four more thrusts with her pump. The tyre remained as flat as ever. "Got your puncture outfit, Sylvia?"

"At home," said Mrs Anstruther, rubbing chapped hands together.

"Not much use there. Where are you going?"

"Just up to Bogger 'All. See if everything's all right."

"I'll give you a lift up," said the constable. "I'll put the bike in the back."

Mrs Anstruther appeared to be making some sort of stammered protest, but it fell on deaf if kindly ears. The officer had the back door of his vehicle open and the crippled bicycle inside before she could form any coherent sort of sentence.

"Visiting the sick as well, are we?" The officer was smiling, pointing to the basket on the bicycle's front. It was loaded with two carrier bags which appeared to contain various items of grocery. From one protruded the neck of a lemonade bottle and from the other the whiskery ends of two leeks.

"Just a bit of shopping," said Mrs Anstruther. "You've no need to go out of your way, you know. I can walk. I like a nice walk."

"No problem," said Pc Costive. "Jump in." And he let out the clutch as Mrs A climbed shakily into the passenger seat as if she had never been inside a vehicle in her life.

"You keep an eye on the Hall, then?" inquired the officer.

"Just see things are all right," said Mrs Anstruther. "Put the heating on for a bit so's the damp don't get too much of a hold. Particularly this time of the year."

"No news of any....?" What was the word he wanted—replacement? Substitute?

Mrs Anstruther saved him the trouble. "Nowt," she said. "I doubt they'll find anybody now. Family's died out, and perhaps that's no bad thing. You get plants like that. Flower good as owt for years, then they just die off. Roots is rotten, see?"

"What'll they do with the house—sell it?"

"Suppose they'll have to." Mrs Anstruther allowed her face to crease into a wink, which was the nearest it had showed to any emotion since the officer had found her. "I dare say that Mr Mahmoud wouldn't be backward in coming forward."

The officer looked a little surprised. "But he's got Mirkin Grange. I mean, that's something like a stately home. But Bogger Hall, well...."

"Ah, it's the prestige," winked Mrs Anstruther. "It's the ancestral home, you might say: the Boggers of Bogger 'All it always was, long before that was built. And if Mr Mahmoud sees himself as Lord of The Manor, then he ought to own the ancestral home too, see?"

"I ought to have a look at it myself," said Pc Costive helpfully. "Just so as to keep an eye on things."

Mrs Anstruther spluttered a cough. "Oh, there's no need to put yourself out, officer . I keep a good eye on it, don't you worry."

"I'm sure you do." It was Constive's turn to wink now. "It goes

40

down in my report, though. Makes it look as if I've got my finger on what's going on. Or in the case of Bogger Hall, I suppose, what's not going on."

"I've just thought...." Mrs Anstruther's hand went to her mouth in alarm. "I don't think I turned the cooker off at home. I'd better get straight back and have a look."

"Tell you what I'll do, then," said the officer helpfully, "I'll run you back, with your bicycle. Then I'll pop out again to Bogger Hall. You give me the key and I'll do whatever has to be done. Switch the heaters on or whatever."

Now Mrs Anstruther looked really alarmed. "I can't impose on you and your time, Robin...." It was first name terms now: Mrs Anstruther was clearly not herself.

"Believe me, Sylvia, it's no bother at all. Some things are more important than just doing the job by the book. We're not put on earth just to follow careers. We're here to help others. That's how we'll be judged." The constable was feeling better now than he had felt since getting up.

"I've just remembered, silly old woman," Mrs Anstruther said. "It's Wednesday, isn't it? And I'm not supposed to go to the 'All till Thursdays. Got it wrong again. Me mind must be going."

But Pc Costive was just getting into his stride. "What'll matter in the end, Sylvia—when I come to be weighed up - is not how many people I booked for speeding, or petty larceny, but how many fellow human beings I helped. Anyway—here we are."

Mrs Anstruther gave another choking sound as Bogger Hall loomed round a bend in all its glory. "Hallo," said Pc Costive. "What's this, then—somebody beat us to it?"

A grey Ford Sierra of the type used by the younger, more desperate type of commission-based salesman, or by newly-made peers of the realm contracting a short-term car hire, was parked up by the gates of the hideous mansion. "Gurp," said Mrs Anstruther, obviously more confused than ever.

"Burglars, d'you think?" Pc Costive pulled in his Land Rover behind the Sierra. There was just room, but not much. "They're getting cheekier, you know. I reckon there's more break-ins during daylight hours these days than after dark. Good job I came, eh?"

"I've never seen it before," was all Mrs Anstruther could find to say. "You want to be careful. A lot of 'em are armed these days, they say."

Pc Costive put on his cap, braced his shoulders, and licked his lips. "We'll see about that," he said. "Got the key?"

As Mrs Anstruther fumbled in the folds of her upper clothing both noticed that her hands were shaking.

"Nothing to be frightened of," said the officer with what was meant to be reassurance. "Most of these chaps are cowards. You just stick with me and keep behind."

He had for a few quite exhilarating seconds contemplated hammering at the front door and shouting to whoever was inside that the game was up, they were surrounded, and to come out with hands on heads. Then it dawned on him that he was not armed. He would rather have liked to have been armed, not because he was particularly nervous, but because he had always wanted to hold a revolver out with two hands like they did on the television. That was another item on the downside of being stationed out in the sticks — no-one seemed to think it was worthwhile giving you firearms instruction. "We'll go round the back," he whispered. "I've blocked 'em in with the Land Rover."

Ducking whenever he passed a side window, Pc Costive led the way round to the back. Mrs Anstruther hardly needed to duck, being too short to be easily noticed.

To the officer's surprise the back door was already open. To his even greater consternation the concreted area around it was scattered

42

with small bits of bread-crust and crumbs from among which a robin, two chaffinches and a blackbird rose with bad grace on being disturbed.

The policeman motioned Mrs Anstruther behind him, flattened himself against the wall, gave the door a poke with is foot, and waited. Nothing happened. Emboldened, he peered slowly round the aperture, but found himself in a sort of lobby or portico from which another door led deeper into the house. He tried its handle. The door gave, but in giving emitted a squeal like an injured animal. The officer held his breath, his heart beating rather faster than he would have wished his superiors to have known.

"Come in," sang out a cheerful male voice from the inside. "Or shut the door. It's bloody draughty in here."

Pc Costive pushed open the door and peered into a large, comfortable, and for the time of the year at least, warm kitchen. An Aga stove radiated pleasantly, the table bore a teapot, a jug of milk, two cups and saucers, and a plate half full of biscuits. Just in the process of climbing to his feet was a man quite unfamiliar to the officer—a middle-aged man of medium height, slightly stooping, slightly greying, with a pleasant, amiable smile and an incipient grey moustache. A man who looked rather less like a burglar than, say, an electronics worker from somewhere like Swindon.

The officer barely acknowledged the man. His eyes were fixed —if eyes half out of their sockets can be said to be fixed—on the other occupant of the kitchen—a middle-aged woman with a startling pallor, raven-black hair only partly covered with a mantilla-like square of black lace. The rest of her clothes were black too but they were set off around the throat by an oblong of white collar such as our clergy wear. Her shoes were sensibly flat and laced, but of a grotesquely large size. Pc Costive stared. Then: "Now then," he said. "What's all this?" It seemed the only appropriate thing to say.

43

7

"Tea anybody?" inquired Norman Gribb hospitably. "Cup of tea, madam, officer? Milk and sugar?" He poured calmly and amiably, as a good host should. The faces of the others, however, were a picture. Pc Costive still stood goggle-eyed, and having taken his cap off at the first sight of a female, stood twisting it now in his hands; Mrs Sylvia Anstruther stood well back, looking as if she was trying to melt into the furniture, or sink down through the floor tiles; whilst the lady in black maintained an almost waxwork-like stillness and silence, looking at no-one in particular but fixing her gaze on the bell contraption high upon the wall which in the house's earliest years had indicated to servants in the kitchen which room the great and good above stairs were summoning them from.

"Perhaps before we go any further," said Gribb pleasantly, "I should introduce myself."

"I think you might do rather more than that, sir," said Pc Costive. "You might for instance explain what you are doing breaking and entering into a dwelling house." Things were not going at all the way the good officer had expected, and he was feeling more than a little put out. He accepted a cup of tea however.

"My name is Gribb — Norman Gribb," said Norman Gribb. "Sugar perhaps? And I am the new Lord Bogger. Of Bogger Hall — which accounts for my being in it. Taking possession, I suppose you might say."

While a pale Mrs Anstruther seemed about to genuflect, Pc Costive did not indicate whether he believed Gribb or not. He turned accusingly to the lady in black. "And this person?" he asked with undisguised hostility. "I've got a very good idea we've met before, madam. Or should I say *sir*?"

"Reverend if you please," said the woman in black. "And of course we've met before. You are Police Constable Robin de Vere

44

Costive, and the lady with you is Mrs Sylvia Anstruther. I am the Reverend Ximenez, Michelle Ximenez, formerly Miguel Ximenez, Vicar of Boggerthwaite."

The new Lord Bogger was nodding enthusiastically, passing biscuits. Pc Costive took two. "Quite true what she says, apparently. She was telling me the story before you turned up. Quite incredible, but then they can do amazing things these days."

"You mean to tell me," said Pc Costive through a mouthful of biscuit, "that you have changed yourself, or been changed, from the Reverend Miguel Ximenez to the female equivalent?"

"Correct," said the lady vicar.

"Does the Bishop know?" demanded the officer, "because he jolly well ought to know. I'm not at all sure that he'll approve. I'm not at all sure that your parishioners will approve. I'm pretty sure I don't approve. Do you approve, Mrs Anstruther?"

Mrs Anstruther had almost reached the stage where she imagined her wish to become entirely invisible had been fulfilled, but the policeman brought her back with a start. "Approve? Well, it's not really for me to say, is it"

"And what are you doing here anyway?" the officer went on. "We've heard this gentleman's story, and it may well be true or not true: we'll have to check it out. But you, madam — what are you doing at Bogger Hall?"

The vicar shrugged , and looked to Lord Bogger as if for support.

"Amazing story," said the new tenant of Bogger Hall. "The Reverend was, until a few weeks ago, to all intents and purposes a man. A male. He had for some years been on that wing of the Anglican Church which passionately believed in the right of women to be ordained within that Church. As we all know, until recently that right was stubbornly withheld — rightly or wrongly — by the Church authorities. The Reverend Ximenez, therefore, decided that a way of forcing the Synod's hand would be to change his own

45

sex, so that the Church would be presented with a fait accompli —
a vicar and a woman in the same person."

"He wouldn't be the first woman round here to be unfrocked,"
said Pc Costive unpleasantly.

"Please don't be coarse, officer," said Lord Bogger.

"Never mind about coarse," said Pc Costive, reddening
nevertheless just the slightest touch. "I want to know what she—
he - the Reverend—is doing on these premises." He stared at the
vicar with no charity. "I've been looking all over for you."

The Reverend took a deep breath. "It was like this, officer. I
needed somewhere quiet while the, er change was taking effect.
Bogger Hall was empty so...."

"So I gave her permission to stay here for a while," put in Lord
Bogger, with the air of someone who thinks too big a fuss is being
made about nothing.

"Is that right, Mrs Anstruther?" The officer turned to
Boggerthwaite's second oldest inhabitant. "You look after the
place: have you seen this....person on the premises before?"

"I didn't realise...." stammered Mrs Anstruther.

"She didn't realise that the vicar was here," interjected Lord
Bogger briskly. "Because on the days that Mrs Struther was due
to visit the reverend would go off on a long walk. So you see it's
really nothing to do with her, is it Sylvia-Anne? What a nice name
that is, Sylvia-Anne. I had an aunt named Sylvia, when I was a lad
and another named Anne. But with you there's two for the price of
one."

"It's all very suspicious, this," said Pc Costive. "I mean, I hadn't
the faintest idea that you, sir, were taking up residence. Did you,
Mrs Anstruther?"

"Gurp," gulped that lady, looking wildy at Lord Bogger.

"I'm afraid there's been an unfortunate misunderstanding. Mr

46

Peel, my lawyer, would appear to have failed to communicate. This does happen from time to time with members of the legal profession, as I'm sure you've noticed in your court work, officer."

"That's all very well," said Costive obstinately. "But how do I know you're who you say you are?"

"You don't, I suppose. I mean, Norman Gribb: it says that on my driving licence. But as to Baron Bogger, well, I haven't had time to get round to having that recorded anywhere yet. You'd better ring Mr Peel. Wait a minute, I've got his number somewhere."

Lord Bogger extracted a pocket diary from about his person, and found Mr Peel's number at the same time as shoving a lightweight telephone across the kitchen table. Costive frowned, dialled, then frowned again while he waited.

"Hallo," the officer said eventually. "Mr Peel? Mr John Peel? Pc Costive speaking, Boggerthwaite Police....Boggerthwaite, sir. B-O-G-....Oh you do know. What about Lord Bogger, then—d'you know him?" The officer slapped a hand over the mouthpiece and appealed to Gribb. "Surely he can't be drunk this early in the day, can he? Keeps singing D'ye Ken John Peel and giggling....Hallo....Yes, about medium height, small moustache, greying hair. No, he doesn't, not at all. Or not as I've always imagined nobility—not having come across all that many, sir.... What? ....Yes I will if you'll hold on." He turned to Norman Gribb, proffering the receiver. "Wants a word with you."

Gribb took the instrument. "Hallo? Gribb....sorry, I mean Lord Bogger here....No, I haven't....What?....No, I am not in trouble with the Law already, as you put it....No, not the brightest of specimens if you ask me. That's not the point: it might have helped if you'd let Mrs Struther know....What? Mrs Struther - Mrs Sylvia-Anne Struther....Oh I see, it's one word. Pity. Sounds much nicer the other way. Anyway, she wasn't expecting me because nobody told her. And that means you didn't tell her. Heads will roll, Peel. A

47

case of hanging, drawing and quartering, I shouldn't wonder. Bye."

Then, looking round the company with the air of a seven-stone weakling who has just humiliated the beach bully, he offered replenishment of tea cups.

Constable Costive responded first. Much as it might be nice, his manner implied, to hang around all morning sipping tea and chatting about this and that, duty called. One thing he would like to know before departure, though, was whether the vicar intended to resume pastoral work "like that".

The Rev. Ximenez gave him the sort of look that Lazarus might have used on someone knocking him up early and asking if he was going to be long with his resurrection. "There will be an announcement in due course," said the vicar.

When the officer had gone, ushering a shaken Mrs Anstruther before him, Lord Bogger topped up his own and the vicar's tea-cups. "I don't think either of us made a deep bosom friend there, old duck," he said.

"He's a funny boy," mused Ms Ximenez. "He is, I believe, not quite the full peseta."

"And the old girl?"

"Mrs Anstruther is part of a very large family indeed" replied the vicar. "I have met her sisters on the fish-quays of Barcelona, on the stalls of a dozen markets from the old Les Halles to Petticoat-lane, and on every back-street corner-end general shop in the world. She is as tough as old boots—the old fashioned, real leather kind, hob-nailed—she knows everybody, trusts none of them, and understands more of their business than they will ever do themselves. She has a nose as sharp as a Toledo stiletto, fingers as sticky as fly-papers, and a heart of pure gold. Well, let's say just twelve carat, but gold nonetheless."

"She knew you were here all along?"

"Mrs Anstruther is the most loyal member of my congregation.

She cleans the church for nothing, she looks after the vicarage for nothing. When she knew I was looking for a little retreat, she gave me the key to this place—your place, I know, but you were not using it. She is a true Christian, our Sylvia. Which is more than can be said for most of the inhabitants of this place."

"Tell me," said Lord Bogger. He was not a practising churchman himself; there had seemed to be little point in a place like Swindon, which God, if He existed, seemed to have left very much to its own devices. In the Bogger Valley things might be different. He would probably be expected to give a lead in such matters, and perhaps he might even quite enjoy it.

"There is only one other old Boggerthwaite standard left," said the vicar. "And that is Mr William Nattrass our verger. Old Billy is a cross-grained, idle, tight-fisted old sot. He detests Mrs Anstruther with a passion, and I believe the feeling is reciprocated. The rest of the village come from all points of the compass and from all walks of life - or all waddles of life in most cases. Some come to church from time to time, but mostly not. Now Stoatholme is a different matter....."

"Ah yes, Stoatholme," mused Lord Bogger, his mind's eye occupied by damp council houses, boarded up windows, and young girls in leather mini-skirts.

"Stoatholme is what you'd call a clergyman's challenge—sorry, clergyperson, I suppose now: it takes some getting used to. Stoatholme if it's anything, is non-conformist, in more senses than one. There was a quite powerful Methodist chapel operating at one time, but just as along the fringes of the old Ottoman Empire there were odd Muslim sects who did not follow the rest of Islam in their attitude towards strong drink so Stoatholme's Wesleyans shy away from total abstinence—quite a long way, most of them, and quite frequently. The chapel is closed, but the Goat and Compasses is well and truly open. I suppose I should stand up in the middle of the Sunny Lea Estate, or outside the Goat, and preach.

Perhaps one day, with God's help, I will, but then again perhaps I won't ...." The clergyperson tailed off and resumed contemplation of the servants' bell-system on the wall.

What rather intrigues me," said Lord Bogger, "is how you came to be a minister of the Anglican Church. There can't be many of you from Spain - or can there?:"

"Very few, I should think," said Michelle Ximenez. "And fewer still of the feminine gender. But I'm not really Spanish at all, you see. I was born in West Ham. My parents went to Spain on holiday years ago and couldn't afford the fare back. My Dad took to the place, got hooked on bull-fighting and Rioja. His name was Nobbs, and you couldn't have a matador with a name like Nobbs, could you? So he changed it to Ximenez. I saw no reason to change it back when I came of age. The Church authorities seem to have some difficulty in pronouncing it properly, so they tend to leave me alone. Suits me."

"And what would you suggest should be the role of the new Lord Bogger" The new Lord Bogger had strolled to the kitchen window and was looking out now on that part of his demesne bounded by the concrete backyard, a row of old dustbins, an empty dog-run and a dilapidated coal-house with a pile of coal before it. "I mean, am I expected to sit up here like the Queen in her palace, and reign? How does anyone reign? There's a limit to the number of bazaars I can open, or meetings I can chair."

"Depends what you want, my dear," said the vicar. Norman was not at all sure about the "my dear" part and busied himself trying to light the pipe he had bought himself in Keswick on his Lakeland arrival. He was one of those fortunate people who can take or leave cigarettes, probably because he didn't really enjoy them. But a pipe—well, a pipe was the sort of thing a rural lord sported, wasn't it? While he—well, while he did whatever it was that lords did.

The vicar was trying to help. "I mean, do you like the country? Do you want to keep it peaceful and natural and non-commercial?

Or...." The rest of her words were drowned out, shattered, by a terrifying roar which seemed to indicate that the skies were exploding.

WHEEEAARRGGHHHH!....Lord Bogger clapped his hands to his ears.

"Right on cue," smiled Ms Ximenez. "As I was saying - if you are a lover of the countryside you'll find, I'm afraid, that these days you have to share it with all sorts of other interests, of which the low flying of aircraft is but one."

Coming from the south of England, where aeroplane noise means a persistent but fairly low-level droning of international passenger jets, usually at a fair altitude, Norman had never before experienced the joys of listening to jet fighters roaring overhead at full throttle at a couple of hundred feet, driven by youths but recently recovered from teenage acne who often had not yet had the time to get round to passing a test qualifying them to drive saloon cars down England's green and pleasant lanes.

WHEEAARRGGHHHH! went another jet fighter.

"What the bloody hell!" said Lord Bogger. Then: "Sorry, vicar, but...."

"You'll get used to them," said the Reverend lady. "If not, a pair of industrial earplugs might come in handy."

"But....we're not at war any more, are we?"

"These lads are traditionalists," said the vicar. "They fly sorties over Scotland, to keep the Old Enemy at bay. Scotland hasn't got an air force that anyone's heard about, and their ack-ack's a bit on the primitive side—mostly sling-shot and bows and arrows."

AARRGGHHHHWHEEEEE! This one seemed narrowly to miss the chimney pots of Bogger Hall, if indeed there were any left.

"I used to ring up the Air Force to complain," said the vicar.

51

"They're ever so nice. They call you sir. They won't call me that any more, at least. Once I complained about night flights and they asked me if I'd made a note of the number of the plane. In pitch dark. Where was I?"

"Country quiet."

"Ah yes - do you want a peaceful countryside, or do you want one full of noise, traffic fumes, screaming kids, motor-bikes and mayhem?"

"I have a choice?"

"Not much, against monsters like those jets. But there are battles nearer home as well."

Lord Bogger nodded. He had managed now to get his pipe alight, and did not want to risk its extinction by neglecting it to talk at any length.

"This village," went on the vicar, "the whole of the Lake District, the total British countryside if you like—is split—down the middle between those who like it as it is, or at least as it was not long since, and those who want to turn it into a marketable commodity like fish and chips.

"There seems to be a mania in places like this to attract tourists", continued the vicar "The councils are all for it: someone only has to mention the word 'tourism' and everyone starts nodding that it's a Good Thing. I've seen a bit of what happened in Spain. Nearer here I've seen perfectly honest little market towns like Keswick and Ambleside grow into nests of touristy shops linked together by permanent traffic jams. And Grasmere! Poor old Bill Wordsworth would turn in his grave. And the parish council here is envious of Grasmere! They keep on about it: why does Grasmere get all the goodies and people only seem to come to Boggerthwaite when they're lost?

"McGurk at the pub's all for tourism, of course: that's what he came here for. To make money out of visitors. But the one to watch is Gladys Loudwater. She's chairman—sorry, chairperson—of the Parish Council, and if she had her way Boggerthwaite would become another Disneyland tomorrow. The sad thing about poor old Gladys is that she'd hardly stand to gain a penny. All she wants is for a grateful Chamber of Trade (which thank God we haven't got yet) to put up a statue of her on the village green as mother of what she thinks is progress. You could have some rare old battles with Mother Loudwater."

Lord Bogger took the pipe out of his mouth. It had failed to keep going in spite of his efforts. "Tell me," he said, still sucking at it, "about this Mahmoud character I keep hearing about. Reckons he owns the place. Is that right?"

The vicar put her head on one side and considered. "Interesting chap, our Arpad Mahmoud. He certainly has social ambitions, but just who's side he's on when it comes to the question of commercialising Boggerthwaite, I really wouldn't know."

"And is Mr Mahmoud on the Parish Council"

"You can bet your life he is," said the vicar. "And he actually attends meetings." Ms Ximenez turned silent for a few moments, looking thoughtfully at Lord Bogger. "I wonder how you two'll get on together. You see, he'd very much like to be you—or at least to have your title. After all, he bought Mirkin Grange from your predecessor. And the Grange is much bigger than this place. Tell you what...."

"What?"

"It's the parish council meeting tonight. The annual meeting as it happens. Which means anyone can go along and see how their elected representatives have been behaving themselves during the year. Why don't you have a look in? Make yourself known. Weigh up the opposition?"

"Are you going?"

The vicar smoothed down her skirt. "I think I'm going to have to.

I've got to come out properly some time, and now that the charming Constable Costive knows what's going on it'll be all round the village like pox round a battalion of guardsmen. So I might as well: it'll give the buggers something to think about, if you'll pardon my Spanish."

8

The Arpad Mahmoud Institute and Reading Room occupies a strategic position in the centre of Boggerthwaite. It stands at the back of the village green almost exactly halfway between St Ethelbogger's Church and the Dehydrated Rambler Hotel. In front of it is a telephone kiosk and beside that a post box and a bus stop. The latter is really hardly use or ornament, since only one bus a day has run through the village in each direction since 1987, two years before the Arpad Mahmoud Institute was, well, instituted.

It was built to replace an earlier village hall which stood down near the bridge, the only building at the lower end of the village to escape intact the Great Bogger Valley Devastation of 1922 when a large part of the village, occupied mostly by workers from Dabster and Tyson's Mill, slowly but inexorably slid into the Bogger Beck which was in full spate after a cloudburst. The foundations of these cottages had been disturbed by the prospecting activities of the then Lord Bogger, who thought he had discovered a thick seam of anthracite beneath them. Lord Bogger was mistaken, but by then it was too late and he was forced into an expensive lawsuit to avoid paying compensation to the hapless residents of the tumbled cottages, most of whom emigrated. Mr Peel could tell you all about it; his father handled the case for Lord Bogger.

The old village hall had been an honest enough building, if a little on the leaky side. But it was built of local stone with a slate roof and at least looked as it had some claim to belong where it was, which Mr Mahmoud's subsequent gift to the community did not. This was a prefabricated structure, its panels pebble-dashed with little light coloured stones which belonged hundreds of miles

54

away, and it had a curious clock-bearing tower with an onion-shaped dome which would have looked grand, everyone agreed, if Boggerthwaite had been in the Lebanon, which it never had been. But the place had electricity and running water, and there were a number of rooms inside so that the Women's Institute could meet at the same time as the Over-Sixties Club held a whist drive (which it never did) and the Youth Club had a committee meeting, which would have been difficult as there was no youth club, let alone a committee.

Anyway, it was big enough for parish council meetings and could easily accommodate far more than had ever been curious enough to want to attend. This evening it was unusually full, and extra chairs had to be borrowed from St Ethelbogger's. It would not be easy to say whether most of the public came to catch a glimpse of the new Lord Bogger or to have a good gawp at their sex-changed vicar, but one way or another both Pc Costive and Mrs Anstruther had done a good job spreading the word.

It being a Wednesday evening, and early in the year, few of Boggerthwaite's weekenders were present, but there was a larger number than usual of folk from the Sunny Lea Estate. "They're mostly from two families," Ms Ximenez told Lord Bogger as they parked as near as they could to the Institute. "There are the Sackvilles and the Wormwalds. The Sackvilles are like human life—nasty brutish and short; the Wormwalds are nasty, brutish but a little taller on the whole. The families are not well disposed towards each other."

In the hall itself the Wormwalds—there must have been nearly twenty of them—occupied the back seats to the left of the hall; the Sackvilles, in comparable numbers, those to the right. Both factions kept up a loud commentary on the looks of those members of the council who had already taken their place behind a long table facing down the hall. In the chair already was a woman who, surely, must be the Mrs Gladys Loudwater Lord Bogger had been warned about. How to describe her? His Lordship considered the question and decided that by far the best way would be to say that in any given crowd Mrs Loudwater would have been the one who most closely resembled every man's idea of a dedicated committee person. Her features were not distinctive (although she might have been quite comely when younger), her colouring did not stand out, and by stature she was neither fat nor thin, tall or particularly short. Yet there was that about her that shouted to the rooftops: "Point of Order!"

Next to her sat a dark, balding, bearded man with bushy eyebrows and a crafty expression. A large meerschaum tobacco pipe was gripped in his teeth, and every few seconds he enveloped the chairperson in a thick cloud of smoke. He appeared to say nothing, but nodded a lot. "The clerk," nudged Mr Ximenez. "Mr Bean—Mr David Bean—a sort of writer chap. Wouldn't trust him as far as I could throw him."

Lord Bogger recognised the beautifully-made but dungaree-clad figure of Ms Georgina D'Arcy, who clambered into the seat on the other side of the Chair as if she was climbing into the control cabin of a very large and awkward JCB. "We've met," Lord Bogger whispered.

"And the next one to her? No? That's Kurt Magersfontein, who farms out on the Thugthwaite back road. Says he's South African, but I have my doubts. Does experimental work with animals, like trying to breed self-gathering sheep and pigs that'll lay eggs so that you'll get your complete traditional English breakfast from the one beast. He's completely potty, but he gives me the creeps, our Mr Magersfontein. The one next to him you'll probably know if you've been in the pub—Jake Otter, our village know-all. Ah, and here we are...."

There was a stirring at the side doorway of the hall, and in walked a dark woman of ample girth, not veiled exactly , but swathed in a heavy black-and-white scarf such as those worn by supporters of Newcastle United. She was followed closely by two other ladies of similar build, complexion and scarves and then by a much younger woman—Lord Bogger guessed she would hardly be twenty—with long blonde hair, an expensive-looking fur coat open enough to show that her skirt was tight, red and very short. She was engaged in cheerfully animated conversation over her shoulder with a short, balding man with a dark complexion, even darker glasses and a moustache which was darker still. His suit was grey and of a boring but pricey cut. "Mr Arpad Mahmoud and Mrs Mahmoud," whispered the Rev. Ximenez.

"What—the young blonde?"

"All four of them," said the vicar. "The blonde's the latest: Mandy they call her. The others arrived with Mr M. He is not, you see, of our religious persuasion."

"Poor sod," said Norman Gribb, who was thinking, for almost the first time since leaving Swindon, of Mrs Renie Gribb, multiplied by four.

The Mahmoud wives found themselves seats in the body of the hall, while their husband smoothed himself into a chair at the top table. He was smiling and nodding all round and kept raising one hand as if to acknowledge applause, of which there was none. Lord Bogger had an uncomfortable feeling that the Levantine gentleman was giving him a good staring although the glasses were too dark for him to be sure.

Mrs Loudwater did the opening in a falsely cheerful manner which might have raised the envy of Dame Edna Everage. She didn't exactly call everyone 'darlings', but the thought seemed to be there. She got Mr Bean the clerk to read the minutes of the previous annual meeting, which he did in tones in which deep boredom and sarcasm seemed to be about evenly mixed. The next item, therefore, was matters arising, which turned out, as is the case with every parish council in the land, to be one, the parking of cars, and, two, the fouling of footpaths by dogs. The first was over fairly swiftly: that is in under a quarter of an hour. The second

57

got people more comfortably into their stride, which was like a giant's, both lengthy and slow.

Mrs Loudwater got in first: "The trouble is that people just do not train their four-legged friends properly. They should develop a sense of public spirit. Privileges bring responsibilities...."

"We all know who the culprits are." This was from Old Billy Nattrass, planted deep in the body of the hall, but unmistakeable in accent.

"Thankyou Mr Nattrass. If I may just finish...."

But there was no question of that once Old Billy got his jaw locked on to a subject. "There's that savage little bitch of Mr Otter's, and also that big daft thing of Mrs Costives' whatever it is."

Mrs Bryony Costive, red-faced, was on her feet oozing indignation. "That is a Bernese mountain dog and it does not...."

"A Burmese mountain dog's got to shit the same as any other," Old Billy interrupted. "It should be kept on a lead, or better still put down."

Mrs Loudwater banged her gavel, or rather thumped on the table with a heavy glass ashtray, which did the job just as well. "Whoever the culprits may be, ladies and gentlemen, they should remember when embarking on a walk to take with them a handy-sized shovel —it doesn't need to be expensive—and a plastic bag, discreetly furled. If the dog cannot be manoeuvred quickly enough to the gutter or grass verge, then it should immediately be scooped up and taken home...."

"You'd never scoop up that big daft Burmese mountain dog," said Old Billy. "It's far too big to get in a plastic bag, and anyway, it'd have your hand off."

"Not the dog, Mr Nattrass," said Mrs Loudwater. "It's her, business."

"And I move *next* business Madam Chair." It was Matty Ouskin,

58

sitting two rows in front of Lord Bogger and clearly in need of a visit to Mr MGurk's establishment.

Mrs Loudwater looked incensed. "When you have lived in this village a little longer, Mr Ouskin, you may realise that democratic debate is not to be stifled like that. As I was saying, the only way this menace can be eradicated is for us all to be public-spirited. If we see a dog fouling the footpath we must remonstrate with its owner. If that doesn't work we should not hesitate...."

"Why has everyone got it in for dogs?" It was Ms D'Arcy, who, being a schoolteacher, presumably felt she could not let her voice rest for too long in case it seized up and became unusable. "What about sheep? What about cows: you can't walk across a field round here without getting you boots covered. Only the other day...."

The man pointed out earlier as Kurt Magersfontein the experimental farmer now climbed to his feet. He was a large, fleshyfaced man with rimless spectacles which reflected back the light in a rather sinister fashion. "I happen to own the fields which Miss D'Arcy is referring to." He had a thick, mittel-European accent far removed from the soft, lilting tones of a genuine South African. "And I do not ask her to walk across them."

"I am not a Miss D'Arcy," snapped Ms D'Arcy. "I am a Georgina D'Arcy or, if you prefer brevity, a Ms D'Arcy. And I think the conditions under which you keep your livestock are absolutely unhygienic. Those poor animals are expected to eat the same grass that they excrete upon. And then we're expected to pay good money for the milk. I only thank God you're not in charge of human beings although I have my suspicions about your past, *Herr* Magersfontein...."

The farmer began to splutter and seethe in a most alarming manner, and might well have gone on to have a full-blown heart attack if Mr Bean, who was also conscious of the time and how many of the permitted hours of drinking were left to the evening,

59

reminded his Chair that there was a proposition before the meeting to go on to next business.

"And I second that." It was Matty Ouskin again, and if anyone noticed that he had also been the proposer, they were fed up enough with dog hygiene to ignore the fact and to pass on to Item, No. Three, which concerned the parish accounts, was extremely boring, but was over before anyone actually fell asleep.

Item No Four, Any Other Business, might have been equally brief if it had not been for Councillor Rory McGurk wanting to know what steps the council was taking to attract tourism to the Bogger Valley. "Why should we slumber away in the past when all other parts of the Lake District are cashing in and making themselves prosperous? Look at Grasmere...." At the mention of which there was a general snarling and hooting from the body of the hall as if Sodom had been mentioned at a congress of the Mothers' Union.

"It's Boggerthit Bleezins soon, Madam Chair." It was Old Billy Nattrass again, but having raised this interesting fact he appeared to have forgotten why he had done so, and sat down again scratching his head.

"My friend is quite right." It was Mr Jake Otter. "The Bleezins are a colourful occasion whose roots go back hundreds of years. Why can't we put on a special effort this year that'll pull in the visitors? I'm sure our Clerk here could write up an article for the Press which would draw folk in from all arts and parts. Make himself a few bob on the side too. We could advertise...."

Mrs Loudwater looked almost amused. "You've heard the financial report, Mr Otter."

"And what does he know about our ancient, time honoured customs anyway?" Old Billy Nattrass was on his feet again, having recovered his thread now that Jake Otter had started.

"Who, me?" said Jake Otter.

"Please address your remarks through the Chair," said Mrs Loudwater.

"Aye, you," Old Billy went on. "Address your remarks through the chair. You've only been here five minutes, and from Birmingham, wherever that is."

"I think I know more about local customs than you do, wherever I come from" shouted Jake Otter. "Do you know the origins of Boggerthit Bleezins?"

"Never mind the horigins," roared Billy. "What do you know about the pig racing we used to have? Or the braffle dancing...."

"Pig racing!" said Jake Otter with scorn. "That's about all you'd be fit for."

"Every Thursday evening in the summer we had pig racing down the main street," said Old Billy. "And braffle dancing. My father was champion braffle player in his heyday...."

"Perhaps the meeting might learn what braffles were," said Mrs Loudwater, trying to retain control.

"Braffles was musical hinstruments," said Old Billy. "Made out of yows' horns. That was the trebles, the yow's horns. Tups' horns for the bass. You blew 'em, and people'd dance. There was wrestlin', gurnin', collie shearin', half-nurdlin'. We had to mek our own hentertainment in them days. There was no such thing as television and these 'ere videos...."

The meeting might have degenerated into the sort of debate any two old men have in any old pub these days when confronted with the question What's Wrong With the Modern Generation? if landlord McGurk had not proposed the formation of a committee of Ways and Means to sort out the tourism promotion question. Matty Ouskin seconded, for the hands of the clock were creeping round, and the motion was carried. Mrs Loudwater then called for nominations, which resulted in the election of almost all the regulars from the Rambler, who debated this question three times nightly in any case.

The meeting was about to wind up when Mr Bean was observed to be having a quiet word in the Chair's ear and nodding down into the body of the meeting. Mrs Loudwater smiled. "Ladies and gentlemen," she said. "It has been pointed out to me that we have in our midst this evening a very distinguished new resident. None other than the latest Lord Bogger of Bogger Hall. That is correct, is it not, my Lord?"

A hush fell on the meeting. Lord Bogger realised that there was to be no escape. So he stood and bowed and smiled and said thank you to Mrs Loudwater, and Matty Ouskin started up For He's A Jolly Good fellow, and even the Stoatholme contingent joined in with loud whistles and sharp, rasping sounds which might have come from traditional braffles for all anyone knew. Some bright spark shouted: "Speech!" and Lord Bogger said he was not much of a speaker but he would try to live up to the standards set by his family in the past, which in turn provoked loud laughter and shouts of "That won't be hard!" from the Stoatholme sector. The meeting then concluded.

It was only as the fag-end of this democratic manifestation straggled out of the doors that Lord Bogger realised that the Rev. Michelle Ximenez was still by his side, looking rather relieved. "Would you believe it," she was saying. "I thought they'd all come to gawp at me and give me a hard time. But I really think nobody noticed. Such is conceit, and such is the effect of the Church upon the public today. "

"Come and have a drink," suggested Lord Bogger, taking the vicar's elbow.

9

"Lord Bogger, please excuse me, but I should be delighted to introduce myself."

The smiling figure of Mr Arpad Mahmoud was advancing on him, hand affably outstretched, flanked by Mrs Loudwater and the Clerk, with Mandy Mahmoud, Wife No. Four, hanging back a bit and yawning. The three other Mahmoud wives were huddled round the exit, swathed in scarves like football supporters after an inconclusive draw. There seemed to be no escape.

"Arpad Mahmoud, at your service," said the dark gent, shaking with a remarkably gentle hand for one so brisk. The smile was friendly enough, but it was still not possible to make out anything behind the shades. Mr Mahmoud checked, tut-tutted. "How impolite of me," he said, propelling Mrs Loudwater forward. The lady needed no propelling but gave Lord Bogger a handshake which would have done credit to a sumo wrestler.

"It has been a long time," breathed the Council Chair, dropping a slight curtsey with the air of a long-suffering Jacobite supporter greeting the late arrival of the King Across the Water.

"Come and meet the wife," smiled Mr Mahmoud, switching his propelling hand to Lord Bogger's elbow. He has worked this joke before, Lord Bogger guessed - many times. "This is Mandy. Say hello to His Lordship, Mandy."

"Hi," said Mandy. She had been chewing something before this speech, probably gum. Now, having made it, she resumed chewing, and fixed a bored gaze on the Reverend Ximenez's figure.

Mr Mahmoud led on. "And Fatima, Scheherazade, and Esmat." All three of the scarve-swathed ladies regarded Lord Bogger with dark, expressionless eyes, nodded slightly, but did not proffer hands.

"And let me present," said Lord Bogger, with just the slightest trace of mischief in his look, "The Reverend Ximenez. The Reverend Michelle Ximenez."

The three older Mahmoud wives bobbed again slightly, Mandy said "Hi", Mr Mahmoud flashed white teeth and bowed, and Mrs Loudwater said rather coldly: "We've met of course."

"I would deem it a great pleasure, and honour," said Mr Mahmoud, "if you would all join us for a little soiree at my place. It would be a pleasure to get to know Your Lordship further."

Lord Bogger glanced at the vicar. Would such an invitation cause her embarrassment? Apparently not by the look of her.

They travelled in what seemed like a whole fleet of vehicles, although perhaps there were no more than three; it was hard to tell in the dark. They were big, powerful, four-wheeled-drive jobs, and none of your Japanese imitations so popular with farmers. There was much opening and shutting of doors by uniformed chauffeurs, and much revving of soft-purring engines. The four Mahmoud wives travelled in one vehicle, Mrs Loudwater in solitary state in another (Mr Bean having managed to effect his escape in the direction of the pub), and Mr Mahmoud himself opened the rear door of the leading vehicle for Lord Bogger and the vicar and followed them in. There was much soft comfort in the back, a smell of expensive leather. Lord Bogger could have sworn a small pennant blew from the bonnet, but could not have told you what device it bore.

"Mirkin Grange is not far," said Mr Mahmoud quietly. "I don't know if you have ever seen the place? Family photographs, perhaps."

"Never," said Lord Bogger. Then, realising that his silence called for some explanation, felt that he had better play along. "It was not, I believe, one of my father's favourite houses." This was, he reasoned, quite true. His father had been a Wiltshire bookmaker, or at least a bookie's runner in the furtive days before the

64

legalisation of betting shops. His favourite houses had been the Dog and Duck, the Crown, and the Red Lion in that order. Mr Mahmoud was not to know this, but he looked a little put out, as far as it was possible to read his emotions in the dimness of the car. "I did not have the pleasure of meeting your father personally," he said.

I don't suppose you had, Lord Bogger felt like saying, unless you were in the habit of passing betting slips in the Gents' lavatories of one of the aforementioned hostelries. Instead: "He didn't like this part of the world at all." That was true at any rate. Old Mr Gribb had probably never heard of the Lake District, there being no race-course nearer to it than Carlisle and Cartmel.

"I believe he preferred a warmer climate," said Mr Mahmoud, apparently somewhat mollified. "The West Indies, I think."

Norman Gribb thought it hardly worth the effort to explain his labyrinthine family connections, or that, from what he had heard, the last Lord Bogger had been barely old enough to have been his younger brother never mind his father.

"It is strange," mused Mr Mahmoud. "I, who was born in a hot country—or at least one comfortably warm—chose to leave it for this. A case of grass being greener, I suppose."

"Oh, I know all right," said Lord Bogger. "Bless me, yes, I know. And it doesn't come much greener than round here." Then, as an afterthought: "Ireland perhaps, or parts of the West of Scotland."

"I love the soft mists," said Mr Mahmoud. "I love the rain. Other people pay out vast sums to escape the wet, to lie on a beach in the sun, and burn. We are never satisfied."

"I take it you don't live in Boggerthwaite the whole time," Lord Bogger probed. "You will travel a great deal, I imagine, in the course of business?"

"Alas, that is true. I have a modest flat in London, another in Paris. It is necessary. But not as necessary as it used to be. I can get much work done from here. I can delegate a certain amount, and the Fax machine is a great boon. Do you not find it so?"

"I believe my secretary has such a contraption," said Lord Bogger loftily.

"Of course," said Mr Mahmoud. "And where were you based before you came as it were, to claim your inheritance?"

"Oh, here and there.," said Norman Gribb. "I have a little place down in the West country where I spent a fair bit of time." He supposed Swindon was sort of West Country if you stretched popular geography.

"And shall you be spending much time here, do you think?"

"Oh, a fair bit," said Lord Bogger airily. *"Noblesse oblige* and all that."

"Please?"

"Duties, old chap."

Mr Mahmoud seemed to understand duties. "A scandalous system," he said. "In my country we have no such thing as robbing the dead through the living. But I say 'my country': I really like to think of England now as my country. But we are home; I told you it was not far."

They were driving now between two large stone pillars which each bore what looked like a rampant rabbit, but was probably some mythic beast belonging to heraldry. Mr Mahmoud caught the direction of Lord Bogger's gaze. "Ah, the Boggerthwaite hares! Properly, I suppose, my Lord, they are part of your heritage, even if I acquired them commercially. Now I have often wondered, why hares? Can you enlighten me?"

"They're not hares really," said Lord Bogger. "They're rabbits. My great, great grandfather's joke, I believe. He had something like 22 children."

"Then perhaps an old ram would have been more appropriate," laughed Mr Mahmoud.

"You are entitled to your opinion," said Lord Bogger stiffly.

The headlights of the vehicle picked out a long tarmacadamised road through a majestic grove of beech and horse chestnut. In full summer leaf they would look magnificent. Just now, in late March, they revealed glimpses through their bare branches of a large Palladian looking building with lawns around and approached by a double flight of stone steps. "Welcome to Mirkin Grange," said Mr Mahmoud with feeling.

A large oblong of light appeared at the top of the steps as the vehicles drew up, and framed in the doorway from which it shone stood a portly, bald-headed figure in black evening-dress—Jeeves to the life. He bowed good evenings all round, then stepped aside to allow the company into the house.

And what a house! Huge entrance hall with the line of the exterior twin staircases continuing its sweep into the upper regions. Twin log fires blazed, one at each end of the hall, and there were dozens of animals' heads around the walls, as if a whole menagerie had butted through to view the human inmates and had got stuck for good. Elks there were, buffalo, zebra and all sorts of wild buck; lions, a tiger or two, you name it.... Only the Boggerthwaite rabbits, or hares, seemed to be missing. "Welcome," said Mr Mahmoud again, beaming now. "Welcome, as it were, to your roots. And to you, Reverend lady, welcome too."

The transformed vicar bowed. "Bless all within," she said.

"Now, after all that talk of dog-dirt and parochial finance, I think a drink is called for" said the host. He led his little party through to the library, where yet another log fire burned brightly and a whole off-licence of drinks stood on tables guarded by three rather nice-looking maids.

"Wine, whisky?" Mr Mahmoud clasped his hands together like an old-time grocer. "I have just the thing to keep this March wind out. Old Sporran, twelve years old. Try some?"

Lord Bogger took a glass. The pale liquor seemed to slip down his throat without any need on his part to swallow. It then started to scald his gullet as if he had foolishly tried to gargle a glassful of boiling disinfectant. "Ugh," said Lord Bogger.

"You like?"

"I think," choked His Lordship, "that it would be no more than the plain truth to say that I have never tasted anything quite like it."

"It comes from a rather special distillery near Inverness," said Mr Mahmoud.

"A special consignment?"

"I own the distillery," said Mr Mahmoud modestly.

"None of my business, of course," said Lord Bogger. "But I'd've thought that would be rather against your religious persuasion?"

"Persuasion?" Mr Mahmoud laughed, showing very white teeth. "Religious? My dear chap."

"But your wives?"

"I am very fond of women, Lord Bogger. So as far as women are concerned I am a Moslem. I am also very fond of old Scotch whisky, so as far as drink is concerned I am a Christian if you like. The best of both worlds." He shook with silent laughter. "You are not married yourself? There is no Lady Bogger?"

Norman Gribb experienced one of those fallings in the pit of the stomach he remembered from a childhood summons to the headmaster's study. "You're right," he said. "There is no Lady Bogger."

"And so no heirs?" Mr Mahmoud managed to look sad.

"None that know anything about it," said Lord Bogger.

"We'll have to remedy that." Mrs Loudwater had seen a chance to get her twopennorth in. "I'm sure there are plenty of eminently suitable young ladies in our little valley. It would be nice to have the home-grown product, wouldn't it?"

Norman Gribb remembered the pair of girls standing by the roadside at Stoatholme, and regarded Mrs Loudwater with a sort of flirtatiousness he certainly did not feel. "I fear that all the eligible ladies around here will already have been spoken for."

Mrs Loudwater simpered.

"And what are your views on the question of tourism, Lord Bogger?" It was Michelle Ximenez, changing the subject, forcing the pace.

"It's not really for me to say is it? Having only just arrived."

"But they've all only just arrived," said the vicar. "Our kind host here is from....well, the Mediterranean. I am from Sunny Spain, and our good Chair-person, if I hear her accent correctly, comes from Liverpool...."

"I beg your pardon, ma'am," said Mrs Loudwater, apparently much offended. "I happen to come from Altrincham, which I think you'll find is in Cheshire."

"The point is, do we want tourists, or not?" The vicar was sticking to her guns.

"But of course we want tourists," snapped Mrs Loudwater. "How else is this place ever going to get anywhere? Look at your church: what d'you get on a Sunday?. Half a dozen of the same old faces if you're lucky and the weather's not too bad."

"You must be very observant, Mrs Loudwater. Or psychic. I've not seen you near the place since Remembrance Day, when you had to go as chair of the council."

"Ladies, now ladies." Mr Mahmoud patted the air with soft, well-kept, much be-ringed hands. And it worked. The man has to be an expert, with four wives to keep the peace between. For a very short, painful moment, Lord Bogger imagined four versions of Renie all sharing the same house with him, and with each other, then killed the notion firmly. He felt he might need all his wits about him, Mrs Loudwater having sidled round from the other side of her host to be closer at hand.

"And were you never married, Lord Bogger?" She was one of those people who thrust their face so close they get quite out of focus. Lord Bogger first drew back his head a little, then finding this insufficient to prevent them actually rubbing noses, took a step backwards and knocked over a small table with a globe of the world upon it.

Lord Bogger did not imagine a slight spasm of annoyance cross his host's face, but it was very short-lived. Mr Mahmoud was smiling again. "Ah, the Pythagorus Syndrome. Give you a lever and you will move the earth, eh? And with you as the lever, Mrs Loudwater."

"Some men need a good woman as a lever," said Mrs Loudwater quite shamelessly. "I trust I always gave good leverage to my late husband, Roy" Lord Bogger knew he was expected to take up the subject and have it developed. He knew it but decided not to play.

Mr Mahmoud must have caught Lord Bogger's mute appeal for rescue. Before Mrs Loudwater could say that her Roy had much admired her way with Irish stew he smilingly suggested that Lord Bogger might be interested in looking at his collection of old English hunting prints. "They would, I think, appeal to anyone to whom our country traditions are important. You will excuse us for a few moments, I'm sure, ladies." And he led a grateful peer out through another door, leaving the chairperson and the vicar with the Mahmoud wives to debate Merseyside accents and tourism to their hearts' content.

"Our Madam Chair can be a little persistent, I know," Mr Mahmoud apologised with the air of a fond dog-owner explaining away his pet's habit of trying to copulate with the knees of visitors.

70

"Anyway, I would much value a quiet word with you."

"Fire away," said Lord Bogger, cautiously sipping a refill of Old Sporran.

"Please?" Mr Mahmoud frowned, then smiled again as swiftly as sun after an English shower. "You know, I have I believe, indicated to you my love of things English. This love started, you may perhaps not believe, as a child some thirty years ago in Port Said, where my father was then resident. I had a little to do with the ships of the British Navy. I was learning English from the newspapers—the Beano, the Dandy—of the sailors. Korky the Cat, I remember, made a great impression on me. Desperate Dan likewise, Pansy Potter the Strongman's Daughter. What a nation, what a literature, which could invent and maintain such characters as these. Above all, Lord Snooty and his Pals. An English milord, with his top-hat and white collar, and his great sense of goodwill towards those under him...."

"Noblesse oblige, as I said," purred Lord Bogger.

"....What other nation—and I had as a young man experienced people from many lands—Egyptian, French, Israeli, American, you name it—what nation could produce such characters? And then I thought: this is not invention. This is reality. There *is* a Lord Snooty. I wanted to know that Lord Snooty. Now I want to *be* that Lord Snooty."

Norman Gribb was back in short trousers in Swindon. He too had loved Korky the Cat, the Bash Street Kids. Lord Snooty and his Pals he had never really understood. Now he began to.

Mr Mahmoud had motioned him to an easy chair, had taken that opposite himself, mentioned nothing about old hunting prints. He leaned forward. "I envy you, Lord Bogger," he said. Only now did he take off his spectacles revealing a pair of very dark and very sad eyes. "I have made in my life much money. It was not at all difficult: one either has a gift for it or one has not. In my own

71

country I could have been a considerable figure. I could have been in government, or high up in international commerce. But I would never have been a Lord Snooty. Here perhaps, I thought, it might still be possible."

"Well, I found it simple enough," said Lord Bogger. For a brief moment he felt like confessing all to this strangely appealing little man, but checked himself with the thought that some advantage might well be gained by saying as little as possible just now.

Mr Mahmoud placed the tips of small but perfectly manicured fingers together, thumbs too, and proceeded slowly to rub them gently up and down between the tip of his nose and his chin, regarding his guest intently over the top of them. "You must know," he said, "that one of the first actions I took on coming to this place was to negotiate with your father..."

"My ancestor, shall we say?" said Lord Bogger, fighting an almost irresistible urge to copy his host's play with fingertips, nose and chin.

"As you please, sir." There was a short-lived flash in those soft, bear-like eyes, a sudden sharp crease of frown above them. This man was not used to being contradicted. "Through you forbear's agent—a Mr John Peel of Keswick—I negotiated the purchase of this property. Once it was the home of your ancient family; the lands too were theirs, the hunting, the fishing, the farms - almost, one imagines, the people themselves. And obligations: what you so rightly call *noblesse oblige.* "

"Indeed," said Norman Gribb as if he had been obliging peasants for years.

"Mr Peel gave me to understand - and this was part of the bargain, to me perhaps the most important part, for I could have bought a big house in many parts of the British Isles—Mr Peel, as I say, gave me to understand that I had also acquired through the purchase the manorial rights of the Bogger Valley. This I find is true only up to a point."

"Really?" Lord Bogger was now rather out of his depth, only wondering how much of the money had stuck to Mr Peel's fingers.

"I am Lord of the Manor," continued Mr Mahmoud. "Which means I have some control—and responsibilities—over the lands. I am not, as I had fondly imagined, entitled to be called Lord Mahmoud. I am a lord but not a Lord. You too are a Lord but not a Lord. I feel regret."

"Jolly hard cheese," said Norman Gribb, choosing a phrase which some instinct told him might be used under such circumstances by a member of the old aristocracy.

"Please?" Then a late flicker of comprehension crossed Mr Mahmoud's features, followed by a smile so charming that the new Lord Bogger could see quite easily how his host had become a man of wealth. "No, I understand. Hard cheese indeed, Lord Bogger sir. I wish for my cheese to become softer, to become as soft and as tasty as the best from the little mountain goats of my homeland. I wish to buy your title." The fingers separated and the hands dropped to Mr Mahmoud's lap.

Now Norman Gribb had not been Lord Bogger long enough to handle this proposition with the sort of ease he felt he should accord with his station. He had on the other hand once been AEU Steward for No. 6 Shop of the factory in which he had worked in Swindon, and he knew that although dice were invariably loaded against his sort there were occasions in which the other side needed something so badly they would make quite unusual concessions. This had been a rare occurrence, but a good shop steward should know how to play the advantage.

"Difficult," said Lord Bogger, pursing his lips.

Mr Mahmoud smiled. "Difficult, I have no doubt. But not, I feel sure, impossible. Money, within reason of course, is not a problem."

Lord Bogger's turn to smile now. "And money my dear chap, is in such a matter, of little consequence to a family like mine. Within reason."

"I am not an insensitive fellow," said Mr Mahmoud, resuming the play with fingers and face. "I realise that the very reason I want your title is the same reason you will be loth to part with it. I know enough of your religion to realise that one does not easily sell one's birthright. Money is really not important."

"Within reason," repeated Lord Bogger. "What sort of figure had you in mind?"

During his years as union negotiator Norman Gribb could never have claimed to have made management look embarrassed. Furious, sometimes, scornful quite often, but never as if he gave real pain. Mr Mahmoud lowered his eyes. "I was thinking," he said, "of something ending with four noughts."

"Five had occurred to me," said Lord Bogger. "With what figure in front of these noughts - nine?"

The calm, seemingly unflappable businessman looked as a calm, seemingly unflappable businessman would look as if suddenly stung on the backside by a large wasp. "I was, I must admit, thinking of a figure at the other end of the scale of digits. It's an awful lot of money."

"It's an awful lot of title." Lord Bogger contrived to look like a man whose bloodline had first been imported into this country by someone on hawking and whoring terms with the Conqueror himself.

"I am not a poor man, as I have indicated," said Mr Mahmoud. "But I have no desire to be a poor lord." He laughed, but his adversary realised there was no humour at the back.

"Details," said Lord Bogger, "are of course negotiable. This is why we employs agents, secretaries, accountants, those sort of chappies."

"Quite so." Mr Mahmoud looked somewhat relieved, as a works manager might look when he feels that he might just get away with giving the toilers of No 6 Shop ten minutes extra tea-break rather than quarter of an hour.

"It's the principle that counts," Lord Bogger went on. "As you must realise, the holder of the thousand year old title does not easily give it up for mere money...."

Mr Mahmoud stopped massaging his features and seemed about to bite an elegant nail. The temptation was overcome, however and the gesture finished as a slight brushing of one side of his moustache.

Norman Gribb ploughed on. "I must tell you quite frankly, Mr Mahmoud, that I shall be quite unwilling to cease to be Baron Bogger...."

It is difficult to describe the look of quiet fury that came over Mr Mahmoud's face. It might have terrified a resistant head of some merely commercial undertaking faced with an appetite for takeover, but Norman Gribb smiled reassuringly. "There is a way, I feel, old chap, which may leave us both in some measure satisfied. I shall have to look into the details of course—or have one of my legal chappies look into them."

"You mean?" Was that just the tiniest hint of perspiration under Mr Mahmoud's hairline?

"I mean this: My main title is Baron Bogger. There is, however, a subsidiary title, but a title nonetheless. I am also Marquis of Stoatholme and Viscount Thugthwaite."

Mr Mahmoud was clearly unaware of this: you could tell by the fresh frown which was as quickly replaced by a flash of beautiful white teeth.

"These titles go back, I believe, merely to the time of Henry the

Sixth—what's that: fourteen hundred and something?"

"Fourteen twenty-two to sixty-one," said Mr Mahmoud. "To be precise"

"Well, Stoatholme upset the king over a matter of messuage or droit de seigneur or some such. Stoatholme lost his head—quite literally—and his property, and title, went to the Bogger who was getting on well with the king.. Or as well as anyone did." Lord Bogger was chatting as if he had known the old chap quite well. "Now as you know, Marquesses and Viscounts precede us barons, but for some reason the Boggers preferred their original title; the marquess and viscount parts were always considered less important. But both Stoatholme and Thugthwaite are titles. Two of these digits, should we say, and just three of the four noughts you suggested?"

"Would I be permitted to sit in the House of Lords?" Mr Mahmoud looked as he might have done had he just emerged from a stiff grilling by Henry the Sixth and wanted to keep just a little of the droit de seigneur.

"I rather doubt that," said Lord Bogger sternly. "But as I rarely attend myself—pressure of affairs of course—I don't see why you shouldn't toddle along instead if it amuses you. No-one would notice, I'm sure."

"Marquis of Stoatholme and Viscount Thugthwaite," breathed Mr Mahmoud.

"Easy on, old chap" smiled Lord Bogger. "Either or. Just one of them: I've got to have something left."

"Stoatholme then," said Mr Mahmoud.

"Subject to confirmation," said Lord Bogger. "I'll get on to old Peel in the morning. He can contact your chaps."

Mr Mahmoud rose. "We must shake hands. That is how these things are done."

"And they're not often done," said Bogger, proffering his hand.

"And something more for celebration," said Mr Mahmoud. He pressed a buzzer on the table beside him and almost immediately there entered one of the ladies who had been dispensing drinks earlier. This one was perhaps not quite as young as the other two, but she had a fine full figure, an impressive mane of chestnut hair, and a ready smile.

"The ladies have gone, sir," she said. "Separately I believe."

"There will be another time, Gloria, to discuss Liverpool accents and Boggerthwaite tourism. For now I think a little of that rather old bubbly would be appropriate."

Gloria nodded, and as she moved slowly and most attractively out, she turned and gave Lord Bogger a quite saucy wink.

10

Mrs Sylvia Anstruther and Old Billy Nattrass had known each other for three quarters of a century. They had been born near each other, had gone to school together, and there would have been few days since when they had not encountered each other in and around Boggerthwaite. Their mode of greeting, you might have thought, would have been polite, if not entirely affable. It was neither.

OLD BILLY: "Squinty-eyed, shuttle-gobbed, shrivel-dugged, hinterfering owd bitch. Thou'd turn cows' milk sour half a mile distant." And Old Billy would make an ancient, secret little sign with his fingers, and spit.

MRS ANSTRUTHER: "Turn the milk sour? How could anyone do that when you've not kept a cow for nigh on twenty years? You've had it too easy, you tight'arsed, piss-headed owd goat - selling off ruined owd byres and hemmels and suchlike to innocent folk from the exterior world."

Mrs Anstruther has a point. Old Billy hasn't had any livestock that anyone's noticed for years. Instead he makes his living hiring out holiday caravans and selling off ancient barns and out-buildings which have become so ruinous over the years that livestock move out of them to keep warm on the open fell. But visitors seem to find them irresistible.

It was Friday morning. The celebrated Bogger Valley rain had thus far held off, which perhaps accounted for the tetchiness of the oldest inhabitants. Such an upset in the established weather pattern tended to disturb them as a sudden onset of the Föhn Wind does something to the nerves of the inhabitants of Alpine regions and makes them snappy.

Pleasantries exchanged, the old couple parted, Old Billy to partake of early refreshment at the Dehydrated Rambler; Mrs Anstruther to keep an eye on the fourth of a list of fifteen weekend cottages entrusted to her while their owners were away in other parts of the British Isles making the money to keep them going. Keeping an eye meant pushing small vacuum cleaners around for about ten minutes in each, turning on central-heating switches, cleaning out grates, and in a number of cases mopping up pools of water under windows, sinks and bathtubs. Mrs Anstruther had a large key-ring attached to the handlebars of her bicycle, and it jingled and clanged like an old gaoler's belt.

Mrs Anstruther was headed for a row of terrace cottages which, many years ago, used to be know as The Slurries, and which were occupied by workers from the Great Mirkin Slate Quarry, which closed in 1928. The cottages fell vacant one by one, decayed as empty cottages in a damp climate will decay, and were bought up en bloc by Old Billy Nattrass in the 'sixties for a rumoured £750 the lot. Old Billy gave the ruins names-Tallyho, Skiddaw, Helvellyn, Scafell and Blencathra—and slowly but surely sold them off as holiday retreats at a profit quite astronomical. Old Billy, in his quiet way, might even have taught Mr Mahmoud a thing or two.

Mrs Anstruther approached 'Scafell' and was about to select its key from her ring when she saw out of the corner of her eye the snout of a large motor-car thrusting over the brow of the hill and making towards her. It slowed, seemed to be searching for something like a sleek but short-sighted animal after prey. As Mrs Anstruther , after three attempts, successfully fitted the key of Scafell's front door into its lock (always an awkward one was Scafell; needed oiling or something) the car stopped, a blast of tinkling music cut off suddenly, and a young, female, and not at all local voice called "Hello!"

Now Mrs Anstruther was far too well bred to whip round and gawp at the new arrival. She had been taught as a girl never to assume that people were addressing her, and that if they were they were probably up to no good. She continued her struggle with Scafell's lock.

"Perhaps she's deaf." It was a male voice this time, loud, rasping and also with an accent far removed from Boggerthwaite's wild and lovely fells. Still Mrs Anstruther did not turn, as neither did the key in the lock.

"Excuse me...." There had been an opening of a car door and Mrs Anstruther could see reflected in Scafell's front-room window —or at least in one of the panes which was not made of quite un-Lakeland-like bottle glass—the slim figure of a young woman in a purple-and-green, very fashionable cagoule, detach itself from the car and approach Scafell's front gate. "I wonder if you can help...."

Even Mrs Anstruther could not keep up the pretence any longer that it could be anyone but herself who was being addressed. She turned slowly, turned the reflection into the reality of a tall, rather willowy young woman with long blonde hair, which she kept tossing back from her eyes. "Yes?" said Mrs Anstruther.

The girl laughed with a sort of relief, as if she had doubted whether the natives had any English at all. She looked as if she might at some time have had awkward experiences on holiday with the natives of the Algarve or Calabria. Her consort, still in the car and tapping impatiently at the wheel, looked the sort who would be unable to communicate with anybody outside the Home Counties. "Ah," said the girl. "Can you tell us if we're right for Boggerthwaite?"

"Aye," said Mrs Anstruther.

What did she mean? You could see the young woman's mind working - aye she could *tell* whether they were right for Boggerthwaite, or aye, they *were* right for Boggerthwaite? These things could be difficult. "We're looking for a Mr Nattrass."

"Aye," said Mrs Anstruther.

"Do you know him?" For some reason the young woman laughed —a high, nervous giggle as if Mrs Anstruther had just cracked a rather risque joke.

"Aye," said Mrs Anstruther. She had turned her attention again to the door, had even managed to turn the key, had given the door a sharp push with a powerful looking shoulder, and now held it open a couple of inches as if reluctant to reveal what lay behind it.

"Well, what does she say?" It was the sharp, impatient tone of the young man again. "Does she know the chap?"

Mrs Anstruther's gaze pushed past the blonde and focused on the owner of the male voice. She saw a pale, plump young man with spectacles and the look of being propped up to the wheel on a cushion or two. "Aye, I know him."

"Then can you tell us where we'll find him?" The young blonde let out another of her nervous giggles as if asking something that might be considered as vaguely improper.

Mrs Anstruther suddenly became quite voluble. "Was it about some property?" she asked with no hint of a smile.

"Well actually yes, it was. Er, is." Again the girl laughed. More of a simper this time, but showing the open mouth of a toothpaste advertisement.

"What is it—some old byre he's trying to get rid of, or the hemmel down by Low Scuttering?"

The young woman turned helplessly to her consort. "Simon," she said, mouth still open from the previous utterance.

Simon climbed from the car. He too was wearing smart new mountain gear and—Mrs Anstruther had been right—he was short: about five feet and only a bit. "We have to meet a Mr Nattrass," he said. "At Boggerthwaite."

"This is Boggerthit," said Mrs Anstruther.

"And-where-might-we-find-mister-Nat-rass?" The man called Simon spoke as if to someone from one of the more backward parts of Estonia.

"I-should-try-the-hotel," Mrs Anstruther articulated in the same measure. "The pub-er-lic-house. Down-the-village."

A telephone chirruped somewhere. Mrs Anstruther knew it was a telephone even if it did not have the full-blooded jangle she had known in earlier years. She was puzzled nonetheless, for she knew of no telephone in Scafell: the couple who used it at weekends—a retired pair from Tyneside who had once been something at DHSS headquarters—said that one of the attractions of Boggerthwaite was that there was no phone to keep ringing.

"Simon Stonechat." (At least it sounded like 'Stonechat') "Ya." The mystery was solved. The short young man had pulled from a pocket of his smart cagoule a telephone handset which he was now speaking into. "Guy - how *are* you?....Boggerthwaite. It's in the Lake District....Ya....We're looking at this little property ....No, not yet....Forty grand....Ya, forty, four - oh grand. I don't see how we can lose....hallo....Hallo....Damn, it's gone out of service. Terrible noise."

WHEEEEAAAARRRRGGGGHHHH!

"Hairoplanes," explained Mrs Anstruther helpfully, without bothering to look up. "You get used to 'em." Simon Stonechat straightened up from the defensive position which had reduced him to around four foot ten, and produced a sheet of paper which, Mrs Anstruther could see, bore the heading of a well-known (to

81

her) Cumbrian estate agency. "Low Scuttering," read Simon. "That's the one you mentioned, wasn't it? Rural detached property, stone built, capable of imaginative conversion. View by appointment Mr William Nattrass, Boggerthwaite."

"Aye, the owd hemmel," said Mrs Anstruther. "Go back the way you came, about half a mile, turn left, you can't miss it. There's a sign up. It says 'For Sale'."

"What about this Mr Nattrass, though? It says by appointment."

"I shouldn't bother about Old Billy," said Mrs Anstruther. "This early he won't know what you're talking about, and when he's had a few pints he'll likely want to double the price. I should go and look at it yourselves first."

The young couple thanked her, he with about as much grace as he might have given to a doorstepping Jehovah's Witness, she with another ripple of tinkling laughter. Mrs Anstruther turned back again to the task of entering Scafell, confirmed in her belief that there was not just one born every minute but quite possibly dozens. She had known this for some nine or ten years now, since Old Billy had begun to buy up and sell almost anything in the neighbourhood where one stone stood yet upon another. Much as she wished him bad luck and a denial of all the good things of life, yet she needed him as he needed her. Every old ruin he sold to a gullible outsider meant prospective work for her.

By dint of following Mrs Anstruther's direction Simon Stonechat and his lady-friend, who was called Tessa, had located the For Sale sign, and behind it the remains of the Low Scuttering barn. Tessa immediately went into a kind of rapture. "Look, Simon - it's got three complete walls!"

"And that pile of stones there," said Simon, "There, among the nettles and things, that'll be the fourth one. Soon get that up again, I should think."

"What about the roof, though, Simey? We'd need a roof, wouldn't

82

we?" The girl looked about her as if the roof might have been left by the roadside intact and ready to slot back on again.

"Shouldn't be a problem, poppet. You can get these plastic tiles now, I think. And anyway, some of the old timbers are still there."

"Simon—beams! We could have real wooden beams, and I could collect brasses from the antique shops—horse brasses and bits of harness, and man traps and ....Simon, we could have a brass knocker!"

Simon said that would be super. He poked around, measuring up with his eye. Eight rooms, he reckoned they could get in there. "Vivian did wonders for Trish and Jeremy at that little place the other side of Keswick. You wouldn't have thought it'd ever held more than a couple of heifers or whatever they call them...."

"Ya—heifers," said Tessa dreamily.

"And now there's Trish and Jeremy and Damien and Lothar...."

"And Agatha, and....what's his name, Simey, the little black one they adopted?"

"Masambula," said Simon. "Something like that. And the dogs, don't forget."

"Simon, we could have dogs too." Tessa in her mind now was Diana the Huntress, striding around with a pack of wolf-hounds to fore and aft. "And you could put all your gubbins in your studio and do everything on that fax machine....Oh look, Simey - squirrels!"

"Squirrels? Where?"

The girl pointed. "Running across those old beams - oh, you've missed them. Now they've gone down those holes at the bottom of the wall! Mmm - squirrels!"

Simon peered. "Yes, there's one! But Tess - don't squirrels have *bushy* tails?"

Within a year - even sooner if the money's handy and they can get hold of some tiles and a rat catcher, Simon and Tessa and their dogs and fax machine will be installed in their converted ruin which they will call Squirrel Garth or some such, and in which they'll play other couples in a similar way—Trish and Jeremy perhaps—compact disc recordings of Richard Strauss's Four Last Songs. Most of the Bogger Valley incomers have the Four Last Songs. Some have even three or four copies - one in the London flat, one in the Porsche, one in Boggerthwaite and one loaned to someone they can't remember.

They don't go in for serious music up at the Dehydrated Rambler. If Dolly Parton or Matt Monro had recorded the Four Last Songs they might have been played, but they didn't and so they weren't . While Jeremy and Trish were having visions of the Good Life over at Low Scuttering, the Rambler's regulars were discussing Lord Bogger, who had just a few minutes earlier been observed to drive off in his hire car after partaking of an early pint of Owd Bogger.

"Seems a nice sort of chap," remarked Old Billy, displaying the most charity about another human being he had shown since Margaret Thatcher had been prised from power.

"Bit on the reserved side, though," said Jake Otter, who had just read for the seventh time that morning and probably the seven thousandth time in his life, the labels on the bottles of whisky ranged behind the bar.

"Reserved?" sneered Old Billy. "You mean he didn't rush to buy you a drink. I'd say that shows common-sense, discrimination. It shows good breeding."

"You'd've thought he'd've shown a bit more interest in his birthright, that's all," said Jake Otter, looking at his watch now and wondering how long he would have to wait before some gullible stranger entered his web.

"Listen," said Old Billy. "That man has a thousand years of

84

noble blood in his veins. Same as my family. We don't have to pretend, like some people. Lordy's a gentleman."

"Why doesn't he talk posh, then?" Jake Otter pounced, then sat back with a small smile of possible triumph.

"Well, that's just what he does do," said Old Billy. "I couldn't understand half the things he said."

"He sounds to me," said Jake Otter, "as if he comes from south-west somewhere. Dorset or Wiltshire way. The sort of country bumpkin way of talking."

"He don't talk like a bloody Brummie, that's for sure," said Old Billy, baring yellow fangs in what was meant to be a flash of humour.

"Oi've never much liked Brummies," put in Matty Ouskin. "We always said they was Walsall people with the brain removed."

"Sure and I think you're all wonderful folk wherever you come from." Mr McGurk, resplendent in white shirt with elastic armlets, red spotted bow tie and braces to match, bobbed up from below the counter, where he had been tinkering with the beer engines, no doubt illegally. "So long as you keep drinking. Now—what are we going to do about this publicity question?"

"Well, Oi'm not in favour," said Matty Ouskin.

"And who are you?" Old Billy wanted to know.

"Who was Wordsworth, you might ask," retorted Matty. "I'll tell you, because you've probably never heard of him. Wordsworth was a poet. He wrote the one about the daffodils. He wrote about the beauty of the Lakes, the solitude of the mountains. When people started invading his space, man, he went bloody ape-shit."

"That's very poetic," said Jake Otter.

Matty ignored the interruption. "If Wordsworth could see what's happened to Grasmere today, he'd freak out in his grave, man.

Coach loads of bloody Brummie geriatrics, buses full of screaming bloody Manchester schoolkids, caravan loads of bloody Dutch and German and Frogs and Eyetalians—none of whom know a line of his poetry. Giftey shoppies, bloody museums...."

"A museum's a very good idea," said Jake Otter. "We could rebuild Dabster and Tyson's old mill, and start striggling flinches again. Visitors love that sort of thing. We could get a couple of old chaps to show how it was all done; we could have tapes of strigglers' shanties, and people could striggle a flinch for themselves and buy it to take home with them. There's an old bobbin-mill like that down Coniston way...."

"Then they could all troop up here and make themselves sick on Owd Bogger and November Owl Pie." It was Geordie D'Arcy, off school for some sort of half-term holiday. She was wearing a very long T-shirt with palm trees all over it, and very little else apparently.

"I suppose you're against it," said Old Billy. "Progressive educationist my arse, if you'll forgive my French."

"Certainly," retorted Geordie. "*Vafanculo*. That's Italian. Pint please, bog-trotting moron."

"Coming up, gracious lady," said McGurk. "Now I think Mr Otter's idea's a grand one...."

"Bloody rubbish," growled Old Billy.

"And I thought Mr Nattrass's idea of a festival - what was it....?"

"Boggerthit Bleezins. We used to have pig-racing, braffle music and dancing...."

"We should have it again," said McGurk. "Someone mentioned Grasmere. We should have...."

"Me," said Matty Ouskin. "I said it was enough to make old Wordsworth turn in his grave...."

"Fell-racing, hound-trails, wrestling, all the fun of the fair. People would come from miles around," went on McGurk.

He was still going on about it over an hour later when Simon

Stonechat and Tessa turned up, still starry-eyed about their prospective mountain retreat. They located Mr Nattrass at the bar, words of financial transaction were exchanged, as was a handshake, which Old Billy seemed to understand to mean that he was entitled by ancient custom to some liquid refreshment by way of consolation for having parted with a precious slice of his heritage. Observing this end of the transaction, Jake Otter coughed loudly and wondered if the newcomers knew of the ancient traditions of the Bogger Valley, like pig-racing and the Bleezins....

"And drinks cadging," interjected Geordie D'Arcy pleasantly.

But Simon Stonechat had not become the possessor of a BMW car, a poser-phone, a giggly blonde, and now the beginnings of a rural pied a terre by buying drinks for any old Tom, Dick, Harry or even Jake in bars. He steadfastly ignored Mr Otter's empty, dangling glass while asking Old Billy about the origins of the Bleezins, of which Mr Nattrass seemed to be extremely vague. Anywhere else on earth this situation would be called an impasse, but the Bogger Valley is different. Suddenly everyone knew all there was to know abut this ancient tradition—how the villagers had from time immemorial paraded round the parish carrying an effigy of Perkin Warbeck....

"Admiral Byng," corrected Jake Otter.

"Aye, Hadmiral Byng," agreed Old Billy, who had never heard of the man.

"Admiral Byng, who lost the British Navy the Battle of Minorca," Jake went on.

"In 1756." Geordie D'Arcy put in her two-pennorth.

Between them all the unfortunate admiral's straw-filled effigy was then taken up to the Buzzard Stone on Great Mirkin Fell, and set alight. On the village green below there were fireworks and feasting, cakes and ale.

"And November Owl Pie for those who want it," said Rory

McGurk. "You haven't tried our famous speciality have you, sir and madam?"

Of course neither sir nor madam had ever heard of owl pie, and both now signified, he by a frown and she by a little ripple of toothy laughter, that they had no intention of rectifying that omission, or certainly not for the moment.

"Then we have our own special Boggerburgers," said McGurk, rubbing his hands together. "or there are jumbo-cumbo...."

"A bag of crisps would be just the thing for now," said Simon, retaining his frown. He had not got where he was by lashing out inordinate amounts of money on the desperate culinary whimsies of rural publicans. He ordered a second half of Owd Bogger, however, and his consort had a mixture of pseudo orange juice and fizzy lemonade. Then the first of the old weekenders started to arrive, and for a while all was smiles and south-country bonhomie and much sloshing of Owd Bogger.

There were Paul and Sadie from Luton - "well, just outside Luton actually" - who were something in accountancy and rented 'Blencathra' next door to 'Scafell'; there were two young men with shaven scalps, black-leather bomber jackets, tight jeans and many metal studs, who were called Stew and Stevie-baby, at least by and to each other: they had possession this weekend of one of the apartments in the Timeshare Stockade which really belonged for most of the year to a barrister called Leslie, or perhaps Lesley; there were Julian and two very short-skirted young ladies called Michelle and Liz, all from Manchester, who rented one of Old Billy's caravans, and there were the old couple from 'Scafell' who immediately set about trying to relieve Mr McGurk of his supply of Newcastle Brown to remind them of home. They all seemed to know each other, and there was much talk of traffic conditions on the M6 and the comparative performances of various types of expensive motor-car. Mrs Pilar McGurk, or at least her head, appeared from time to time unsmiling and wreathed in steam at the hatchway above the Carvery, and portions of her various delicacies were served and consumed without any apparent ill effects.

Mr McGurk was in his element. It was for this sort of activity that a merciful and omniscient Deity had created him, and every time he served up another plateful of indescribable gunge with a smile as broad as a prize estuarine crocodile, he mentioned the growing plans for putting the Bogger Valley on the map.

"What you need's a sponsor, old lad," said one slender youth with an earring and a crisply-ironed checked climbing-shirt. "I shouldn't think I'd have much trouble getting our lot to cough up a slice."

"Really?" Mr McGurk smiled even more broadly—as if he really didn't know that his customer was a recently bankrupted garage proprietor from near Watford.

"What you need's publicity, dear," breathed a jolly-looking woman with a deep, comfortable bosom and a Somerset sort of accent. "I know quite a few chaps at the Beeb, and they're always looking for this sort of thing."

"You don't say?" beamed Rory McGurk, as if he wasn't at least ninety per cent certain that the nearest the good lady came to acquaintanceship with any broadcaster was the unrequited wink she gave nightly to Trevor MacDonald in the privacy of her own sitting-room.

"What you really need," said a man who could easily have doubled for Alf Garnett, both in looks and voice. "Is patronage. And I mean noble patronage. Haven't you got any nobility round here—a duke or something?"

A new light of hope entered the publican's always hopeful eye. "Nobility," he mused. "You know, I do believe we have the very thing."

11

Lord Bogger stooped to re-tie a bootlace, then straightened to look about him. It was a glorious morning, the first that year that held some promise of Spring. Cloud still lay in patches in the valley, but the tops were clear, and from where he stood halfway up Great Mirkin Fell, a matter of about twelve hundred feet, he could see the whole panorama of the Lake District mountains. If he had known their names Lord Bogger would have recited them to the morning as if praising their magnificence—Blencathra, Helvellyn, Fairfield, Great End and Glaramara, the Langdales and Scafell. He felt quite humble and yet monarch of all he surveyed.

Lord Bogger resumed his climb. He noted that the track up this fell could hardly be called a proper footpath—just an intermittent line of gravelly patches among the springy turf and the clumps of dead golden bracken. There were no empty beer-cans or soft drinks bottles, no abandoned cigarette packets or discarded toffee-wrappings. Only the occasional faint imprint of a Vibram-soled boot in the mud indicated that he was not the first human being to try the ascent, and that he was probably not lost. Across the valleys, he knew, already at nine in the morning the more fashionable heights would be receiving their first pilgrim-lines of the day. There would be crocodiles of walkers on Great Gable, queues forming on Skiddaw, transistors drowning the babblings of skylarks. Yet he was alone, and gloriously so.

Things seemed to be falling out well for His Lordship. He had found that Bogger Hall contained just about all the necessities of life. There was all the bedding he would ever need, the kitchen was well stocked with the necessary utensils, there were hundreds of books in the library, including several shelves devoted to football and cricket, and, best surprise of all, a quite respectable cellar of good claret and an impressively - cobwebbed array of old port. All he needed was to stock the refrigerator with solids and he would pop over to Keswick to get these when he felt like it. But not today.

Today was a day for celebrating freedom. Today was a day for feeling the mountains—his mountains—alive under his feet. In his other life Norman Gribb had never seen a mountain, had looked at nothing higher than the low, rolling hills that fringed Salisbury Plain. But he had seen the Alps on television, and when not scoring imaginary goals against Manchester United, was an avid reader of books on Himalayan exploration. Why, then, had he never just got on a train, or taken the car, up to Scotland or North Wales to see high ground for real? He did not know the answer, for now he was a different man.

He was grateful at least that his uneventful life had left him comparatively fit. He had more or less given up cigarettes some years before, and now only smoked (or rather most of the time sucked) his new briar pipe, and he did not over-eat. So, although unused to propelling himself up anything much steeper or longer than a flight of stairs, he was agreeably surprised to find that he could tackle the present gradient quite easily. His calves felt it a little, but his wind seemed sound enough. "The assault on the North Face of Great Mirkin," Lord Bogger said to himself, but out loud. "The peak that time forgot." A pair of fat little Herdwick ewes a few yards away stopped chomping the grass to look at him. Then they looked at each other, and if sheep had eyebrows, would no doubt have raised them. Then they continued their everlasting meal. Lord Bogger was evidently reckoned harmless.

Below him in the valley the Bogger Beck wound like a silver thread, and Boggerthwaite village crouched along it, St Ethelbogger's Church steeple prominent, the mosque-like dome of Mr Mahmoud's village hall rivalling it. The pub on the other side of the village-green plumed up a column of smoke, fuelled no doubt with last night's soggy beermats and the remains of uneaten portions of November Owl Pie. Dogs barked down there, wanting to be out, but there was no movement among the ranks of large cars parked outside the weekend cottages, the Timeshare Stockade, and the caravan compound of Old Billy Nattrass. Most weekenders were late risers, and the pub would not be open for a couple of hours yet.

Further off, Lord Bogger could just make out his own Bogger Hall: one day he would have to see about the garden. One day. For while he had been quite keen on gardening back at Swindon, he realised now that it had only been a means of getting himself out of the house and away from Renie. Someone else could do this garden: he could afford it.

It was not until he got to the first line of crags that the view opened up to include Stoatholme, and he wondered what, if anything, was going on down there beneath the uniform slate roofs and behind the pebble-dash. Could it really all be as hopeless as it looked? Or did it have a life of its own, unfashionable, but active in a way that Boggerthwaite would never be again? He must look in at the Stoatholme pub one night. Matty Ouskin might like the change.

The crags he was now confronted with were not at all formidable —just a rank of outcrops of slatey rock with foot and hand holds almost as regular as a short flight of stairs. Clumps of bilberry grew between them, as did two or three stunted rowan trees, not yet in their full white blossom. Lord Bogger had read somewhere that rowans were reckoned lucky, and he reached out and touched the twisted branches as he scrambled up.

The slope evened out a bit above the rocks, and now there were stretches of slatey scree before the next rise, which was topped with a large boulder. Lord Bogger was almost disappointed that the hummock above the stone appeared to be the top of the fell. He was just getting into his stride and did not want the walk to end. Well, it didn't have to end if he didn't want it to. He could surely go on down the other side, or on to the next fell, although he had no map and had not consulted one before setting out. It would be all right. You couldn't get lost up here unless the cloud came down, and there was no cloud any more to come down - just a huge sky of brilliant blue fringed by the sunlit mountains. Lord Bogger began to sing:

> Oh the grand old Lord of Bog
> He had ten thousand men:
> He marched them up to the top of the fell,
> And he marched them down again.

He stopped, suddenly aware that he had not to his knowledge sung anything since The Lord's My Shepherd at his father's funeral. There had been a grand turnout of Swindon's betting fraternity that day, and Renie hadn't attended, having regarded her father-in-law with the same degree of approval as a would-be pedigree poodle views an old tom-cat.

Lord Bogger slowed as he drew near the big rock, exaggerated the difficulty of his progress, bent almost double and putting on a painful gasping for breath. He scrabbled his way up an easy crack in the boulder, heaved himself erect as if facing a battery of cameras, and bellowed: "I claim this peak in the name of her Majesty....No, dammit — in the name of Lord Bogger, of Bogger Hall."

"Do what, pet?" The voice was female, very close, and totally unexpected. Lord Bogger looked down the other side of the rock. A face—a rather pleasant woman's face —was tilted up to look at him.

"I'm sorry," Lord Bogger said. "I hope I didn't make you jump." Then he laughed: it seemed about the only thing he could do.

But the woman appeared not at all disturbed. She remained seated, her back to the rock, and took a long draw on a cigarette. "Feel free, pet," she said. "I just hope Her Majesty's not disappointed, after all your effort." She had a local voice, deep and quite attractive.

There was something familiar about that face, thought Lord Bogger.

Then, as the breeze stirred her fine head of chestnut hair, he remembered. She was one of the three women serving the refreshments at Mr Mahmoud's the other evening. The one who had given him a refreshingly saucy wink. Gloria — that was it. "We've met, haven't we?" said Lord Bogger.

"Champagne," said Gloria. Her face, still tilted up to look at him, was getting the full benefit of the sun, making her half-close her eyes, a sort of double wink. Then: "Are you going to stay up there all morning? Or do you come down to earth from time to time?"

Lord Bogger looked at his feet, as if wondering how they came to have got him to his present statuesque position. "Oh, er, well...." he said, and slid down to the ground beside the woman.

"This'll be your first time up here?" Gloria's eyes were fully open now, a confident, frank pair of eyes, greenish, with golden-brown flecks.

"It is," said Lord Bogger, not knowing quite what to do with his hands. "Do you come here often yourself?"

In the black uniform she had worn the other evening, with the neat little white pinafore, she had not looked at all the outdoor type. But now, dressed in fleecy cagoule, cord jeans and boots, she seemed quite at home on the fell. "That's not a very original line, is it?" she smiled. Then, in case she might have hurt his feelings: "But yes — quite often really. Though it's not usually as clear as this." She took a final draw on her cigarette, then flicking it with her finger-nail, sent it flying in a long arc over the top of the boulder behind her.

"It's — well yes— it's a grand morning," said Lord Bogger. "Let's hope we get more of it." For the first time for years he wished he had a cigarette to occupy his hands, which were hanging quite loosely down beside him, rather foolishly he thought.

The woman said nothing but regarded him frankly, with a half-

94

amused look on her face. She had full lips, slightly parted now, and her teeth, Lord Bogger noticed, were a little protuberant. Just a little, but attractively so. "This is the Buzzard Stone," she said after a little while.

"The, er...." said Lord Bogger. "Oh, really?"

"The story goes there was once a buzzard ....Do you like fairy stories?"

Lord Bogger indicated with a gulping sort of sound and a nodding of the head that there was probably nothing he liked better.

"Sit down then. Make yourself comfortable." Gloria patted the turf beside her and fished out a cigarette packet while Lord Bogger settled himself. "Ciggy?"

Lord Bogger was about to say that he didn't smoke, but checked himself. "Please," he said, and fumbled for matches.

"Now then: once upon a time. There was this buzzard. It was a very big buzzard and it was called Barnaby. It used to sit on top of this rock. The people for miles around were mortally afraid of it because it preyed on the lambs, and when it had finished all the lambs it had this look in its eye which told them it might start on them next. Being superstitious folk they dared not kill the buzzard, but something had to be done because while the crop of lambs was getting smaller and smaller, the child population was getting bigger and bigger, there being not much in the way of things on telly to occupy their minds in those days. So — too many mouths to feed, and not enough lambs to feed them with. So one day a farmer called Luke, who had lost more lambs than most, and whose wife had regularly presented him with triplets, had the bright idea of making a gift of one of the latest of his broods to the buzzard. To....what's the word I'm looking for?"

"Propitiate it?" suggested Lord Bogger.

"Propitiate it, yes. Just testing. So he left the infant with the buzzard, and lo and behold, his lambs were left alone. Well, the

95

idea caught on like wildfire. Every day some father or other would climb up here with a new-born child and leave it with the bird. They had a ritual. They used to walk three times round the stone chanting: 'Barnaby Buzzard on thy stone/ Stop us setterin again'."

"What's 'setterin'?" Lord Bogger wanted to know.

"Search me!" Gloria laughed deeply. "But it must have had a little something to do with having babies, don't you think?" And she looked sideways at Lord Bogger as if wondering whether he knew about such things. "Anyway, the buzzard grew bigger and bigger, the population grew smaller and smaller and easier to feed, and the lamb stocks grew so big that the farmers made a lot of cash selling them. So everyone was happy." She stopped, and gave Lord Bogger another searching look, as if expecting a response.

"An early form of birth control," suggested the peer.

"Well, an early method of population control without losing the enjoyment."

Was there just a touch of suggestiveness in Gloria's look now? Norman Gribb had not had much experience of such things.

"I'll carry on," said Gloria. "All went well until one night, a farmer from over Stoatholme way, called Wormwald, who was jealous of all the prosperity round here, shot the buzzard. As a punishment his wife immediately gave birth to quads and carried on doing so every year. And that's how Stoatholme got as big as it is and why there are so many Wormwalds still causing trouble. Silly, isn't it?"

"What about the other tribe — the Sackvilles, isn't it?"

"I'm a Sackville," said Gloria.

Lord Bogger looked a little startled again. "I'm sorry."

"Why sorry? What's wrong with the Sackvilles?"

"No, I didn't mean that...." His Lordship was almost stuttering.

Gloria laughed, patted his knee for reassurance. "Don't worry," she said. "If you could answer that question — what's wrong with them — it'd take all morning."

Lord Bogger felt as if he wouldn't really have minded that. "What I really meant...."

"Anyway, I'm not really a Sackville. Not a proper one. I just married one."

If faces really can be said to fall, then Lord Bogger's dropped. He hoped it wasn't noticeable, but he could feel it. "Oh," was all he could think of to say.

"Married," repeated Gloria, eyes laughing. "Past tense. *Was* married."

"Oh," said Lord Bogger again. "I'm sorry."

"No you're not. Why should you be? You didn't know him." She paused just a little. "Don't know me for that matter."

"What happened?" Lord Bogger was all concern.

"To the marriage? It just disappeared. Gradually melted away until it slid down the plughole. Well, perhaps gradually's not the right word...."

"Where is he now?"

"Gary?" The woman shrugged. "Durham, last I heard."

Durham? Lord Bogger had heard of Durham. Gary would hardly be at the cathedral. The university, perhaps?

"Durham Nick," explained Gloria. "G.B.H—Grevious Bodily Harm. At least, the Law called it G.B.H. In Stoaty they just call it sticking one on a Wormwald. As natural as drawing breath. I'm from Thugthit myself. I was a Nattrass."

"Any relation?" Lord Bogger had only to cock his head down in the direction of Boggerthwaite.

"Good lord no," laughed Gloria. "I'm a Thugthit Nattrass. No

97

connection. I live down at the Grange now, though. Little flat by the sawmill." She indicated with a nod of her head this time the other side of the hill, and Lord Bogger could see the forest of tall chimneys, pepper-pot turrets and crenellations that sprouted among the trees of Mr Mahmoud's domain. "Your old family seat. You wouldn't like it though, I bet. You're lucky old Paddy took it off your hands."

"Paddy?"

"Paddy. Arpad. My boss. Or the Marquis soon, I believe."

Lord Bogger frowned. "He shouldn't have said anything yet. It's not all signed or sealed."

"He didn't say a word," laughed Gloria. "I just had one little shell-like ear to the door when you two were talking."

Nosey bitch, thought Lord Bogger. "How very enterprising," is what he actually said.

"Well, that's my story, for what it's worth. How about you—do you think you're going to like it here?"

Lord Bogger didn't hesitate, which wasn't really like him. "I'm sure of it," he said.

"Why?"

"It's different. I mean it's not like most of the Lakes — over-commercialised, too crowded...."

Gloria's face went serious for the first time since their meeting. "Then you want to see they keep it that way."

"I'm not sure I can do all that much on my own."

"But you're not on your own, pet. There's me." she paused again, threw her cigarette end after the earlier one. "Seriously, though, there's a lot down there would turn it into a bloody Blackpool if they knew how to."

"So I gather. I had the dubious pleasure of meeting Madam Loudwater, if you remember."

Gloria nodded. "Gladys Loudwater is a cow of the first order of cud-chewing beasts. She's in cahoots with that Irish racketeer down at the pub. Most of Stoatholme would be on their side because they think there'd be work if the place was developed. Not that they'd know what to do with work if a slice of it jumped off the roof and hit them on the head. But to be fair they haven't had a great deal of experience of it, bless 'em."

"What about, er, Paddy?"

"I think when he was much younger Paddy would have cut his grandmother's throat if he thought she'd swallowed a fiver. But he's not interested in money now — well, not so interested. What he wants is to be a fine old English gentleman. Well, he told you, didn't he?"

"The Marquess of Stoatholme," mused Lord Bogger.

"So, if he thought that building a replica of Blackpool Tower on top of this fell, and turning the path into a second Golden Mile would get him in the Birthday Honours List he'd do it like a shot. But you may have saved him from all that. He's got the idea that a true British gent lives well away from the sources of his income. He wants Boggerthwaite to himself."

"Well, he hasn't got it to himself," said Lord Bogger. "Not any more."

"I think he'll be on your side. He respects you. It's nothing personal of course. To him you're a blue-blooded English aristocrat." She turned and gave another of her bold and searching examinations. "Some time you must tell me how it happened, and how you picked up that delightful little Wiltshire accent. Would I be right if I said Swindon way?"

"Never heard of it," said Lord Bogger, and for the first time in this strange woman's company he felt easy enough to give her a proper smile.

"You're still staying at the pub, aren't you?" Gloria wanted to know.

"Not for much longer. One slice of November Owl Pie is fine, but if I eat any more of it I'll look like a bloody owl. And his beer is like something that's been filtered through a cat. I don't know how he gets away with it."

"But he does, doesn't he?" said Gloria. "Even during the winter. Those weekenders and Timeshare people wouldn't know a decent pint if they saw one. They'd drink the boilings of my old Gran's knickers if you told 'em it was real ale." She stopped. "What do I call you? I've been rabbiting away for the best part of an hour now and I don't even know your name. And I'm not going to call you 'My Lord' or whatever it is."

"It's Norman," said Lord Bogger. "And I don't really care if you don't like it: it's the only name I've got."

"I think it's wonderful," cooed Gloria. Then: "I wonder where they got names like that from. I'm Gloria, by the way."

"Gloria in extremis. Perfect."

"Thankyou, kind sir. We were talking about that awful pub. You know it used to be quite nice when I was a kid. But then the whole village has changed. If McGurk and my horrible old name-sake get their way it'll be one huge caravan site, full of dreadful computer salesmen and accountants' mates. Norman, you've got to stop them. Has he sounded you out yet?"

"Not properly. Or rather I didn't let on about how I felt. He's trying to get me on his bloody committee, but I changed the subject quick."

"Join it," said Gloria, very serious now. "Let 'em think you're all for it, and that way you'll find out what they're plotting."

"Boggerthwaite's Fifth Column, eh?"

"Do what?"

"Ah, you're far too young, my dear."

"You'd be surprised," said Gloria. "Fair, fat and forty."

100

"A wonderful age. I can give you a year or two. Not many, but say eight or so."

"Forty-eight. A dangerous age. With a bit of luck." And she roared with laughter.

"And you've got a lucky face," said Lord Bogger, quite amazed at his own confidence. "Are you working today?"

"No. Saturday's my day off."

"Then, how about a conducted tour of Bogger Hall?" Lord Bogger felt a boldness mounting inside him that he had never known for years, if ever. He climbed to his feet and held out his hand.

"What a perfectly grand idea — Norman." And Gloria reached out her hand in turn to be helped up.

12

Mrs Gladys Loudwater sat at the little checkout of her village shop like an old hen on a clutch of eggs. Monday was not usually a busy day: the weekenders had all raced off back down the M6 the previous afternoon — not that they bought much at the best of times, but lived out of their car boots, stoked up in supermarkets down South. The few remaining locals, like Pc Costive, the vicar when he was himself, Dr Rhoid and the others mostly took a weekly trip to Carlisle or Keswick and plundered the big stores there; it was cheaper that way. Mrs Loudwater relied on the immobile — the likes of Mrs Anstruther and Old Billy Nattrass, and the people at the Timeshare Stockade and the caravans who needed the odd tin of beans or loaf of bread not considered worth travelling any farther for. It was this low state of trade which made Mrs Loudwater hold with passion to the view that what Boggerthwaite needed was Tourism.

The ad hoc Tourism Committee proposed by Mr McGurk was due to meet for the first time that evening, and Mrs Loudwater was full of ideas that had tossed around in her head between waking (at five) and rising (at seven). There was the revival of the Boggerthwaite Bleezins of course, with its effigy burning and the racing of pigs (though where they would get pigs from she had little idea: all her bacon and other porky products seemed to come from Denmark these days); there was the traditional dancing in the streets, though again she wondered who would be any longer familiar with the old tunes and figures if such had ever really existed. There was Jake Otter's idea of re-opening Dabster and Tyson's Mill, but this was surely a long-term project, and one they would need to raise extra money for. She had made a note on the pad by her bedside that morning: "Mill Museum money? County Council? British Heritage? Arts Council? British Telecom? National Lottery?....Lord Bogger?"

What they really needed was to make the whole thing national, if not international. Perhaps they ought to twin with some foreign town and have exchange visits. Somewhere nice and warm like the South of France or one of the quieter Spanish costas. Though who would want to visit Boggerthaite when they were used to the Mediterranean sun, Mrs Loudwater was not at all sure. Besides, the local voters would jib at the idea of spending money on sending her abroad; or her and the clerk: he'd be bound to get in on any freebies going.

This was him now, shambling up to her door with that foul pipe of his belching smoke like the Flying Scot of her youth and wearing an old army greatcoat that would have disgraced a scarecrow. He would want an ounce of tobacco (well, it wasn't an ounce any more, was it? something in grammes.) a four-pack of beer and half a pound of sausages. Mrs Loudwater did not really like Mr Bean. He was too clever by half (or thought he was), and she had the not mistaken idea that he was laughing at her most of the time. Still he was a fairly assiduous Clerk, wrote the letters on time and all that, and she needed him.

"Good morning, gracious lady," sang out Mr Bean cheerily,

102

although it was no such thing: the Saturday sunshine which had cheered Lord Bogger on the fell having collapsed the following day into the usual ruin of high winds and heavy showers. Mr Bean looked more cheerful than usual, a dangerous sign, and was flapping a large envelope about under Mrs Loudwater's nose.

"Fame at last, most exalted chairperson," said the Clerk. "Look."

He placed the envelope down on her little cash counter. It was a large envelope of pale green, hand-addressed in violet ink, and bore a large number of stamps which appeared to have emanated from Australia. It was addressed to the Lord Mayor, Boggerthwaite, England, Europe, and it was already open.

"How did you get hold of this?" Mrs Loudwater sounded not at all gracious.

"Tot Titmuss just brought it." Tot Titmuss was the district postman based on Thugthwaite, a man whose knowledge of the most private goings-on and intimate predilections of the people of the Bogger Valley was unrivalled. Not a sparrow fell you might say, without Tot knowing about it, though he usually had rather juicier bits of knowledge to impart.

"Why did he give it to you—you're not a Lord Mayor?"

"I'm sure it has not escaped your notice, Madam, that we are without a Lord Mayor. For the present, anyway."

"But I am Chair of the Parish Council, and that's the nearest thing."

"Exactly," said Mr Bean, re-lighting his pipe and filling the little shop with a choking, sulphurous reek. "So knowing what a busy chairperson you are I felt it incumbent upon me to save you the trouble of digesting it." In any case, he might have added, Tot Titmuss had had it open already and had made an imperfect job of re-sealing it. He was usually expert at this sort of operation, but Australian gum must be of a different quality to ours, and the tampering showed.

"Anyway, what is it?" Mrs Loudwater wanted to know. "An appeal from one of their crackpot religious outfits — what do you call them?"

"Evangelicals are what Madam Chairperson probably has in mind, although they're mostly American. No, nothing like that. Why don't you read it?"

"That's extremely civil of you considering it was addressed to me in the first place."

"Turn again Loudwater, Lord Mayor of Boggerthwaite," chanted the council clerk. "I had a great-uncle went to Queensland. He was one of whom it was said that he preyed upon the finer feelings of young women. A bounder, as they used to say."

But Mrs Loudwater had extracted the letter and was reading, "Read it aloud, then," said Mr Bean. The manner of her reading voice never failed to convulse him with silent laughter. Mrs Loudwater was not aware of this, and so read aloud.

'The Court House Boggaburra, New South Wales,' began Mrs Loudwater, 'Dear Lord, It has long been my desire — indeed you might almost call it a lifetime's ambition (a lifetime devoted to public service and the betterment of the lot of my Fellow Man) — to go one day in search of my Roots.

'You will see from my signature....' Mrs Loudwater peered at the handwritten scrawl at the foot of the letter. 'William Hudspith Wordsworth, Senator, mmm."

"Go on," urged Mr Bean, keeping his face as straight as he could.

'You will see from my signature that I bear a name not without honour in the realms of the Poetic Heritage of the English-speaking nations. Indeed, the late William Wordsworth, of Grasmere, Westmorland was, apart from being a versifier of no mean merit, my own great-grandfather several times removed.

'I am a plain-spoken man— you do not get far in Australian public life if you are not— and I have to admit that, alas, my branch of the family is not in strictly legitimate descent.

'It would appear that my illustrious forbear, being in the habit of

104

taking long and energetic upland walks in search of inspiration, once strayed over from Grasmere to the Bogger Valley, where he wrote the following stanza:

> My heart leaps up when I behold,
> The valley of the Bogger.
> Long may its rills and clemmits bold,
> De dum, de dum de....

'The manuscript, which has been in my family's possession for generations, is unfortunately incomplete. I have myself tried for years to think of a suitable rhyme for 'Bogger' without success, and can only assume that the Poet had a similar difficulty.

'It would appear that the Great Man was, on his rambles, not always entirely given up to his Muse. For it was in the hamlet of Boggerthwaite that he met a young gatherer of 'simples' called Letitia. She was apparently also a lady of some literary bent, for William left her with a much-annotated copy of his Lyrical Ballads as well as a pair of identical twins named Dorothy and Hudspith. It is from the latter that I trace my ancestry.

'It is with much joy, therefore, that I am now able to announce my intention of visiting personally the rills and clemmits of the Bogger Valley which so inspired the Poet, and gave me my proud birthright. I expect to arrive in three weeks' time, and would be personally indebted to you if you could forward the address of the nearest Hostelry. There does not appear to be a Hilton in your neighbourhood, but no doubt you have your own good reasons for this. Yours ancestrally, etc., etc."

"There's a bit more," said Mr Bean.

"Ah yes: 'P.S. Perhaps you will also be able to tell me, (a) what a clemmit is, and (b) whether simples should not read samples."

"What they call a turn-up for the book, eh?" urged Mr Bean.

"It's quite amazing," said the Chair. "I mean, I was just wondering how we could drum up some international interest, and Australia will do quite nicely, won't it? Three weeks, eh? The Bleezins will have to be brought forward a bit. And do you know what clemmits are?"

"I haven't the faintest idea," said the Clerk. "But Jake Otter will make something up, don't worry."

13

At about the time the Ways and Means (Tourism) sub-committee of Boggerthwaite Parish Council was assembling in an inner room of the Dehydrated Rambler, for which Mr McGurk declared he would make only a nominal charge, Lord Bogger and Matty Ouskin, Bard of the Bogger Valley, were drawing up in the hired car in the rutted mud car park of the Goat and Compasses, Stoatholme.

Lord Bogger had not been invited to the Sub-Committee meeting. Mrs Loudwater had been all for asking him along, but the Clerk had persuaded her otherwise. The more they decided among themselves, he said, the less chance there would be of dissension or interference. The committee had powers to co-opt, and the best thing to do would be to present Lord Bogger with as near to a *fait accompli* as they could get, but at a somewhat later date. While his name might look impressive on letter-heads, handbills and publicity material, his presence at an early meeting might place a dead hand on the whole project. Mr Bean had once read Machiavelli's *The Prince*, and considered himself something of an expert on governmental intrigue, even if it was only locally governmental.

So Lord Bogger had settled his bill at the Rambler that morning without hearing of the meeting. He had spent the day in Keswick re-stocking his fridge with the able assistance of Gloria Sackville, and now he felt he had earned a proper pint. He would have invited Gloria along, but she was working late, helping Mr Mahmoud to entertain a partly of German businessmen, and anyway the Stoatholme pub was not one which she felt at home in, or rather perhaps too much at home, considering the number of other Sackvilles who were likely to be giving it their patronage. Some other time, perhaps.

But Matty Ouskin was delighted to go along. They sold Stella lager at the Goat and that would make a pleasant change from McGurk's gnats'-piss, as he poetically described it.

It was quite dark when they arrived, but Lord Bogger could see that the same incomplete old banger was still propped up on the forecourt, the price on the windscreen having dropped a fiver to £50 since his last sight of it. Lights were on in the bar, but the curtains were drawn, making it impossible to judge how busy or otherwise the place was, although a steady muffled drum-beat indicated that someone was alive within. On a strip of wood above the front door, quite brightly illuminated, was a sign which should have read: 'Gordon Bertram Howard McNally, licensed to sell ales, wines, spirits and tobacco.' But some wit had changed 'ales' to 'alas'; such is local pride.

"Another son of the Emerald Isle," commented Lord Bogger. "Have they taken over all of the pubs round here?"

"G.B.H?" said Matty. "No, he's a real Paddy. Used to play for Glentoran. McGurk's no more Irish than Boris Yeltsin. He comes from Manchester way. His name's Jimmy Pringle or something. Wrong image for a pub like that. So it's in his wife's name, which is McGurk, her coming from the Philippines, which by all accounts is full of McGurks."

"It's a strange old world," said Lord Bogger, opening the latch and nearly falling flat on his face down the step cut immediately behind the door, no doubt to deter foolhardy strangers.

"Mind the step, sir," said a voice so rawly Ulster you could only have cut it with a very powerful chain-saw. A wave of rough guffaws lapped round the bar.

"Thankyou for the warning, and good evening," said Lord Bogger genially. The laughter died out.

The bar reminded him at first sight of one of the less well-appointed drinking shops provided for the hard lads of the Yukon Gold Rush days. It was by no means as packed as in the adventure story illustrations of prospectors' bars Lord Bogger remembered from his youth, but it was by no means slack either. It was a very long bar, stretching off right and left of the door, and the clientele divided distinctly into two — a knot of some twenty men and youths down one end, and a roughly equal number at the other. The middle space—about four yards of it—was completely empty of customers, and it was to this area that the apparently practised hand of Matty Ouskin guided him. Nobody in the bar was saying a word, but all were watching.

Behind the bar, and directly facing them, was a beefy man with a broken nose and a mouth which displayed in an unnerving grin a very incomplete set of very yellow teeth. The effect of beefiness, boxer's nose and hooligan's fangs was spoiled somewhat by a thatch of peroxided yellow hair which hung long upon weight-lifter's shoulders, and more than a touch of mascara around the eyes. A double brassy-looking ear-ring hung from one lobe. Lord Bogger had never been sure of the symbolism of ear-rings. "Pint of Stella, please," he said.

"Pint of Stella for Matty, yes," said the gargoyle behind the bar. "And?"

"And a pint of Bass for me." Still dead silence from both ends of the bar.

"No Bass," said the yellow-haired tough.

"It says Bass outside," said Lord Bogger.

"It says fuckin' Oxo on the buses, but it doesn't mean to say they sell it."

Oh, a smart-arse. But a big smart-arse with hands like shovels. "Owd Bogger?" ventured the lord of the same name.

"And a pint of rat's vomit for sir. That'll be three pounds and sixpence." Then, out of the side of the mouth to Matty: "Pal of yours?"

"One of the best, Gordon." Matty swallowed a quarter of his

lager like a horse after a hot gallop. "A real gent. And I mean that. He's a genuine gent." Then to Lord Bogger: "Mind if I tell him who you are?"

The bartender glared. "I know who he *is*, son. I just asked if he was a pal of yours."

"Most certainly," said Matty.

"Then welcome," said the bartender. "I'm McNally," and shook hands across the counter. It was like having a hand caught in a hydraulic press.

"And I'm Norman," said Lord Bogger. "I don't stand on ceremony." Almost at once he wished he hadn't said it.

"We don't stand on ceremony either, pal," said Mr McNally. "And if you hadn't told us your name we'd've made one up, don't worry." And he went off to change tapes on a music centre, the drum-beating cacophony having just ceased.

"The only trouble with this pub," said Matty Ouskin in the quietest voice Lord Bogger had ever heard him use, "is that it's hard to get any real crack going. Those down there...." and he rolled his eyes discreetly to his left, "....are the Wormwalds. And those...." Eyes to the right. "....are the Sackvilles. And never the twain shall meet, not in here. You see them beams?"

There were lots of beams—big, black, oaken timbers— apparently holding up a sagging ceiling which had turned orange with the patina of generations of tobacco smoke. But two larger ones stood out, running fore-and-aft across the pub from the front wall to beyond the bar, one on each side of where they were standing. "The Wormies," Matty went on, "keep on the other side of that one; the Sackies the other side of the one behind you. If you wanted to speak to someone in one lot, the others would have it in for you. Neutrality is not an easy state. Sometimes in here I feel like a one-man Switzerland."

Both Sackvilles and Wormwalds had resumed their own tribal

conversations now, Lord Bogger having apparently ceased to interest them. "What happens when they want a pee?" he whispered.

"Oh, they've got that one sorted. It's through that door in the corner down the Sackville end, and there's a sort of neutral corridor along the wall. So long as you don't stray too far out of that you're OK. The bogs are no man's-land as well. It's an unwritten rule, but there's never any bother. They're all too scared of Gordon there."

Gordon there, having changed one drum-thumping tape for another—or maybe replaced the first one with itself; there as no way Lord Bogger could tell one from the other—was amusing himself by landing a series of swift karate chops on the shelf below the spirits' optics. Exhausting this little diversion, Mr McNally served two Sackvilles with a pint of lager each, and then a mixture of strong cider and vodka to a large lady of the Wormwald clan. Then he wandered slowly back centre-stage, ear-rings bobbing.

"Matty here will have told you what the set-up is in this establishment." It was more a statement than a question, as if the rules had to be handed to each newcomer. "Someone suggested that I ought to change the name to the Belfast Arms, but we get no trouble now. You should have seen it before I came. A fight ever night, blood everywhere."

"Why don't they get on?" Lord Bogger asked.

Mr McNally shrugged. "Sure, they just don't like each other. Now come on—if you were down that end of the bar...." He indicated the Sackville sanctuary. "....and looked at the folks down that end you wouldn't like the look of 'em, would you? But if you were one of *them* looking at one of *those*, you'd like the look even less. It's always been like that, as far as I can gather."

"But what happens if a lad from one family starts taking a fancy to a girl from the other. That must have happened, surely...."

Mr McNally looked horrified. "Never, sir. Never on your sweet life. And if you were a young girl from either side looking at one of them young no-hopers from the other, wouldn't you just feel the same? Either side, I mean. No, as far as I know they bring in fresh blood from other spots—Thugthwaite mainly. Some nice young lasses from Thugthwaite, if you like that sort of thing." And he tossed back his mane of hair and winked lewdly.

"I know," said Lord Bogger, and immediately wished he was better at keeping his mouth shut.

"You *know*, do you?" Mr McNally stared disapprovingly as if his customer had said something derogatory about the beer.

"Tell me," Lord Bogger said, trying to change the subject. "If I wanted to come in here and talk to one of the Sackvilles, say...."

"Ah, but you wouldn't would you?" said Mr McNally with the look of a master logician. "Unless you were a tax man or a probation officer. Nor the other lot, either. I'm telling you." And he wandered off down to the Wormwald end again to serve two pints of Snakebite, a revoltingly murky-looking drink achieved by mixing more or less equal quantities of bitter beer and strong cider, a thing no man with any regard for his liver should ever attempt.

"What happens at Christmas?" Lord Bogger asked, more by way of witticism than as a serious question.

"Ah now, Christmas is different," said Mr McNally. "Christmas they all have a truce. The Sackvilles move down to the Wormwald end, and vice-versa. They still don't talk to each other, but they change ends, like half-time at a football match, and they keep those ends till the following Christmas."

"I thought you were going to say they play football in no-man's land here. Like in the First World War."

Mr McNally looked puzzled, as if his new customer was not right in the head. "Now why on earth should they want to do that?" he said, and wandered off again without waiting for an answer.

Glass empty, Matty Ouskin searched his pockets long and hard, came up with a fifty pence piece, and then a minute or so later, with a twenty and two fives. "That won't do it," he said, scratching his head, as if trying to work out where two fat rolls of bank-notes could possibly have got to.

"I'll do it," said Lord Bogger. "I'll have a pint of Stella please, Mr McNally, and a pint—no, make that one of those Snakebites."

A grin which could only be described as 'wolfish' split the publican's face. "I'm sorry, sir, I can't serve you one of those. You have to be under twenty-one and present a certificate of insanity." Then, patting Lord Bogger's forearm, called to one of the Wormwald lads who had just been about to raise a Snakebite to his mouth. "Here, Blocker, give his Lordship a taste of that stuff. I want him to know how horrible it is."

The lad called Blocker, a six-foot young thug with cropped red hair and a face full of acne, advanced over the imaginary demarcation line and handed his glass to Lord Bogger without a word. Lord Bogger thanked him. "It's all right, like," said Blocker amiably. "Puts hairs on your chest, like."

Lord Bogger stared at the murky potion, then took a sip. Never in his life had he tasted anything quite so foul—not even Rory McGurk's version of Owd Bogger. But a thousand years of strong Bogger blood coursed through his veins. He smacked his lips. "That," he said, "has something. Let me buy you another, young man."

"All right, like," said young Blocker Wormwald, and went back to his side of the family line. Mr McNally looked amused.

Next there was a rumbling in the ranks of the Sackvilles, a stirring as in a hive of bees. "Here, mate," yelled somebody. "Try a drop of this."

He stood, a thin, weasely lad with pop-eyes and a pig-tail, a fetid-looking glassful raised, until Mr McNally signalled him across his line as a referee will call on a football substitute. Then the youngster proffered his glass. "Try that, mate," he said.

Lord Bogger did. He closed his eyes, swallowed, and the floor seemed to shift beneath his feet. "Excellent," he breathed. Then, remembering the awkward etiquette of this unhappy place: "Would you get this gentleman a replacement, Mr McNally?"

"That's Throttler, by the way, " said McNally. "Real name Thurston. The Sackvilles all go in for fancy names."

"Know what that is, mate?" Throttler stared at Lord Bogger without blinking. "We call 'em rotweilers—a bottle of Special Brew topped up with vodka"

"It's bite's worse than its bark, eh?" said Lord Bogger.

"You what?" said the pop-eyed youth.

"Never mind," said Lord Bogger. "Good health."

And the young Sackville returned to the boozy bosom of his family, like a single-combat warrior rejoining his ranks.

"You should be in the United Nations, Norman," said Matty admiringly. "I've never seen anything like that before."

"Can't have civil war in my patch," grunted Lord Bogger. "Unruly subjects and all that. They'll have to get to love one another, or there'll be heads banged together. God, this stuff is foul."

Mr McNally said nothing, just leaned back against his shelves and sucked his jagged teeth. His attention span seemed to be about as short as his temper probably was.

"When I first came in here, " said Matty Ouskin, wondering how he was going to get a third pint without paying for it. "It freaked me out, man. I wrote a poem about it. Want to hear?"

"Go on," said Lord Bogger. "It might take the taste of this stuff away."

Matty took a deep breath.

> "I wandered lonely as a cloud,
> Into the Goat and Compasses.
> I drank in that bleak no man's land,
> Then wandered lonely out again."

"I say, that's really very good," said Lord Bogger. "You'd better have another one. Then we'll wander."

And somehow he managed to finish his dreadful drinks.

14

Jeremy Blink-Howell, ace reporter (his description) of the Bogger Valley Bugle (with which is incorporated the Thugthwaite Mercury, Registered at the GPO as a newspaper, price 25 pence), parked his battered little Mini on Boggerthwaite Village Green and sighed.

It was Tuesday morning, the day he did his calls in the village. He sighed because trying to get news out of Boggerthwaite was usually about as productive as squeezing the proverbial stone for blood. Whist drives seemed to be a thing of the past, the vicar had been away for weeks, no-one had died for years (there being hardly anyone left to die who mattered), and even the monthly Women's Institute reports were written up on her husband's station typewriter by Mrs Bryony Costive, and posted in with a second-class stamp. Jeremy Blink-Howell was an ambitious young man who wanted to be a foreign correspondent on the Daily Telegraph, and Boggerthwaite gave him the hump.

It was, as is usual in the district, a cold, drizzly morning. Jeremy was not a great lover of the mountain scenery, but if he had been his spirits would have fallen even further than they had got, for not one of the surrounding tops could be suspected, never mind seen. The young man checked his red-and-yellow spotted bow tie in the car mirror, reached for his trilby hat as he ducked out of the door, belted his fawn trench-coat tightly about him and pulled up the collar as he faced the elements. Jeremy had seen several ancient Hollywood films about ace reporters, and what garb was OK for them would do very nicely for him as well, thankyou.

The calls, he knew, could quite as easily, just as non-productively, and equally frustratingly be done by telephone from the office in Keswick. But that way no mileage could be charged, no lunch, and he would be found something even more boring to do, like compiling the local soccer round up, by Bert Ballast, his dyspeptic Chief Reporter. Even Boggerthwaite on a wet Tuesday was better than Bert Ballast's company. Besides, even if no news was forthcoming, he could sit on a stool in the Dehydrated Rambler with an orange-and-lemon cocktail and pretend it was rye whisky and he Humphrey Bogart.

First call was to Mrs Loudwater's little shop. Jeremy had found in the six months or so that he had been doing the Boggerthwaite calls, that the Chair of the Parish Council did at least try to produce news even though she didn't know what news was and there was no news anyway. At least she had enough vanity to try to get the village (meaning herself) into the paper. This morning she was brimming over with enthusiasm.

"I've got a scoop for you, dear," she began. Everything was a 'scoop' to her. "Boggerthwaite goes International." And she began at great length to tell him of the forthcoming visit of Senator Hudspith Wordsworth from Australia, how a special committee had been formed to open the district up to tourism, how the Boggerthwaite Bleezins were to be revived...."

"How d'you spell that?" Jeremy wanted to know.

Mrs Loudwater told him. "That's colloquial of course, dear. The Bleezins go back so far that they didn't have a standard spelling for them. Anyway, we're going to burn Admiral Byng in effigy....What? B-Y-N-G...."

"No, effigy," said Jeremy.

Mrs Loudwater told him—or at least had a stab at it which sounded confident enough. "We're going to have pig-racing round the Green—traditional again—folk dancing, fireworks we think, and possibly a carnival procession." Mrs Loudwater told him this and much more, for they had worked far into the night at the committee meeting the previous evening.

"And we have a new Lord Bogger....Yes, isn't that exciting: another scoop for you, dear. My word, the Bugle'll be a big edition this week....What? No, I can't tell you a lot about him, except that he seems quite nice. No side on him at all, when you think of his ancestry. But then his father....But of course no, it wasn't his father, was it? Did you know the previous Lord Bogger, dear? I hadn't the pleasure myself. Somebody was telling me the other evening that he was West Indian or something, though that seems hardly possible, does it? Anyway, you'd better go and see him yourself.

"The other thing, dear, is you really must go and see the vicar. I think there'll be another scoop there, very much up your street." She would have gone on, but Jeremy's head was beginning to spin, and he had more calls to make.

Police-constable Robin de Vere Costive, usually a model of taciturnity, rounded off an account of how there was no news again by saying with much mysterious winking: "I'd have a look in at St Ethelbogger's if I was you, lad. Though how you'll print the story I don't know." Both Mr Magersfontein the farmer and Dr Rhoid the village GP said much the same. Still Jeremy was not particularly keen. For the past five or six weeks no-one had answered his knock at the vicarage, and this morning he had almost made up his mind not to bother. He had never been a great admirer of the Rev Miguel Ximenez, finding him uncommunicative to the point of almost complete Trappism.

The drizzle had intensified by the time he made his way up the vicarage path. There was a light on in one of the windows, and a bicycle propped up beside the front door: the vicar did not own a car. Jeremy adjusted his damp trilby, straightened his collar, and pulled the bell handle.

....

Some fifty minutes later Jeremy Blink-Howell was sitting bolt upright on a high stool at the long bar of the Dehydrated Rambler. To say that he looked a different ace reporter from the one who had arrived in such low spirits just a couple of hours earlier would be to understate an utter transformation. There is a moment in a man's life, an occurrence, after which he is never the same again. It doesn't happen to everyone: it happened to Paul of Tarsus on the Damascus road, it happened to Pythagorus in his bath (or was that Euclid?). Now it had happened to Jeremy Blink-Howell at St Ethelbogger's vicarage.

He was in a state of high excitement. He had forgotten his usual predilection for orange and fizzy lemonade and had ordered himself a large whisky. A true reporter—he knew this from the media studies course at his polytechnic—could, indeed often had to, work under all sorts of difficulties and distractions. So he ignored the bonhomie of Mr Rory McGurk and started to write.

When he had finished he read over his copy, swallowed the remains of his drink, and made his way across the green to the telephone kiosk. But it was not the number of the Bogger Valley Bugle that young Jeremy rang. And he completely forgot to call on the new Lord Bogger at Bogger Hall.

15

High dignitaries of the Church of England are not generally supposed to be readers of our popular tabloid press. They do not dive into their local newsagent's on their way to mattins and eagerly buy the Sun, the Star, the Mirror and suchlike. Yet somehow they get to know about the contents of such publications: how else could

117

they be at all familiar with the varieties and quantities of sin in the rest of the community which it is their job to fight with all their might?

Certainly they were very soon aware on the morning following Jeremy Blink-Howell's visit to Boggerthwaite of the splash story in the Daily Brute. "Sex-change Vicar Says No Regrets" it said in letters which would have been six inches high, all of them, if the format had been bigger. Underneath were two photographs. One showed a serious, unsmiling, black-bearded clergyman, captioned 'Before', the other a rather tarty looking woman with black shoulder-length hair and a lipsticky grin which bore the word 'After'.

> Pretty, curvaceous Michelle Ximenez (42) shocked the church of England last night by celebrating Evensong in a Lake District village church.
>
> Nothing wrong with the form of service—just that the previous time it was celebrated Michelle was a MAN.
>
> Last night she mounted the altar dressed in a tight-fitting black blouse, black pleated skirt, black stockings and black high-heeled shoes. On the previous occasion, as the Rev Miguel (Michael) Ximenez (42), he wore plain cassock and surplice.
>
> Said dimple-cheeked Michelle (36-28-34) : "I changed sex as a protest. I defy the church to unfrock me." And there was much more of the same.

The story was not exactly as Jeremy Blink-Howell had dictated it, indeed he had not been able to muster sufficient bravado to ask the vicar for her new vital statistics. But the staff men on the Brute, much practiced, had done all that over the phone. Or guessed it.

Now it may be a matter of some mystery to the general public how a reporter on a quiet local newspaper suddenly transforms, as surely as Miguel into Michelle, into a rampantly sensational digger-out of lurid if not scatological details. It is really quite simple: young staff-men on the smaller papers in the provinces are paid only a modest amount, but there exists in most offices a tradition known as "lineage". This is nothing to do with the sort of lineage which turned Norman Gribb into Baron Bogger by a devious route, but is a term of reckoning going back to the time when newspaper hacks were paid so much a line for their stories. It is a perk of the job that, once they have supplied an item of news to their own paper, they can supplement their income, sometimes quite significantly, by selling the same story to the nationals.

Normally the items should first appear in the local paper. This is only fair. But there are stories and stories, and Jeremy reckoned that there was absolutely no chance that a journal such as the Bogger Valley Bugle was ever going to publish the news that a potty village vicar had decided to change sex, even if his/her motives were of the highest. So he had felt no compunction whatever in getting straight through to former Fleet-street. There are at least two ways of doing this, and Jeremy's mind had been in something of a turmoil when deciding which might be the better. He could phone the story to all the likely papers in the land, one by one, which would take time; or he could offer it exclusively to one, which would be the work of a few moments and might bring in a very respectable sum indeed. Jeremy chose the latter, and as the Daily Brute at that time was reckoned the most lavish in its rewards to those who served it well, he rang the Daily Brute. Later he would ask for a job.

One man who was even less pleased next morning than any of the bishops of the Church itself, was Mr Bertram Ballast, Chief Reporter of the Bogger Valley Bugle. Mr Ballast held the rather unfashionable view in these days of market forces that by seniority and ancient custom he was the channel through which any lineage should go. So that when he had read the story his first suggestion to young Jeremy was that he might as well go and seek that permanent job on the Brute right away.

Meanwhile in Boggerthwaite itself opinions were, as usual, well split. Pc Costive told Mrs Loudwater that the vicar should be run out of the village; the Chair wasn't so sure, but then she had been rung up by two other tabloids earlier that morning and had high hopes of seeing her name in them on the morrow. "There's no such thing as bad publicity, dear," she told the officer. "You want to bet?" he replied.

Ms Geordie D'Arcy was ecstatic. Failing to get through to the vicar by phone she sent her a greetings card depicting Botticelli's Birth of Venus by hand with the message: "Right on, new sister! The support of all true feminists is with you." And got her friend Muriel the sculptress to sign it as well.

Lord Bogger did not read the papers, and so the first he heard of it all was a phone call from the vicar herself. "I think I'd rather like to see you," she said gloomily. "It might be a case of seeking sanctuary."

Lord Bogger was not best pleased, as he was finishing a delightful late breakfast with Mrs Gloria Sackville. Among a number of very pleasing accomplishments the lady was turning out to be quite a skilled cook. So Lord Bogger snorted.

"I think you're going to be involved whether you like it or not," said Ms Ximenez. "After all, the living is in your gift. You are my patron."

"*Noblesse oblige*, I suppose," grunted Lord Bogger. "All right, come on up."

Fifteen minutes later a scraping sound on the wall outside the kitchen announced the arrival of the vicar's bicycle, and a knock at the back door of the Rev Ximenez herself.

She said nothing to start with—just handed a copy of that morning's Brute to Lord Bogger. His eyes went wide as he took in the front headline, then widened further as he read on. "Well," he said finally. "They wanted Boggerthwaite on the map, and you've certainly got it there." He handed the paper to Gloria, who had been pouring the vicar a coffee.

"Not quite what they had in mind, though, is it?" said the vicar.

"How did they get hold of it?"

"Our local reporter, Jeremy. Not the brightest lad, I always thought, but I can see now he's going to go far."

"Did you tell him....well, all that? Vital statistics and that sort of thing?"

Ms Ximenez looked down at herself, as if noticing her changes for the first time. "No, but I suppose he could guess pretty accurately. D'you know, I've never actually measured myself."

"They'll be wanting you to pose for Page Three next."

It had been meant as a grim sort of joke, but the vicar's face told another story. "Oh, they've been on about that already. Three of them, on the phone this morning."

"Think of the cash you could pull in for the church roofing fund," smiled Lord Bogger.

"The answer-phone's a great boon in times like these," said Ms Ximenez. "The phone's hardly stopped ringing. But it won't put them off for long. Have they not been on to you?"

"I don't think anyone knows about me yet," said Lord Bogger. "And I'd rather things stayed that way. How did they get the pictures?"

"I gave young Jeremy a copy of some old snaps, and he took one of me when we'd finished chatting." The vicar paused. "I didn't mind, you see. The whole reason for my changing was to get publicity for women's right of ordination. It just seems I've gone about it the wrong way."

"Anyway, you missed the boat, didn't you?" said Lord Bogger. "They've got it now. As far as I can make out the Church is full of lady vicars. Or vicaresses."

Ms Ximenez looked down at her sensible but rather large shoes.

121

"I can't pretend I hadn't always wanted a change. I suppose I might have done it anyway, but I thought I'd got a good and Christian reason. The powers-that-be would probably call it a sin, though I never looked at it that way...."

"Has the Bishop been on to you yet?"

"Not yet. I dare say this has all been a terrible embarrassment for the poor dear. I just had no idea it would be like this."

"Well, serves the buggers right," said Lord Bogger with a smile. "What do you think, Gloria?"

"Exactly," said Mrs Sackville. "I think they're a pack of narrow-minded, sexist old fossils. If I wanted to be a vicar, why shouldn't I be?"

Lord Bogger smiled dreamily. "Because you're not pure enough. But in principle...."

"They'll all be up here in no time." The Rev Ximenez had a hunted sort of look. "It only takes five hours from London in a fast car. Less from Manchester. I don't think I can cope with it all." She paused. "And I didn't wear high-heeled shoes: I had these sensible ones on."

"Difficult," said Lord Bogger, not particularly helpfully.

"Mind if I say something?" Gloria had produced her cigarette packet and failed to pass it around.

"Please, dear," said the vicar.

"The way I see it there are three things you can do. One, you can go missing again, run away from it until it all blows over; two, you hold a press conference, make a statement, and put up with it until they get tired of you. I mean, unless you try to seduce the Rural Dean or take a lesbian lover there's not a lot more mileage in the story. Three, you can sell the story to the highest bidder, and clear off the church restoration debt. You're bound to have a restoration debt—all the best churches have. What you really need is a good agent."

"I think Gloria's right," said Lord Bogger after some reflection, which involved the filling and lighting of his pipe, there being apparently no cigarettes on offer. "But let the buggers sweat it out for a while., You're welcome to stay up here a day or two...."

Gloria shook her head. "It won't take them five minutes to find out that you're the patron, Norman. Then they'll be up here like a pack of wolves. If I can borrow your bike, vicar, I think I'll just pop down to the village and see what's happening. I'll report back."

And so, buttoned up most attractively against the foul Bogger Valley weather (or so Lord Bogger thought) Gloria Sackville sped on her way. It was a quarter past eleven.

16

It is a commonly-held belief among the newspaper reading public, or at least among many of those people who stick faithfully to one paper only and take what they read as a sort of gospel, that there is a great deal of rivalry between those who gather the news for their edification. This is true only up to a point.

Many reporters would sell their grand-children, never mind their grandmothers, for a good story, and cut each other's throats to get anywhere near the sources of information, but this is usually only a last resort, for they are on the whole an amiable, lazy lot, and spend a lot of their time in each other's company, if only to keep an eye on each other.

And so by midday most of the press crew detailed by their various news-editors to sort out the Boggerthwaite sex-change caper had installed themselves in the bar of the Dehydrated Rambler, proprietor Rory McGurk Esq., a most delighted man. Having drawn a blank at St Ethelbogger's vicarage, having listened to an effusive character assassination of the vicar by Mrs Loudwater, and having got themselves thoroughly wet in between times, they were comparing notes and preparing for what might be quite a long siege. The photographers had taken shots of St Ethelbogger's in the dismal light and were now kicking their heels and telling each other that the weather was bound to pick up after lunch. Till when they were getting stuck into the plates of November Owl Pie and Boggerburgers and chips, for it is a phenomenon of newspaper workers that while the reporters, even in these days of dull conformity and mineral water, will fasten themselves on to any glass of gin and tonic available, the takers of photographs are by and large men who like to keep a head clear of alcoholic fumes and a belly full of solid grub. This is handy for reporters who can cadge a lift with them without having to worry about breathalysers and suchlike.

Gloria Sackville was not by any means an habitue of the Rambler, being a woman of quite sound common sense. But on this morning she approached the bar with all the familiarity of a regular. Skilfully avoiding the toothy insincerities of a happy Rory McGurk, she ordered a glass of sweet cider—for even the Rambler can't do much harm to such an ersatz production—and found herself a high stool between two jaded looking individuals who by their distinctly un-rural clothing had to be members of the hacks' brigade. "Not a bad morning," she commented to the one on her right—a lank-haired young man with a pale face whom you would not trust even if he were trying to give away a second-hand car.

"You must be joking," said this shifty-looking character in a voice which should have been wheedling gullible old provincial clergymen into a London clip-joint. "I'm bloody perished." Then, swivelling piranha's eyes on to our Gloria: "Come from round here, do you, love?"

Gloria Sackville admitted this, rather shyly, but there was just the hint of a fluttering of eyelashes too.

"You'll know this vicar character, then," said the shifty young man. Gloria noticed that the person on her left was leaning in to catch any gems that she might let drop. She didn't turn to look at him, but watched his reflection in the mirror. He didn't look shifty in the same way as the other: he had the look of a fairly prosperous farmer—all red face and big innocent blue eyes. Gloria knew she could trust him even less than the first.

"This vicar character?" echoed Gloria. "Which vicar character would that be?"

"This Ximenez cove," pronounced the reporter with some difficulty. "The one that's changed his sex."

"Oh, our *vicar*," said Gloria, and smiled a broad country-girl's smile.

"That's right. Know him, do you?"

"Her, you mean," corrected Gloria.

"So they say. Seen her lately?"

"Just last night," said Gloria. "As a matter of fact."

The red-faced man was leaning so close now that Gloria felt her glass to be in danger, and so shifted it to safety.

"Where was this, then?" persisted the lank-haired young man.

"Where was what?"

"Where did you see the vicar person?"

"Oh, Michelle you mean. Why, by the bus stop."

"Of course," said the reporter, with the air of a general preparing for a long siege. "Say anything?"

"Who, me?" Gloria looked all innocent bucolic defensiveness. "I just said by the bus-stop. That's where I saw the vicar."

The reporter would have rolled his eyes into his cranium and tapped the bar-top with his finger-ends if he had not been inured by years of working with idiots to making a great show of patience.

"No," he said. "I meant, did the vicar say anything? To you, if you're with me."

Gloria gave a little frown, as if trying to work out how she could be with the vicar at the bus-stop at the same time as sitting in a bar with her questioner. "She said good evening," came out eventually.

"Nothing else?"

"And it was— a right good evening," said Gloria, warming to her subject. "We'd had no rain at all since about eleven o'clock in the morning. Well, just a shower round about three. But no, it was grand weather. Aye." She looked along the bar to where Old Billy Nattrass was deep in conversation with a group of extremely bored looking hacks. "Wasn't it grand weather yesterday, Billy? These gentlemen were asking."

"Champion," agreed the old farmer, pausing long enough for two of his company to escape.

"Aye," said Gloria, and took another deep sip of her cider.

"Did he—er, she—say where she was going?" said the farmer-faced reporter.

"Who would that be, pet?" Gloria was all amiability.

"The vicar. Did he—she—say where she was going? On the bus."

"Aye, now she did, come to think of it." Gloria frowned deeper.

"And?" The first reporter was trying to get back in.

"Keswick," said Gloria after a great show of unusual concentration. "Aye, I'm almost sure it was Keswick. Had to be, I suppose, since that's where the bus goes."

"Keswick, eh?" said the two reporters, almost in unison.

"Mind, it'll stop at Stoatholme if you want it to. And Thugthit. After that there's not a lot—just a few farms, but the farmers has all got motors these days."

"She didn't tell you what she was going to Keswick for, did she?" asked the lank-haired scribe.

"Or whether she was staying there long?" added his colleague.

"Aye, now you mention it," said Gloria, draining her glass with a great show of its being empty which would have done credit to Jake Otter, who was in the process of doing much the same thing in the company of two more reporters who looked so bored they had failed to offer a refill.

"Have a drink," suggested the lank-haired man.

"Another cider?" said his red-faced rival.

"No—too gassy," giggled Gloria. "Could I have a gin and tonic, d'you think?"

"Sure," said the two in chorus.

"A large one," said Gloria demurely. "A single's hardly enough to cover the bottom of the glass."

The drink served, the two reporters glared daggers at each other. Both attempted to pay, and Rory McGurk would have taken both lots of money if the farming type had not slid his away out of reach in the nick of time. "You were saying, dear?" he prompted.

"Cheers," said Gloria. "On holiday, are you? We don't get many visitors this time of the year. Easter they start...."

"I'm sure. Now...."

"Then there's another long gap till Whit. Or what used to be Whit. It's Spring Bank Holiday now, isn't it? I don't know why they have to muck about with the calendar."

"Beats me too," agreed the red-faced reporter. "Now, the vicar. You were saying he—she—said something else. About what she was going to Keswick for. Do you remember?"

"Oh yes. She said she was going on to London. And I thought it must have been somewhere like that because she had this bag with her. What d'you call them—an overnight bag, isn't that it?"

"London?" said the red-faced man, pop-eyed now. "Are you sure?"

"Positive," said Gloria.

"Oh Christ!" said the lank-haired man, tossing back his locks and finishing his pint of Owd Bogger.

"She said she was going to see someone on one of the newspapers. The Sun, was it? No, that other one—the Brute."

"Did she say anything else?" The red-faced man was looking at his watch with the jerky movements of a man who suddenly realises that he is going to be lucky not to miss his train.

"Aye. She said they were going to give her a holiday. It sounded dead romantic. They were going to take her away somewhere. A safe haven, she called it. In hiding, like. She didn't know where. The West Indies, she thought, but I said no, it couldn't be that. It's all cricket there. I've never been, mind. In fact, I've never even been to London."

Gloria looked into the mirror behind the bar and treated herself to a broad wink. Both her gentlemen had already gone, and the rest of the bar was clearing rapidly.

17

Next morning former Fleet-street exacted a terrible revenge on Boggerthwaite. 'Rural Rip-Off,' screamed the Daily Monster and hung on to its splash headline a long story about Old Billy Nattrass's barn conversions.

'RSPCA Hits Out at Owl Abuse' yelled the Daily Grub, and roasted Rory McGurk for the proud speciality of his house.

'Work-shy Wordsworth in Lakeland Dole Scam' bellowed the Inquisition, and printed a number of incomplete poems from the pen of Matty Ouskin, 'at £500 a line of taxpayer's money'.

The Daily Excess carried a three-column photograph of a furtive looking Arpad Mahmoud attempting to hide his face as he climbed into one of his Range Rovers, followed by a brace of mature rotweiler dogs. 'Is this man playing the game?:' the heading read, and went on to report that the Bogger Valley's new Master of Foxhounds had strange and un-English ideas as to what constituted a fair fox-hunt, Helicopter gun-ships were mentioned, as were radar and ex-Soviet machine guns. Mr Mahmoud had, it read, no comment to make on any of this. The picture caption read: 'Gone to earth.'

Farmer Kurt Magersfontein got his desserts, just or not, on the front page of the Daily Scrounge. According to this crusading organ, he was a former SS guard at one of the nazis' worst concentration camps. 'They called him the Laughing Hyena,' it revealed. 'Mr Magersfontein, today experimenting with live veal calves on his farm, had nothing to say.' Except, one imagines, to his lawyers.

"Baby Bloodbath Orgy" screeched the Daily Beast. It had uncovered the legend of the Buzzard Stone, a place of black magic, leylines, Druids and human sacrifice. Its hilltop site, it revealed, was to be the setting for the Boggerthwaite Bleezins, a traditional orgy participated in by local leading lights who should have known better. 'Ban the Bloody Bleezins!' roared the Beast.

'Sex-change Vicar Hounded From Pulpit,' accused almost every paper except the Brute, which had gone strangely quiet on the subject.

Mrs Gladys Loudwater stood with the morning's newspapers spread out before her, and scratched her head. "I must say it isn't quite what I'd hoped for," she admitted to Mr Bean the Council Clerk, who appeared to be trying to fumigate the pet-food shelves of her little shop with his tobacco-smoke.

"All I can say," said that worthy, "is that my conscience is clear. None of that came from me." This was not strictly true, only that he had managed to keep his name out of it all, except on several cheques which he hoped were already in the post. They would be addressed to him post restante at Carlisle, to escape the curiosity of Tot Titmuss the local postman. Mr Bean, as has already been remarked, had not read his Machiavelli for nothing.

"I think you'll have to write to them all for apologies," said Mrs Loudwater. "And the Press Complaints people. Put the record straight."

Mr Bean nearly choked on his noxious pipe. "My dear lady," he said when he had recovered a little. "That would be about as much use as pissing against the wind. They'd make us look complete Charlies."

"But....but we can't let it go unchallenged," said Mrs Loudwater. "Surely." What she was really miffed about, her clerk knew, was that she had only got one mention in the whole of the morning's spread, and that had her name spelled "Loosewater" and described her as "plump, motherly postmistress", no mention of her chairmanship of the council.

"You said yourself that there was no such thing as bad publicity," coaxed Mr Bean. "At least we're on the map now. People'll be getting their road atlases out right now, all over the country, trying to find Boggerthwaite."

"Yes, the place famous for profiteering property-developers, black magic, phoney poets, bent clergymen, war criminals and cruelty to animals." Mrs Loudwater was working herself into a fine state of outrage. "Couldn't we work in a murder or two?"

"You might start with young Jeremy Blink-Howell," suggested the Clerk. "He got the ball rolling in the first place."

"What about Lord Bogger?" Mrs Loudwater said suddenly.

"You want to bump him off too?"

"I mean, I wonder what he thinks about it all. It's time we roped him in. He might have some ideas."

Lord Bogger did indeed have some ideas, though not along the lines that the Chair would have approved. He too had bought the day's crop of papers and had read them all with no little pleasure in the company of Mrs Gloria Sackville and the Rev Ximenez. "I say," commented His Lordship, "What an interesting little place we live in. I had no idea there was so much variety."

"If you were a tourist would you want to come here?" asked Gloria.

"I'm damned if I would," said Lord Bogger with a happy chuckle.

At which point the telephone rang. It was Mrs Gladys Loudwater.

18

"Admiral Byng," said Ms Georgina D'Arcy in a loud but not unmusical voice. "Now, have any of you any idea who Admiral Byng was?"

Sixty-seven eyes rolled around in various attitudes of utter incomprehension. It would have been tidier to have been able to say 34 pairs of eyes rolled, but this would not have been strictly accurate. Little Garth Wormwald, aged eight-and-a-half, was the possessor of only one eye. In most schools this affliction would have made him the butt of all and sundry, but Garth was big for his age, the owner of an exceptionally violent temper, even for a Stoatholme Wormwald, and something of a popular entertainer. For his missing eye—lost in some long-forgotten playground fracas with a posse of Sackvilles—had been replaced by a replica made of glass. It had belonged to his paternal grandfather, the still legendary "Gouger" Wormwald (1925-79), and Garth's parents, against objections by doctors and hospital specialists, had insisted on its being passed on, in spite of the fact that it was a pale shade of greeny-grey which did not match the deep innocent baby-blue of its natural neighbour. Garth Wormwald could, and often did, remove his glass eye and roll it around his desk top and the floor, where it made his female classmates scream and cling to each other in fascinated terror.

Garth, it seemed, didn't know who Admiral Byng was, or is, and neither did anyone else. Ms D'Arcy smiled grimly. She had expected at least three or four of the smarter-arses to have mentioned Bing Crosby, but it seemed that nobody had heard of him either.

"Admiral Byng—Admiral John Byng—was in charge of a fleet of ships sent to relieve....Now hold on. Have any of you been to Majorca for your holidays?"

Mark and Debbie Wormwald had, it seemed, been to Majorca the previous year. Their Daddy could afford it, because their Daddy was a skilled motor-mechanic with a speciality which made him in much demand for swiftly altering the looks and performance of cars belonging to person or persons unknown. Encouraged to expatiate on their holiday impressions of the Balearics, Mark Wormwald said that Majorca was grot.

Not discouraged, although she had enough experience of these children to be forgiven for being in a state of permanent pessimism, Ms D'Arcy said that was a pity, because it really was quite beautiful in parts. Deborah grimaced horribly to her mates and made a noise like a young hippo being sick.

"Now the next island to Majorca is called....anybody know?"

One hand shot up. It belonged to Elvis Carstairs, a member of one of the families tributary to the Wormwalds. Elvis Carstairs was a creep. "Please Miss, the Isle of Wight, Miss," said Elvis.

"Not quite, Elvis, but a jolly good try, dear. No, it's the island of Minorca—Min-or-ca. Say it, all of you: Min-or-ca. That's right."

Georgina D'Arcy herself had been quite expensively educated somewhere in Buckinghamshire, and had achieved a quite respectable two-one in psychology at university. Yet she still clung to a method of teaching long ago abandoned by her more realistic brethren. Geordie D'Arcy had the optimism of a dog and the heart of a lion.

"Right, now in seventeen hundred and fifty-six—that's a long time ago, isn't it?— in 1756 Minorca belonged to the British—to us. But we were fighting the French at the time....Does anyone know why we should be fighting the French? Emmanuelle?"

Emmanuelle Sackville, conceived after her parents' mutual viewing of a video of the same name, said it was because the French were a pack of froggy poofters.

"Not quite, dear," said Geordie. "It was because they were threatening to attack Minorca. And Admiral Byng was sent to drive them off. But they drove him off instead...."

"Silly sod," said someone at the back, quite possibly another Sackville judging by the way the rest of that tribe and its supporters were rolling about with laughter. Ms D'Arcy didn't want to know.

"The French drove off the British and Admiral Byng was tried by court-martial....Anyone know—no, never mind.... and shot for cowardice. At Portsmouth. Anyone know where Portsmouth is? Halfway down Division One. Yes, very good, Craig, thankyou."

Ms D'Arcy looked around her class. She felt very close to relieving her feelings. She gritted her teeth and muttered to herself: "You'll get to love Admiral Byng, you little bastards, before I've done with you." Then something snapped and she spoke out loud: *"Il est bon de tuer de temps en temps un amiral pour encourager les autres."* She paused at the end, ear cocked, quite prepared for someone to shout out "Voltaire" or "Candide" or both, but no-one did. It would have been quite like the perverse little monsters though.

Geordie D'Arcy needed such moments of quiet vengeance from time to time. They did no-one any harm and made her feel better. They were soon over as well. Now she was back in the real world again. "That's what you need to know about Admiral Byng," she said to the class. Then, raising her eyes slightly above it: "Would you like a few words now?"

She was looking to where Lord Bogger stood at the back, listening and marvelling not at the vagaries of the British educational system, but that there was any educational system left at all. He cleared his throat, a murmuring rose from the class. He had never faced a mob of children before, not even the softer variety in his native South, and certainly nothing like this bunch of Cumbrian assassins. The murmuring swelled. Lord Bogger's mouth was dry and he felt like poor Admiral Byng must have felt when he realised he was to be the politicians' scapegoat. But a thousand years of noble blood cannot let itself be thinned by a pack of Stoatholme yobs. Crecy came to mind, Agincourt too. "Right," he said loudly. "Sit down and shut up."

To his great surprise the children did just that. You could have heard, if not the dropping of a pin, then at least that of a two-inch nail. Ms D'Arcy gave him a glance which mixed respect and encouragement.

"Right," went on Lord Bogger. "We're going to act out the story of Admiral Byng. We're going to have ships and guns and sword-fights and an execution, and then fireworks....Who said that?"

The silence of the lambs had been broken, fairly softly but quite unmistakeably, by the utterance of the word "bum-holes". It had been followed by a titter of laughter.

Lord Bogger followed the direction of several spiteful gazes and located the stalwart form of Garth Wormwald, he of the glass eye. "Right," said Lord Bogger. He marched into the thick of the class, grabbed young Garth none too gently by the scruff of the neck, and hauled him to his feet. "I've got a job for you, big gob," he said.

"You get your hands off me," protested the one-eyed lad. "You're not allowed to touch me."

"I am Lord Bogger," said the peer in a voice so severe it shocked even its owner. "And I'll touch anybody I want to. And I'm not just going to touch you, lad. I'm going to have you shot. You're Admiral Byng, right? Go and stand out at the front."

Garth Wormwald made his way to the front, covering his defeat with a grin. A little cheer went up from the Wormwald faction, and a volley of hisses and cat-calls from the Sackvilles.

Lord Bogger went back to his place at the back of the classroom. "Now," he said. "We'll want a British Navy and a French Navy. They were sworn enemies, weren't they? So it shouldn't be too hard to match it here. You, Admiral Byng, what's your name?"

"Hadmiral Byng," said Garth Wormwald with a smirk.

"You're a fast learner, Byng," said Lord Bogger. "I think I'm going to enjoy seeing you shot. What's his other name, kids—the one he uses when he pretends he's human?"

The class told him—or at least the Sackville part of the class did. Right, said Lord Bogger, if Admiral Byng's a Wormwald, it's only right that the other Wormwalds should be the rest of the British Navy, and the Sackvilles could be the French.

"Er, Froggy poofters!" yelled Emmanuelle Wormwald, and the ranks of the Sackvilles looked far from suited.

"Don't forget," said Lord Bogger. "That the Frogs won. OK?"

....

"You should have been a teacher," said Geordie D'Arcy a little later over a pot of tea and something a little stronger as a supplement. "Or a lion tamer."

They were in what went by the name of the Staff Room, a pokey space hardly bigger than a broom cupboard, whose thin walls shivered to what sounded like the Third Battle of Ypres which was going on outside, around and above them. There had been a Bogger at Third Wypers, His Lordship was sure, and no doubt he had acquitted himself well. "They've reduced strong and healthy school advisers to nervous wrecks," said Geordie. "They chased a police superintendent who was supposed to be giving a talk on road safety, and the vicar never dared come near the place. When he was a man of course."

"And you?"

Geordie D'Arcy laughed, and rolled herself a cigarette. "Oh, I love the little sods, They've at least got a bit of life about them. It's just a pity there's nothing for them when they leave."

"So we're doing the right thing?" Lord Bogger didn't sound at all sure.

"What else could we do?" Geordie pulled on her roll-up like a navvy. "There are no kids in Boggerthwaite—well, none to speak of except Darren Costive the copper's son. He wants to be a ballet dancer, poor little sod. No, this'll give 'em something to get their teeth into."

"Hardly National Curriculum, though?"

"Look, I gave all that crap up years ago. This'll get their imagination going. Already this morning they've learnt there's somewhere called France; never mind the Balearics. They'll make the ships up on a couple of old lorries, courtesy of parents. They'll make the costumes. They'll build the effigy of old Byng, and setting light to the bonfire they might find just as much fun as trying to set light to the school. And they'll wake bloody Boggerthwaite up a bit."

"I think you may well just have made the under-statement of the year," said Lord Bogger. "Cheers."

19

The day of the Boggerthwaite Bleezins drew rapidly nearer—all too rapidly for Pc Robin de Vere Costive. He was used to an even tenor of life—gun licences to be inspected from time to time, and weekend shenanigans on the Sunny Lea Estate to avoid. The remainder of his time he spent helping the water bailiff keep an eye on the welfare of the fish stocks in the Bogger Beck, and since there hadn't been an actual water bailiff since before the war, this meant quite long periods of solo and uninterrupted conservation work on his own behalf.

But the Bleezins! As Pc Costive received it, the village was to be turned into a cross between the Notting Hill Carnival and the 'Prentice Boys' March in Derry. Traffic would have to be controlled, crowds directed, enthusiasms of unforeseen proportions curbed. Tourist attractions might be all very well for the likes of Mrs Loudwater, but they did not promise to make the village policeman's lot a happy one.

Pig racing, for example. Where were the pigs to come from? Once in Boggerthwaite, how handled? Where would the pig transporters be parked? What would the RSPCA have to say? What about animal rights protesters? Who would round the beasts up once they had finished their emulation of Lynford Christie? Then the prospect of thirty-five hooligans from Stoatholme School being let loose with fire and sword, egged on by their terrible parents, seemed to the good officer tantamount to opening the gates of Broadmoor. Thugthwaite Silver Prize Band had been mentioned, and Pc Costive's last recollection of this mob of musical alcoholic bruisers, at the funeral of their chief trombonist at St Ethelbogger's in 1989, still gave him nightmares. Don't ask why: anyone who remembered the way Barmy Bill Bowman had been regarded, on or off the trombone, would have known there would be a certain amount of exuberance. The local cottage hospital would have borne this out.

Someone had suggested a contest of athletics, in which Stoatholme Football Club (known far and wide as the Stranglers) would fight—no, sorry, play, an eleven scoured from the gutters of Penrith, Keswick, and even the west side of Carlisle—any place where players were no longer allowed officially to exercise their art. Pc Costive had felt like ringing up the Ministry of Defence to ask for a company of the SAS to help him keep order, but didn't know quite who could be contacted with such a request.

And then there was the question of Senator William Hudspith Wordsworth from Australia. Pc Costive had once tried to intervene in a discussion between three Australians and a chap from New Zealand in Earls Court. He had not been entirely successful. The good constable wished with all his soul that Senator Hudspith had never been born, never mind imagined himself a descendant of the late William Wordsworth, poet, of Grasmere.

20

The brown monotony of the Simpson Desert, or was it the Great Sandy Desert, slid by five miles beneath the jumbo jet, a gnat's eye view of a huge plate of burnt polenta. Senator William Hudspith Wordsworth, of Boggaburra, New South Wales, regarded it without enthusiasm. The only break in the sameness of the view was the very occasional patch of green, which might have been a chunk of pasture, a lump of discoloured rock, or maybe an insect in his eye. Once or twice there had been tatters of cloud far below, whose shadows thrown on the desert reminded him of kangaroos at play. What a boring hole Australia was! All right if you liked swimming, rugby football or sheep, but for a man of culture it wasn't really worth a light. Mind, the senator had not done at all badly out of it, materially, having built up an agricultural plant-hire business left to him by his father, the late Roger Hudspith Wordsworth. But he wondered now what his really renowned ancestor would have made of it. OK—there was plenty of commercial culture in Sydney these days—much variety of music and all the rest. But if you were a man of solitude, a creator, what would you find to write about in the interminable grotty suburbs or out in the bush, wandering lonely as a cloud between one heap of sheep-shit and the next, with not a daffodil in sight?

Senator Wordsworth ('Hud' to his friends) had never been to Britain. Myra, his wife, had: in fact she had been born there, at somewhere called Stockton-on-Tees, which the senator imagined must be somewhere cultural like Stratford-upon-Avon, otherwise why all the hyphens? Myra was not accompanying him on this trip. She said that England was a cold and windy dump full of pale, sick-looking people, and she wouldn't shed a single tear if she never saw it again. "The Old Country" was the right term for it, said Myra. It was bloody geriatric. Besides, she had her bowls tournaments.

Her husband had made diplomatic noises of regret that he had to be without her company, but not too many in case. He was in fact quite excited to be on his own. Myra's idea of culture was the next instalment of 'Neighbours' and poetry was something that rhymed between pictures of flowers on greetings cards. Wordsworth—*the* Wordsworth— she said, was a randy old goat who slept with his sister. 'Hud' often wondered where she had got this idea from, as she knew absolutely nothing else about the poet. "Anyway," she had said, "you watch yourself, Hud. You look like the old bastard and I don't want you to be acting like him." She believed in this family resemblance simply because the senator had told her about it years before. She would have had no way of checking it out except by looking at the old frontispiece engraving by Lipton after Haydon's portrait, and she would not have bothered much with that. In fact 'Hud' didn't look like his ancestor at all, apart perhaps from the beaky nose and the thinning hair, but 'Hud' fancied he did, and that was enough.

So—he was away from Myra, away from Boggaburra, away from New South Wales, and before very long he'd be right out of Australia altogether, footloose and fancy free. For the umpteenth time since he had received it he pulled out from an inner pocket the typewritten airmail letter, smoothed it, and read:

High Mitherins, Boggerthwaite, UK.

My Dear Senator,

It is my dearest wish to respond adequately to your kind letter. Suffice it to say that the news of your intention to visit the 'cradle of your forebears' has created quite a flutter in our little 'dovecot in the hills'. A hundred thousand welcomes!

By a marvellous coincidence—or perhaps the workings of Divine Providence (you do not state whether you are a Believer) your visit occurs during the celebration of our chief festival of the year, the Boggerthwaite Bleezins, in which, after our long winter, the forces of darkness, as symbolised by the short days, are pushed back and overcome by the advent of Spring. Your ancestor would have put it a thousand times better, of course, but the Bleezins, we are all convinced, will give you something to remember for the rest of your life....

"There you are," said the senator, prodding the typesheet with his finger. "The good old Boggerthwaite Bleezins." He pronounced the place-name to rhyme with 'bait' and he was addressing a tall, heavy-bosomed young lady who sat between him and the porthole chewing gum. The young lady was reading about the British Royal Family in a primary-coloured magazine and snorting from time to time. To the senator's friendly sally she merely remarked "Oh yeah?" without lifting her eyes from her page.

"Ever bin?" the senator asked next.

The young lady shifted her gum to the other side of her mouth. "Where?"

"Boggerthwaite," said the senator.

"Where?" as if he had uttered some obscenity.

"It's in England. You going to England?"

The young lady looked at the senator for the first time during the exchange, and frowned rather irritably. "Why?" she said.

"Well," smiled the senator, "It'll be my first time, you see, and I thought if you knew it at all you could show me round a bit."

The young lady did not answer straight away. Instead, she removed her wad of gum, bearing the imprint of her beautifully white teeth, screwed it into the corner of the plastic box which had contained the first meal of the flight, and of which she had consumed, Hud noticed, every last little bit, dumped the tray on the floor, folded back the shelf on which it had rested, wriggled back as far as she could in her seat and raised one perfectly-shaped sun-bronzed bare leg to rest the dimpled knee against the back of the seat in front of her. Then: "Git lost, Dad," she said before closing her eyes.

The senator sighed, but it is not like a full-blooded Wordsworth to repine for long in the face of an early rebuff. London was still the best part of 24 hours away, and 24 hours is a long time on an aeroplane. He resumed reading his letter.

We have taken the liberty of working out an itinerary for your stay in our little 'haven of peace'. You are of course not bound by any part of it: it is merely for your guidance, but we trust you will be impressed with what the Bogger Valley has to offer.

Bleezins Thursday (April 23). Five pm, Flight 1501 from Sydney arrives Heathrow-London Airport. Overnight in our capital city at your own convenience.

Bleezins Friday, 6 a.m. Train from London Euston to be met by a small delegation from Boggerthwaite Parish Council at Penrith, 11 a.m. Please be wearing something red in your button-hole as we lack a picture of you and we do not want to risk embarrassing delays...."

The young lady in the neighbouring seat shifted her position with a grunt and changed legs, forcing the senator's attention away from his letter for a moment and causing him to groan inwardly.

Twelve midday. Arrive at Boggerthwaite. Civic reception at the Dehydrated Rambler Hotel, followed by lunch at 1pm. Two pm, motor tour of the Bogger Valley, afternoon tea at the home of Mrs

G Loudwater, Chair of the Parish Council. Six pm, assemble at the Dehydrated Rambler for evening of Poetry and Fun, followed by supper and soiree at Mirkin Grange, home of Arpad Mahmoud, Esq., Lord of the Manor. And so to bed.

"I'm to be the guest, you see," said Senator Wordsworth to his neighbour, who had the most amazing pair of breasts he had ever partly glimpsed in that land of amazing mammary development he was now quitting.

"Good for you, sport," said the young lady, shifting brown legs yet once again. "Now, jist sod off, will yer?"

Senator Wordsworth sighed. The manners of young people today, he reflected, left much to be desired. He turned again to his letter for another taste of an older, more elegant way of life.

Bleezins Saturday. Gala football spectacular between Stoatholme United and the Lakeland All Stars. Concert by Thugthwaite Silver Prize Band. Grand parade and carnival 2.30pm. The effigy of Admiral Byng, constructed by local schoolchildren, will be transported to the foot of Great Mirkin Fell, where it will be carried to the Buzzard Stone by the attendant Byngers and there set alight (weather permitting). This will be followed by a grand 'Byngburger Bar-bee-q' on the village green.

At the conclusion of our little festivities, we hope that you may want to stay on for a while in our 'Land of the Lakes', and you can be sure that you will not lack willing guides to 'show you around' its many delights.

You may also be interested to learn that the missing line of your esteemed ancestor's Boggerthwaite poem has now been supplied by our own 'Poet Laureate' Mr Matthew Ouskin, as follows:

'My heart leaps up when I behold,
The valley of the Bogge
Long may its rills and clemmits bold,
Be hymned in Wagga-wagga'

We hope you appreciate this little linguistic whimsy, and that it will help to cement further relations between the UK and its young Antipodean Offspring.

Yours ever, Gladys Loudwater (Mrs), Chairperson Boggerthwaite Parish Council.

"D'you mind?" said the young lady in the neighbouring seat.

She had stood up now. Long dark brown hair tumbled over shapely shoulders. One dimpled bare knee was poking quite insistently into the senator's thigh. "Need the loo," explained the young lady as he stood to let her past. He shivered as soft, warm contact took place between her extraordinary bosom and his chin. The young lady gave no thanks, but the senator felt that in some respects he had been amply rewarded without words.

"D'you mind?" It was one of the stewardesses this time, come to collect up the detritus from the first meal. She leaned across him in order to retrieve his young neighbour's plastic tray, discarded chewing gum and all. She was a brave stewardess, or perhaps lacking somewhat in experience, but she jumped nearly a foot in the air as a hand belonging to Senator Hudspith Wordsworth found her shapely backside and gave it an appreciative squeeze. Yet she was able to retain some dignity. "That is not part of the service, sir," she said icily. "So piss off."

21

Whatever the rest of former Fleet-street believed about the whereabouts of the Rev Michelle Ximenez, the Daily Brute knew for a fact that they had neither abducted her nor persuaded her in any way to put herself under their wing. In fact they had seen neither hide nor hair, cassock or chasuble of her. If newspapers were capable of being offended, then the Brute would have been licking its wounds. "The buggers grumble about falling church attendances," remarked Desmond Cardington-Sprott, the bluff, hard-bitten news editor, at the lunchtime editorial conference which took place by custom in the Rabid Jackal, the paper's pet wine bar. "And they treat us like shit. After all the publicity we've given them."

His assistant agreed with him. But then attractive, green-eyed, red-haired Minette Mendoza (38-24-36) agreed with everything he said (or suggested). Breathed 26-year-old former pop-star Minette: "Ungrateful bastards."

"They're always after public money to repair their rotten roofs, bolster up their bloody belfries, and get rid of death watch beetle in their putrid vestries. If this bloody clerical bimbette played along with us she could afford to build a whole new bloody cathedral."

"Absolutely, Des," murmured long-legged Oxford Graduate Minette. "You're so right."

"Bergholz is the man," said the news editor suddenly.

"Wow! Absolutely right on!" said his lovely assistant. "I'll see to it."

And so it came to pass that a rheumy-eyed, badly shaven, indeed quite grubby little man, apparently well past his middle years, came to take up residence on the public bench outside St Ethelbogger's Church, Boggerthwaite. Stan Bergholz (36-44-46) was the Daily Brute's star reporter. He specialised in assignments that even the low-life employees of the other tabloids forbore to touch. He cared not for personal discomfort, hunger, cold, wind or rain. He was said to be worth a fortune.

From his public seat (presented by Arpad Mahmoud Esq., in commemoration of Commonwealth Day, 1993) Mr Bergholz commanded a view of both St Ethelbogger's Church and its vicarage. He could also see the front of the Dehydrated Rambler, but the place seemed to hold no attraction for him. If he ate at all it was from some secret store of food about his well-wrapped person; if he drank it must have been from puddles. Or so Mrs Sylvia Anstruther remarked to all and sundry. Mr Bergholz's one apparent concession to creature comforts was a fondness for cigarettes. These he rolled himself from time to time from a battered old tin of tobacco, and the grass around him was fairly covered with very short dog-ends and a small timber-yard of spent matches. How he had got where he was no-one seemed to know. He just appeared one morning and did not go away.

Police Constable Costive couldn't stand the sight of him. He was a clear case of a loiterer with no visible means of support, but he wasn't at all sure what he could do with him. There was a cell

144

in the police house, but Mrs Bryony Costive made it quite plain that there was no way she was going to have an old tramp like that fouling up her home. Besides, in winter she used the cell as a sort of indoor kennel for Rudi, her Bernese Mountain Dog, and her husband knew better than to cross her in canine matters. "And think of the effect it'd have on Darren," she said to clinch the matter.

The officer tried the personal approach with Bergholz. "I'm going to have to ask you to move along, old son," were the actual words he used.

The old son rolled his eyes and said: *"Nicht verstehe."*

"That's all very well," said Pc Costive. "But I don't want to see you sitting there next time I'm past. OK?"

"Wie bitte?" said Mr Bergholz, and rolled another cigarette.

He was still there the next morning when Mrs Anstruther arrived to have a look at the vicarage. The rooks were cawing in the trees behind it, the daffodils fluttering and dancing in the grass verge before it, and clumps of crocuses still showed, though well past their early best. Even a pale, watery sun appeared from time to time. Springtime in the Bogger Valley. Once the daffs had gone, thought Mrs Anstruther, there would follow a few indifferent weeks of what people still called summer, though it wasn't, of course, not like when she was a girl, and then they'd all be on about Christmas, and it would be winter again. Winter—the Bogger Valley's natural season. You knew where you were with winter.

Mrs Anstruther regarded the old tramp out of the corner of her eye as she propped her bicycle before the vicarage gates. Mr Bergholz reciprocated, though it was hard to tell what he was looking at.

Mrs Anstruther was not long inside the vicarage, it not being one of her regular cleaning days, and in any case there was no-one there at present to clean for. She tidied one or two things the vicar

145

had put out of place before beating her retreat, took two bottles of milk off the step and put them in the fridge, then changed her mind and transferred them to a plastic shopping bag. Then she picked up a few items of mail from the doormat, sorted the junk from the letters that looked at all important, and having secured the door behind her, carried both the mail and the two bottles of milk to her bicycle and popped them in the basket up front. The old tramp was still on his seat.

Now Mrs Anstruther, for all the hard life she'd had, and for all that her April thoughts kept dwelling on the imminence of Christmas, was at heart of kindly soul. She registered the tramp's presence, put one foot on her bicycle pedal, and scooted over towards him. "Like milk, do you?" she asked.

Mr Bergholz raised his battered old hat and twisted his unbeautiful face into a smile. "That really is uncommonly decent of you, madam," he said, even standing to receive Mrs Anstruther's offering.

His eyes, of course, took in the bottles of milk, but they lingered rather longer, if Mrs Anstruther had but noticed, on the handful of letters beside them.

"Vicar away, is he?" asked Mr Bergholz, deferentially.

"She," said Mrs Anstruther. "Matter of fact yes, she is."

"And you're keeping an eye on things, eh?"

"I've always cleaned the vicarage, as a matter of fact," said Mrs Anstruther, and, peering more closely: "Are you getting enough to eat?"

"Oh, yes, certainly, ma'am," smirked Mr Bergholz. But his cold, yellowish eyes were trying to decipher postmarks on envelopes. "Where's the vicar, then—on holiday?"

"Visiting friends, I believe," said Mrs Anstruther stiffly.

"And you forward her mail, do you?" Mr Bergholz had punched

146

loose the foil top of one of the milk bottles, and started to swig from the neck.

"I look after things," said Mrs Anstruther. "And I mind my own business." And she set her bicycle in motion again.

Mr Bergholz viewed her retreat with a sardonic look. "Minding my own business," he said to himself. "Now that's something I just never could do—thank God."

Mrs Anstruther's cycling figure grew smaller as she reached the Stoatholme road. Mr Bergholz produced from one of the many folds of his overcoat a pair of small but extremely powerful binoculars. He was rewarded a few moments later by the sight of Mrs Anstruther meeting another woman on a bicycle. She was younger, plumpish, but quite attractive, with rich chestnut hair. A few words seemed to be exchanged, then the older woman handed over the batch of letters and cycled off again down a farm track. The younger turned her machine out the way she had come and moved off. It was time for Mr Bergholz to take Pc Costive's advice and move on, which he did with a speed and agility surprising in so unathletic looking a figure.

....

"Quite a trawl," said Gloria Sackville some ten minutes later, fanning out the batch of letters before the Rev Michelle Ximenez in the kitchen of Bogger Hall. Lord Bogger used the kitchen quite a lot. It was warmer than the rest of the rambling old house, and he had not yet got the hang of the central heating.

The vicar took the mail. "Three bills. The rest look pretty harmless. Or do I speak too soon?" She peered at one of the envelopes with more than usual suspicion, then opened it. "Looks churchy." She sniffed the expensive looking notepaper. "Yes—the odour of sanctity."

She frowned as she began to read, and her frown grew more intense the further on she got. "Well," she said eventually, "They certainly don't hang about." She handed the letter to Lord Bogger. "The Rural Dean," she said.

Lord Bogger read aloud for Gloria's benefit:

Dear Reverend Ximenez,

My attention having been drawn to certain organs of the popular press, it is with deep regret that I read about the state of affairs prevailing at the present moment in Boggerthwaite Parish. Of course, until I hear your side of the story I refuse to accept at face value all that has been written about you. Unfortunately you seem to have made yourself unavailable. Repeated telephone calls have failed to elicit any response, and a personal visit by the Bishop's Secretary and myself this morning likewise drew a blank.

I must ask you, for the sake of your flock, to contact me as soon as possible. Meanwhile I must insist that you cease *pro tempere* the performance of your pastoral duties.

In the earnest and prayerful hope that we shall see a speedy solution to this apparently sad affair. I remain, etc., etc.

"Well, looks like what they call the bullet, me old darling," said Lord Bogger.

"I shall defy him of course," said Ms Ximenez. "I shall celebrate Mattins on Saturday, which is St Ethelbogger's Day—I'll bet you didn't know that—and if they want to stop me they'll have to drag me from the altar."

"Wouldn't it be better to hang on a little longer," suggested Gloria. "Until things die down a bit?"

"No—my congregation has a right to know what's going on. I shall tell them, and I think they'll understand."

"Both of them," said Gloria under her breath.

Exactly what it was that prompted her to look up at that moment towards the window she could not have explained exactly, but she was in time to catch a blurred glimpse of the head and shoulders of a rather unsavoury looking old man. She was at the back door before you could say Stan Bergholz. "Can I help you?" Gloria asked.

The disreputable looking man, who was still trying to recover breath expended on an unaccustomed uphill trot, gave an ingratiating leer and raised his hat. "Wondered if you 'ad any odd jobs, marm," he wheezed. "Just to help us earn a crust, like."

Gloria switched on a smile in which those who knew her would have detected little merriment, or mercy. "I do believe we have," she said. "What are you like at splitting logs?"

Mr Bergholz leaned against the door jamb, the picture of a man who was not good at splitting logs. His muddy eyes probed past Gloria. "Not so good as I am at what you might call, well— ecclesiastical tasks. You get my drift?"

"Like grave-digging, d'you mean?" asked Gloria. "Mucking out old crypts?"

"Digging, yes, in a manner of speaking," said Mr Bergholz. "Uncovering the truth, I suppose you might say. I'd like a word with the vicar, sweetheart."

Gloria Sackville's nicely-shaped eyelids remained un-batted. "I'm afraid you're barking up the wrong tree, old dear," she said. "If you're after a vicar, why don't you try a vicarage, perhaps?"

Mr Bergholz smiled sadly. "You know, I had thought of that. Alas, I drew a blank—as I think you'd realise."

"Then it's not your day," said Gloria. "You've just drawn another one. Now if you'll excuse me." She was making to shut the door against Mr Bergholz when the Rev. Ximenez came out into the porch from the kitchen. Lord Bogger was behind her, but if he had been trying to restrain her, he had been unsuccessful.

"It's all right, Gloria," she said. "The gentleman wants to see me I take it?"

"Gentleman is very nice," said Mr Bergholz, uncovering his grimy scalp yet again. "But it may not be quite accurate. Bergholz is my name—Bergholz of the Brute."

149

22

Arpad Mahmoud Esquire, the embryonic Marquis of Stoatholme, was taking the air on a morning of rare sunshine. He had strolled through the grounds of Mirkin Grange, down the long drive towards the road, a brace of rotweilers at heel. The first buds were burgeoning on the avenue of beech trees and the rhododendrons and azaleas were having a good burgeon too. Birds were twittering in all the bushes and a great host of daffodils swayed in their thousands on the open patches of lawn. Mr Mahmoud took deep lungfulls of air and expelled them as slowly as he could. "Oh to be in England," he said, softly but with feeling. "Now that April's there."

To an unknowing observer Mr Mahmoud would have appeared to be at leisure, a man with no worries about toil. In fact already that morning (and it was still only eight-thirty Greenwich Mean Time) he had received very satisfactory fax messages from agents in both Hong Kong and Beirut which would be netting him the equivalent of the fruit of many years' hard graft on the part of most of us. Life was good, and Mr Mahmoud appreciated it.

Again, one not in the know would have believed Mr Mahmoud to be alone. He appeared to be, but he was not. A number of the larger shrubs, and one or two of the more mature trees, served as cover for men in Mr Mahmoud's service. Gardeners, he called them, but they were leaner and much fitter than the general run of horticultural servants, and those who know about these things would have pronounced them to be members of the Korean race, all quite probably called Kim something-or-other. Each carried a small walkie-talkie with which he conversed from time to time with his fellow gardeners. Only God, they and Mr Mahmoud knew what they carried out of sight tucked snugly in their armpits. Mr Mahmoud, of course, knew they were around, but he was usually unaware of their precise whereabouts. He liked to preserve his feeling of solitude even if it was only an illusion.

So he did not expect to see one of the 'gardeners' — rather a bright young lad, too, who was almost certainly called Kim—so far forget himself as to be quite visible from where he, Mr Mahmoud, was walking. The man was peering over the shoulder of a clump of flowering currant and watching something intently through a pair of binoculars. He then appeared to say something into his walkie-talkie. Mr Mahmoud followed the direction of the man's gaze, and there, round the first bend in the avenue from the front gates, located the most extraordinary looking vehicle he had seen since his days of early struggle in Port Said.

It was of no recognisable make, but seemed to have collected parts and styles from a dozen different types of vehicle and almost as many decades—a real mongrel of a truck. Some of it was blue—perhaps the greater part of its bodywork. But there was also some bright yellow, some green, and a large amount of red which could have been rust. A canvas awning somehow attached behind the cab gave it a sort of covered wagon look, and it farted and belched loudly with great bursts of blue smoke. Mr Mahmoud's two rotweilers growled, then bounded forward to greet it. Mr Mahmoud was about to call them off but was saved the trouble by the sudden appearance in great leaps over the tail-board of the truck of two large dogs of no breed known to the Kennel Club or indeed any zoo. One was black, shorthaired, with pointed ears and a fluffy tail that might have looked better on a chow; the other was like a short-legged wolf, only yellow. The pair met the rotweilers head-on, and after a few fang-baring flurries, full of sound and fury, Mr Mahmoud's dogs turned and disappeared into the rhododendrons, tails well down.

The vehicle stopped, one door opened with a loud creak, and the driver eased himself out of the cab. He was a big driver, well over six foot, and dressed in spite of the earliness of the year in a torn yellow singlet, blue jeans and leather boots with high heels. The absence of any covering on his arms permitted an uninterrupted view of a fine collection of tattooed emblems which covered every inch of flesh and were on their way down through the armholes as if to invade the torso. There was plenty of torso, particularly just above the belt. The man had an unkempt thatch of yellow-brownish hair so long that it obscured some of the designs on the upper parts of his arms, and a fine growth of stubble which covered a rather slack jaw. A squashed nose and two bright blue, innocent eyes completed a face which had more in it of amiability than aggression. "Hi," said the man. "I'm Haitch." The aspirate was most pronounced.

Mr Mahmoud put his head on one side and studied the man. "I'm sorry?" he said. He had noticed three or four of his 'gardeners' converging, but motioned them to wait.

"Haitch. It's short for 'Arry."

"I'm pleased to meet you," said Mr Mahmoud. "On such an exceptionally fine morning too. Have you come far?"

"Just from Blackpool, like. Set off yesterday afternoon. Kipped in a lay-by on the old A5."

"And to what do I owe the honour of your appearance here at Mirkin Grange?"

The newcomer considered the question as if it merited a lot of thought. "Dunno really," he said eventually. "It's these ley-lines, I suppose. Linda reckons you're on one. Oh, you haven't met Linda. Linda!" He shouted the name as if its owner was a mile or two away instead of occupying, as Mr Mahmoud now became aware, the passenger seat in front of the truck. Linda opened her door and started to emerge.

Now Mr Arpad Mahmoud, in the course of a not uneventful life in some of the more exotic parts of the world, had come across a fair number of extremely attractive women. Never, he realised now, but never, had he clapped eyes on one quite so gorgeous as Linda.

She must, he reckoned, have been about twenty-two (as against an estimated forty or so for Haitch), petite, but beautifully developed, particularly where Mr Mahmoud best liked development, in the thorax and the posterior. She had long, rather shaggy hair, very dark brown, and people who knew about hair and its dressing would have told you that its apparent wildness was really the result of much careful grooming. Linda was wearing a tight-fitting long dress of white spots on maroon, and had no shoes—or stockings for that matter. So, altogether a very juicy little package, you might say if you wanted to sound sexist. But that would have missed the whole point—which is that she had a face of quite extraordinary loveliness. Deep dark eyes, fine bone structure, a full mouth with a smile to captivate any male it landed upon, and altogether an expression of total sweetness, with the promise of a temperament both sensual and intelligent, in short a paragon. "Ullo," said Linda.

Mr Mahmoud, who had been about to lead up to having the intruders thrown off his property, was himself completely thrown instead. "I, er....welcome to my humble....er, to Mirkin Grange."

"Ley-lines, wasn't it, Lin?" Haitch was peering about as if ley-lines were like telegraph wires, strung up above the ground on a series of poles.

"Ley-lines, that's right Haitch," said the girl, in a broad London accent. She smiled, fixed Mr Mahmoud's eyes with her own, even seeming to penetrate the darkness of his glasses. "You interested in ley-lines, then?"

Mr Mahmoud struggled with words, but the girl went on: "Lot of people don't know about ley-lines, do they? But I suppose you do or you wouldn't be living here, would you?"

"My dear young lady, I had no idea...."

" 'Ow old's the 'ouse?" asked Linda, gazing past Mr Mahmoud

153

to where the turrets and battlements of the Grange peeped through the trees, the Union Flag fluttering over all.

Mr Mahmoud puffed out his chest a little. "The original Grange was erected in the thirteenth century," he said. "But most of what you see now is about a hundred years old."

"You need summfink a bit older than that for ley-lines," said Linda thoughtfully. "Prehistoric really." She sounded a trifle disappointed, like an interested house-buyer who has just learned that the drains have fallen in.

"I could show you around," said Mr Mahmoud brightly, and Linda could see that behind those dark glasses beady eyes were busy removing every stitch of the rather inadequate clothing she was wearing.

"Oh, there'll be summfink," said Linda. "Some old burial site or whatever. I can feel it. Haitch can feel it too, can't you Haitch?"

Haitch was busy scratching one armpit with quite intense concentration. "Right from the start, doll," he agreed.

"We saw about it in the paper, like," said Linda. "The Buzzard Stone and that. It said ley-lines. And you can feel 'em, you really can."

"You have been up to the Buzzard Stone?" Mr Mahmoud sounded surprised. "So early already?"

Linda nodded. "First fing," she said. She sounded like a small, serious girl who has actually *seen* fairies at the bottom of her garden.

"Yeah, we read about it, like," said Haitch, switching the raking activity of his fingers to that part of the upper trouser which bowling cricketers use to polish the ball on. "In the paper. Ley-lines, it said, and we're always after ley-lines. Stonehenge, we go to; we go to Glastonbury. But it's really heavy there. Get moved on."

"Oh it's something terrible, the harassment," agreed Linda. She pronounced the last word with the accent on the second 'a'.

If Mr Mahmoud had the slightest inkling of what the pair were talking about he failed to show it. In view of what was to happen later it is most probable that he didn't have a clue. But he did like the look of Linda and was already wondering how she might fit in with Fatima, Scheherazade, Esmat, and of course Mandy. Mandy wasn't going to like it, he knew that.

"We checked it out on the map," Linda was saying. "If you draw a line through the Buzzard Stone to that stone circle outside Keswick it goes on the other way to that one at....what's it called? Then there's that place near Penrith—Long Meg, in't it? The line from there to that old abbey place—you know—crosses the other line right here at Mirkin Grange. So it must have been a very special place."

"It's a special place to me," said Mr Mahmoud. "Cost me a lot of money."

But Linda didn't seem impressed by the financial side of things. She was looking around at the park now with great intensity. "Wot's that?" she said suddenly.

"What, dear lady?" said Mr Mahmoud.

"That rock. There." Linda was pointing. Then she was away.

Mr Mahmoud saw only a boulder lodged at the foot of a slope and almost totally hidden by surrounding trees and shrubbery. Obviously considered immovable by the layers-out of Mirkin Grange's gardens, they had done the next best thing and hidden it.

The two dogs which had seen off Mr Mahmoud's rotweilers reached the stone first, and were giving it some cocked leg treatment before flushing out one of the 'gardeners', who scowled and retreated. Linda went up to the stone, her hands held out in front of her like a stage sleep-walker. Indeed when Mr Mahmoud joined her it was to find that she had her eyes closed as she passed her hands over the rock like a blind girl feeling a stranger's face. At first she was tense, frowning with concentration. Suddenly her

155

face relaxed. She opened her eyes, a beautiful smile came to her lips, and she was breathing deeply, a woman aroused. Mr Mahmoud was most uncomfortably fascinated by the sight. Mandy just wouldn't have to care. Mandy would do as she was told.

"Yes," Linda was saying in a voice deep and full of certainty. "Oh, yes, this is it." And she stroked the rock as if expecting it to come alive for her. Which, judging by her expression, it may well have done.

"You got it, Linda?" Haitch was looking at her as he might have viewed a terrier locked on to a rabbit.

"I can feel it, Haitch. This is definitely it."

"What can you feel?" Mr Mahmoud wanted to know.

Linda switched her gaze, as if recognising him after years away. "Oh, the Forces," she said. "The Energy. Touch it. Feel for yourself."

Mr Mahmoud would very much have liked to have felt Linda's own forces, but there would be time for that later. He placed his hand on the rock. He felt nothing—just a rough, cold hardness. "It is like a vibration," he lied, beaming as if in discovery. "Is that what you could feel too?"

Linda did not answer. She had taken Haitch by the arm and was leading him away slowly, but out of earshot. Haitch was nodding in some sort of agreement. "Can only try," Mr Mahmoud heard him saying.

Linda was back again, all young girlish smiling charm. "Can we stay?" she was asking, eyes full of promise. "Just for a few days?"

Mr Mahmoud's heart nearly missed a beat. Oh come into my parlour, little fly, he found himself thinking. "Of course, my dear," he found himself saying.

"You'll probably hardly notice us," said Linda, beaming gratitude. "We won't make a mess."

156

"My place is your place," said Mr Mahmoud magnanimously.

"It's just that...." The girl dropped her eyes for a second, and when she lifted them again they were more appealing than ever. "It's just that there's a few friends of ours as well. Psychic archaeologists, you know. Intuitives. They'll be ever so interested. That be all right?"

"Of course, my dear," said Mr Mahmoud. "Now let me show you round the house."

Somehow Haitch appeared to have been excluded from the invitation. But it seemed hardly to worry him. As Linda was led away up towards the big house by Mr Mahmoud, arm round waist only a little lower, Haitch was clambering back into his truck, tinkering with some sort of radio transmitter. There was a crackling, then: "That you, Alf? (crackle) Haitch here. (crackle) Yeah, big Haitch. Look, we're at that Mirkin place. It's OK to pull on. (crackle) Yeah, great. Right mate—see you all later."

23

Ms Muriel Korbishley was in Mrs Loudwater's shop, looking for this and that on obscure shelves, as happens these days. Not so long back she could have approached Mrs Loudwater directly, asked for a packet of raisins, a tin of bamboo shoots and half a pound of mushrooms, and got them. Not any more. Mrs Loudwater sat behind a flap, till by her side, waiting like a spider in its web for customers to bring their chosen wares to her notice. The Chair was talking to Mr Bean the Clerk, and to Mr McGurk from the pub, and had quite forgotten Ms Korbishley rooting around behind the packets of tights, pan-scourers and lavatory paper.

Ms Korbishley, Geordie D'Arcy's friend, has been mentioned before, but not materialised. Here she was then—a dumpy women of about thirty, black-haired, black-browed, heavy-hipped, broad-shouldered as perhaps befits a sculptress, dressed in dark blue salopettes and a purple shirt, with green Wellington boots encasing

157

her lower legs. Ms Korbishley habitually said little—well, she didn't need to be otherwise with Geordie around—but she was a very good listener.

Her name I spell with a K—Korbishley—in the almost certain knowledge that no-one of that arrangement of letters exists to take me to court. If there is a Ms K, then I must assure her that my character in no way resembles or is based upon her. Not that there is anything vicious about her—just a touch or two of eccentricity.

She listened now, while still absent-mindedly plucking this and that package from the shelves and transferring it to her wire basket, like some spring bee at flowers. She listened, and she heard what sounded like a discussion of the plans for Boggerthwaite's big day, the Bleezins.

"Well, D-day minus one, and everything seems to be tiggety-boo." It was the voice of the Parish Clerk at its most unctuous pitch of self-satisfaction.

"Even the weather...." began Mrs Loudwater, then checked.

"Perhaps it's better not to say anything about the weather. Tempt fate."

Ms Korbishley selected a tube of toothpaste, examined it for organic suitability, then rejected it in favour of another of hideous green.

"I must say I'm not a hundred per cent happy." It was Rory McGurk, sounding like a man who has lost sleep. Ms Korbishley pricked up ears.

"What's up, luv?" asked Mrs Loudwater.

"And I'm not the only one," Mr McGurk went on. "I was talking to young Costive, and it's giving him nightmares."

Mr Bean was chuckling. "Poor bugger, he hasn't got the imagination to have a wet dream, never mind a nightmare."

"Now," cautioned Mrs Loudwater. "Now, now." and pretended to be shocked.

"He's worried about Stoatholme," Mr McGurk went on.

"Ah well," put in Mr Bean. "He wouldn't be the first."

"I mean," said Mr McGurk, "they're all very well where they belong, down Sunny Lea and round the Goat and Compasses. But they're going to invade. They'll take over the Bleezins if we're not careful."

"Democracy, Rory," said Mrs Loudwater.

"Absolutely," said Mr Bean.

"The last time I let any of 'em in the Rambler was chaos. A darts match. I was young and innocent at the time."

"Must have been a while ago," said Mr Bean.

Mr McGurk ignored him. "It was supposed to be a friendly match. Friendly? They started off fighting amongst themselves, then when our team turned up they closed ranks and had a go at them. Absolute bedlam."

"I remember when we first came," attempted Mrs Loudwater. "Boggerthwaite was heaven. We'd settled in before I saw Stoatholme, and I nearly...."

"The next time," bulldozed Mr McGurk," was the Remembrance Service. When the vicar first came here. Remembrance? They remembered all right. They did the Second World War, the First World War, the Boer War. Right back to Agincourt that lot went. They remembered all right. They're a bloody menace."

"Now I'm sure they'll enter into the spirit of the thing this time." Mr Bean sounded optimistic. He re-lit his pipe, puffed it, and spoke down its stem. "Democracy, as I said."

"Democracy's all right," said Mr McGurk. "If you'd just left it to Boggerthwaite. But whose bright idea was it to let that lot of apes into it? They wouldn't have noticed if you hadn't told 'em."

"Now we had to let the children in," said Mrs Loudwater. "They're doing the tableau. They've put a lot of work in, I believe. Anyway, Miss D'Arcy's looking after them."

"That's what I'm really worried about," said Mr McGurk in tones truly sepulchral.

Muriel Korbishley waited until the little meeting dispersed, then paid for her purchases cheerfully. That evening she reported back to her friend.

"Right," said Geordie D'Arcy grimly. "I think we know how to deal with that attitude."

24

It was not in Mr Bergholz's nature to spend money lavishly. Not that there was any shortage of the stuff where the Daily Brute was concerned, but their man was a reporter of Spartan disposition with regard to himself and about as free with gifts to others as the manager of a small-town Yorkshire bank. Most of his breed, having picked a ripe plum like the Rev Ximenez, would have whisked her away with many sugary blandishments to some extremely discreet but wickedly expensive hotel where food and drink would have been out of the reach of most people except for members of parliament being entertained by Arab sheikhs in search of arms favours. This food and drink would have been less for the delectation of the captive than of the reporter. Much of their working lives was sustained by fish-and-chips and hamburgers, and many of them, if dissected, would have resembled chunks of streaky bacon, from the alternation of fat times and lean.

But Stan Bergholz was not like that. He positively enjoyed fish and chips, and could go for two days or more on a bacon sandwich and a cup of tea. So, having been surrendered to by Ms Ximenez, he whisked her off not to Claridges or the Ritz, but to a small private hotel in a back street in Keswick. It had no bar, the rooms were very much not *en suite*, and it smelt of cats and Lancashire hot-pot, known colloquially in Cumbria as tatie-pot. But it was a discreet hotel and it was very cheap.

Again, most London reporters would have transported their prisoner either in their own car, or in a local taxi, regardless of expense. Or rather because of *expenses*, which could be doubled by getting the driver to present an abominably heavy but purely fictitious bill and then tipping the man rather over the going rate. Not Bergholz. "It's such a lovely day, my dear," he said to the Rev Ximenez, "that it would be a shame to miss the sun. You do like fell-walking, I gather?"

As it happened the Rev Ximenez loathed and abominated fell-walking, or any perambulation of more than a few yards. But she was so relieved at having given herself up at last, to have put an end to all the secrecy and furtiveness of the past few weeks, that she agreed. She had a pair of boots left over from a charity walk she had been obliged to take part in the previous Easter, and whatever other changes her body might have undergone since then, her feet had stayed the same at size nine-and-a-half. Not particularly large for a man, but not doing much for assumed femininity. The vicar laced the boots on heartily enough, however, and with a few things packed into a small rucksack loaned by Gloria Sackville, strode off with Mr Bergholz over the fell.

"Well," said Lord Bogger when they had disappeared in the general direction of Keswick (a good ten miles away as the crow flies and the rambler sweats), "I don't see what else we could have done."

Gloria nodded. "Poor lass, she couldn't go on living in hiding like that for much longer. Besides, she gets in the way."

"It isn't," said Lord Bogger, "that I have a particularly great sympathy for transexuals, but that I have even less for the hidebound nanny-goats who run the Church. The poor old rev might have got her timing wrong, but at least she had a go."

161

Gloria smiled as Lord Bogger rather absent-mindedly stroked her flank. "We could go for a walk too; it's such a lovely morning. I wonder if they've got a map and compass."

"And a whistle to blow six blasts on? I rather doubt it."

....

As things turned out the big-footed lady vicar and the old reporter had no need of such mountaineering aids. They were an oddly-matched pair, and not such as one is normally likely to meet on our Lakeland fells: she with black mantilla and modest skirt above the hideous boots, he with dirty, bulging mackintosh and green wellingtons, which he had 'found' in Lord Bogger's porch. Yet they appeared to be getting along well enough together, were deep in conversation most of the time, so that they hardly seemed to notice the steepness of the fell-side or the roughness of the occasional patch of scree they had to cross.

"You must," said Mr Bergholz after they had been going for just thirty minutes and had not yet got halfway up on to the ridge, "you must think that I and people like me—reporters and such-like—are a pretty undesirable lot." And he cupped his hands to light the latest in a chain of hand-rolled cigarettes.

"I hardly know you," smiled the vicar.

Bergholz coughed long and deeply. "Not much to know, I suppose. But you'll think we're a pretty useless bunch."

"Every creature has its place in the scheme of things," said the reverend mildly. "We can't all be eagles or lions: some have to be jackals and woodlice."

"Thanks," said Mr Bergholz. He was quiet for a few more paces, then, thoughtfully: "I'd've liked—or rather sometimes I think I'd've liked—to do something really good. Like Mother Theresa or someone...."

"Then perhaps you ought to do what I did, and change."

162

"I'm not changing my sex for anyone," said Mr Bergholz, a trifle indignantly. "But my outlook—I think that needs changing."

"But you're doing what we might call a necessary evil, aren't you? You're exposing wickedness, bringing down tyrants, championing the little man."

Mr Bergholz sighed, and the exhalation had little to do with all the energy he was expending. "I used to believe that. I still tell myself sometimes that I'm some sort of instrument of the Avenging Angel, a kind of Robin Hood—righting wrongs, revealing the truth. But...."

Ms Ximenez paused and looked back. She realised she was beginning almost to enjoy the walk. "Look at that view," she was about to say, but realised that her companion had not once looked about him, could have been walking down some featureless, gritty freeway on the outskirts of Milton Keynes for all the impact the landscape and the weather were having upon him.

"Look," she said instead. "About this story. What I want you to write is quite simple...."

25

Old Billy Nattrass was a man not often touched by confusion. In his younger days there had sometimes been decisions to make— how many shearling lambs to sell at the mart, whether to attempt to repair a length of drystone dyke or to bodge it up with a few yards of pig-netting—but since he had switched from the farming of livestock to the manipulation of the property market life had become even simpler, Until recently, that is. For as the day of the Boggerthwaite Bleezins drew nearer Old Billy's confusion took root and started to grow.

The main trouble was that he could not decide whether he was for the celebrations or agin them. It was true that he had first mentioned the Bleezins themselves, but what they had really been like he could not have told you. He had vague recollections of some sort of carnival when he was a lad some seventy years before. But pig-racing? Pig-racing had been mentioned, it's true, but whether it had been fact or fiction was something else. Of course Jake Otter had piled in, pretending to know all there was to know, though how an incomer from Birmingham or wherever it was could have any idea baffled Billy Nattrass.

What use would the Bleezins be anyway? At some time or another, in the pub, he had lent his voice in support. But why? The idea was to attract tourists, but what use were damn tourists to him? He could rent his caravans, sell his ruined farm buildings, without trying to bring in more of the half-arsed sods from the South. Bloody McGurk was all for it, of course—to sell more of his lousy beer; the old cow Loudwater wanted it, naturally, to make her feel more important. God, Billy told himself, if there was any one woman he hated more than Sylvia Anstruther, it was that jumped-up bloody old Liverpool tart Loudwater.

And yet....Something in the dry recesses of his old brain told him that as the oldest Boggerthwaite inhabitant he should be able to turn support of the festival into some advantage to himself. After all, he had practically invented the idea of the Bleezins, and his cross-grained pride would not let him give the benefits over to the likes of Jake Otter. Even if there were no old barns to be sold as a direct result of it all, no leaky caravans to be let, why, there would be free drinks enough if he played his cards right. He only wondered what Lordy felt about it all.

He wasn't exactly disappointed in the new Lord Bogger....Well, yes he was a bit. There had been no contact. It obviously wasn't his place as a commoner to do the approach. That was up to Lordy, and Lordy hadn't obliged. Although Old Billy had only seen the last holder of the title—the absentee one—two or three times in his life, yet he remembered that one's father—the thirteenth baron, wasn't he? The original 'Lordy' of his youth. He had been a great one for going round visiting the tenantry. Some folk had said it was nosiness, but Old Billy hadn't seen it like that at all. While the old Lord might quite inconveniently drop into a cottage without warning, and no doubt kept his eyes well open, he didn't always automatically raise rents at any signs of lowly affluence; indeed he had been known to settle medical bills in needy cases, and had seen more than one bright lad through schooling that would have been out of the question without his patronage. Forelocks had to be touched, of course, but that did no harm: what else were forelocks for? Anyway, the new Lordy hadn't put himself out yet, enough to call, or to offer him a drink in the pub, or just introduce himself. And he should have done. Old Billy didn't much like to entertain really seditious thoughts, but it irked him the more because they were occurring. He was the oldest native of Boggerthwaite, and the new Lord Bogger ought to have recognised his importance in the village pecking-order. Mr Mahmoud did. Mr Mahmoud always greeted him with a friendly smile, and had once even given him permission to take rabbits from his warren down by the Bogger Beck. (He had done so anyway, but it was nice to be invited.) Mr Mahmoud was a gent, for all he wasn't a proper English toff.

Old Billy was musing along these lines as he strolled that fine morning on a leisurely tour of some of his outlying ruins, in various stages of conversion to dwelling-houses of a sort. He rounded the corner of the lane which led to Mirkin Grange, and a sight met his eyes which filled him first with astonishment, next with irritation, and finally with a pleasant anticipation of malice capable of being turned to his own enjoyment. He stared once more at the amazing sight which caused this rapid succession of emotions, then turned and hurried off to find the local guardian of Law and Order.

....

Now Police Constable Costive had not had a pleasant morning that far. Ominous predictions in his mind as to the likely outcome of the imminent village festivities had been all but ousted by an event nearer home and even more ominous. Just before breakfast the telephone had rung and announced the arrival of his mother-in-law. She had travelled up to Keswick overnight and wanted picking up. Not at some reasonable hour later that day, not after breakfast, but now, right away.

Mrs Stella Jekyll, Bryony's Mum, was not totally unexpected. There had been rumours and portents of her visit for some weeks, rolling around like distant thunder and growing louder. If he had had the imaginative eye to see, Costive would have noticed crows and ravens rising. Now the storm had burst.

Pc Costive made a half-hearted attempt to suggest that his wife should go and collect her mother herself, only to be met with a look which suggested he had taken leave of his senses. Rudi the Bernese mountain dog had to be exercised, didn't he? And before that Darren had to be got off to school. Darren himself was in a state of high excitement. His grandmother was an enthusiast of the ballet: she *understood* Darren. "Can't I go with you, Daddy?" the child asked. "And pick Grandma up?"

"What's the matter with her—has she fallen over again?" His father was showing just what a state of frustration he was in. "Get yourself off to school, lad—and take your ballet skirt with you."

Which was cruel. The boy's lip quivered and Bryony snuffled, which, being quite a tough woman, was as near as she ever came to crying. And so at the indecent hour of nine o'clock her mother was collected from Keswick bus station. The son-in-law was resplendent in full uniform, leading one or two of the younger people who had had the pleasure of Mrs Jekyll's company in the coach all the way up from London to conclude that she had been arrested.

"Bryony has told me all about your festivities," Mrs Jekyll said. "I dare say it'll be the high-spot of your year." Which meant, as the good officer well knew, that life in the country must be even worse than portrayed by the Archers, and why had he not got himself—and more importantly her daughter—out of such a backwater? Mrs Jekyll, widow of a brigadier in the Pay Corps, lived in Camberley, loved it, and wondered why everywhere else wasn't like it. That is all anyone needs to know about the lady. "I did think you'd be away from here by now," she remarked as she settled into the police Landrover and watched the straggly suburbs of Keswick slide by. "It can't be good for Darren to be stuck out here." And without waiting for a reply, which she knew would not come: "Any juicy murders, then?"

'Police-officer's Mother-in-Law found drowned in Lake District river: son-in-law suspected.' Pc Costive could see the headlines swim before his eyes as he crossed the bridge over a river whose name he had no idea of. "Pretty quiet," he grunted.

"No promotion, I suppose?" Mrs Jekyll fired next, and again without waiting for an answer: "Bryony's father was just a second-lieutenant when we married, but he was a captain within two years. He had *push* you see."

Push. The young constable devoutly wished he was able at that instant to lean across the front of his mother-in-law, gently open the passenger door, and not so gently push the woman out of the Landrover. Never again, he told himself, would he fail to sympathise with, or at least see the point of view of, any murderer who should cross his path. Up to now it was true there had been none, but you never knew in a spot like Boggerthwaite. He risked a glance at Mrs Jekyll's face in the mirror. She was, he had to admit, a striking-looking woman even at—what would she be: sixty? Sixty-five? Raven black hair only slightly dusted with grey, high cheekbones, a face cleverly rather than heavily made up, but above all a mouth set to show with no shadow of a doubt that its owner was used to getting her own way and intended that this state of affairs should continue. Bryony was not unlike her mother in looks, and the officer found himself wishing he had made a longer, closer inspection of the older woman before taking the matrimonial plunge.

167

"How is Mitzi?" Mrs Jekyll didn't at all want to know, but was shaping up for another little snipe.

"You mean Rudi, don't you?"

"That great brute of a dog, whatever its name is. I can't think what possessed you to get a beast like that. It must cost a fortune to feed."

"It's Bryony's dog actually," said the constable. "Nothing to do with me."

"She probably felt she needed protection," said the mother-in-law. "Stuck out in a God-forsaken place like that, and with you never at home proper hours."

And so it went on. By the time Pc Costive reached the Boggerthwaite police house all thoughts of his fears for the Bleezins had melted away. Until Mrs Jekyll revived them. "I suppose we'll see precious little of you over the weekend, what with this carnival nonsense." Then, spotting her daughter at the gate, leapt out and enveloped her in a fierce embrace of the sort given by fond relatives on their loved-one's release from ten years in a Cambodian lock-up. Pc Costive slipped away to find his fishing tackle. He needed relaxation and he needed peace.

So that on only his third cast in the pool below the old Dabster and Tyson's mill dam he was far from pleased to behold the malevolent horse-face of Old Billy Nattrass. The man reared up almost like a horse above the reeds, and leered.

"It's a good job somebody knows where to find you," said Billy. "when you're needed, which is not often. "

Pc Costive thought for a moment how well Old Billy and his mother-in-law might have got on together. "Sod off, Billy," he said. "If you've nothing better to do."

"*Me* got nothing better?" barked Old Billy rather ungrammatically. "What about *you*? You're supposed to be looking after the Law hereabouts.. The Peace of Her Majesty the King." Adding "God bless her," as he freed one old boot from a patch of mud and positioned himself so that he could look down on the village policeman.

"What is it, Mr Nattrass?" asked Pc Costive, with the air of a man who tries for a lie-in when everyone else is awake and raring to go about their unnecessary, noisy business.

"Don't you keep an eye on your patch, then?" Billy pressed on. "Don't you keep your eyes open? Bloody fishing! The bloody Martians could have landed here for all you care. My uncle was police officer here before you were ever thought of. Nothing happened he didn't know about. He was a proper policeman. We had three murders in two years, and he nabbed the lot. Hanged two on'em and all. He earned his money. People were safe. He didn't spend all his time fishing. When he did fish he caught summat worth catching."

This last sally cut the officer to the quick. "I'll ask you once more, Mr Nattrass. Otherwise I'll have you nicked for wasting police time."

"I shouldn't be doing your job for you, you know," Old Billy said. "But if you were to take a look down the Old Mirkin road you'd see summat you ought to be doing summat about."

"Perhaps you'll tell me what you're talking about, Mr Nattrass." Pc Costive had lost the battle for peace and quiet. He was winding in his line and climbing on to the bank.

"I'll show you if you like." Mr Nattrass was consulting a large old watch from his waistcoat pocket. It was getting on for opening time. "If you get a bloody move on."

"This had better be important," Pc Costive said ominously, though the last thing he really wanted was anything of any importance bigger than a bicycle without lights, although unlit

169

bicycles at 10.30 in the morning would not normally be part of his fight against evil.

"The Ghosts of Hideon!" Old Billy breathed. "It's a hinvasion."

"You what?"

"The Hosts of Gideon. It's a hinvasion. Wait till you see."

Pc Costive's attempts to follow the old man were made somewhat difficult by reason of his not having thought it worthwhile to take off his waders, so that he flip-flopped along the road like some sort of aquatic creature out of its element. "If this is your idea of a joke," he snorted.

"No joke," said Billy. "Just look at that."

Pc Costive did as was suggested. What he saw reminded him of nothing less than an engraving in a book on the South African War he had been given as a boy by an ancient army relative. The Great Trek of the Boers was all there before him, strung out along the lane, except that instead of draft oxen and horses there was a long line of motor-vehicles in various states of dilapidation. One of them seemed to have stuck, quite blocking the road, and a sizeable crowd had collected around it—unkempt looking men with beards and long hair, girls dressed more for convenience than for propriety, small children more or less naked, and dogs—dozens upon dozens of dogs of all shapes, sizes and degrees of ferocity. Half a dozen radios, each tuned to a different pop-music station, were competing with the barking of these dogs. The young policeman, never the possessor of the healthy ruddiness one expects in rural guardians, turned quite pale.

"There you are," said Old Billy triumphantly. It's all yours." And he set off to celebrate opening time.

"....hands across the sea....cementing relations within our great Commonwealth of Nations....links in the British Empire....pride in our forbears....rich cultural heritage....right good Cumbrian welcome...." The words went on and on. Some of them registered, but not very much; others didn't register at all.

In truth Senator William Hudspith Wordsworth, of Boggaburra, New South Wales, was feeling far from his usual ebullient self. If asked, he would have blamed jet lag, which would have been a euphemism for an energetic night-out in London after a 24-hour flight from the other side of the world.

"....old nation salutes its young descendant....blood thicker than water....the rills and clemmits of the Bogger Valley....right good Cumbrian welcome...." Sometimes the voice was a woman's with, if the Senator had been able to distinguish such niceties, a rather broad Merseyside accent. Other times it was male—probably from the middle-aged, slightly stooping guy who had been introduced to him as Lord Bogger a thousand years ago at some bloody draughty railway station. The Senator wished deeply that the voices would stop.

It had been an abominably early train that he had been required to catch. In fact, he remembered now, he had only caught it by dint of not having gone to bed all night, at least in the sense of retiring for the purposes of rest and relaxation. He had found himself out on the street in the first cold light of morning minus quite a large amount of money, though incredibly the overnight bag, containing passport, credit cards and tickets, had somehow remained in his possession. Where his larger items of luggage had got to the senator hadn't the faintest idea.

Eventually Mrs Loudwater showed signs of finishing. She was not an entirely happy person either. At Penrith Station the senator had only been identified, having forgotten to stick a red flower in his buttonhole, by his apparent seniority above the rest of the train load. Two old farmers' wives, one clergyman, and five or six young back-packers had emerged from the train. Then a man, bleary-eyed, rumple-suited, looking entirely lost. They had claimed him — Mrs Loudwater, Mr Bean and Lord Bogger—pushed him into the back of Mrs Loudwater's Japanese saloon, and driven him to Boggerthwaite. Some of them—Mrs Loudwater in particular— had tried to point out the beauties of the countryside, but Senator Wordsworth had seemed no match for his ancestor. He had come to life a little only when the egregious Mr McGurk had passed into his hand one pint of Owd Bogger, which he had received as a sponge receives water. And then he had another. "Bloody funny sort of beer, this," was all he had said.

And then Mr Bean had done the introductions. There weren't many there: Jake Otter, of course, and his collie; Old Billy Nattrass, fresh from assisting the Law; Jeremy Blink-Howell with his tape recorder and notebook; Matty Ouskin, Dr Rhoid, Tot Tyson, and a couple of weekenders who had managed to get away from the South more quickly than most. Muriel Korbishley was there, but unusually not her friend Ms D'Arcy. Mr Magersfontein came in, but drank only soda water. Mr McGurk did the opening.

"What'll youse all have? We have the best ale in the whole of the Lake District." Which was a damnable lie. Then Mrs Loudwater had occupied a space at the end of the bar which commanded the rest of the room, and she had beamed all round in spite of her deeper feelings, and had started off the official welcome. Matty Ouskin had a part in this. As well as having supplied the missing line to the poem introduced by Senator Wordsworth, he had composed a Welcome to an Antipodean Cousin. And we quote:

> He wandered lonely as a cloud
> Across the Southern Seas,
> Until at last he came to rest
> In Bogger's vale of ease.

Kangaroos and didgeridoos
All vanished from his mind,
And in their place the gladsome grace
That Wordsworth left behind.

There was a polite ripple of applause, which the senator joined in rather too late, and then came a dreadful hiatus which he realised was meant to be filled by a contribution from himself. "Speech!" they were saying, "Speech!"

On the latter part of his aeroplane journey, the young lady next to him having managed to find herself an alternative seat, he had in fact jotted down some notes for just this sort of eventuality. But an extensive groping in his rather empty pockets failed to produce them. "Layzn genmn," he began at last, voice quavering as it had never done at any election rally back in Boggaburra, the sweat standing out from his forehead as it had never done in the tropical heat of Christmas Down Under.

He was saved by an extraordinary noise from the car park. It was as if the Monte Carlo rally, the Rangers v Celtic Football match and a pop festival of Woodstock proportions had all decided to happen at once outside the pub. Senator Wordsworth's halting efforts were drowned as the front doors burst open and admitted a crowd of people of whom the kindest thing that can be said is that they were unconventional. There were broad-brimmed cowboy hats, kaftans, beards, tattoos enough to cover a battalion of young soldiers, leather jackets cut off at the shoulders, bikinis, dresses of medieval length, nose-studs, pony-tails, ear-rings, worn-out denim jeans, and lots and lots of hair except on the skinhead section. Some played ghetto-blasters, many laughed, and all shouted. Matty Ouskin, who had spent the previous eight months hacking his way through *Barnaby Rudge*, was to say afterwards that it all reminded him of the Gordon Riots, but nobody seemed to know what he was talking about.

The throng entered the pub like a leak of water through a hole in a dam, spreading out to fill every available space, and pressing up against the bar. Some wanted twelve pints, others only six or eight, but all wanted drink. Mr McGurk was sweating with the dilemma of it all, his distaste for his visitors fighting a losing battle with his natural cupidity. He gave a despairing glance to Mrs Loudwater and started to pull beer.

"I say, this is a private function," said the Chair of the Parish Council. But only expert lip-readers would have understood above the hullabaloo what she was trying to say.

"That'll be nine pounds exactly," Mr McGurk was saying to a large, bald-headed, bearded man in leather clothes who had ordered six pints. "Sir."

The bald man smiled, revealing jagged fangs and stumps like a wolf well past its best. "Do what?" he said in an accent that seemed to have originated in one of the nastier parts of Cardiff.

"Nine pounds exactly," repeated the unhappy publican. "It's one pound fifty a pint."

"That's not what they told us," said an even larger young man with a floppy-brimmed hat and a moustache which straggled down each side of his mouth like a pair of rats' tails.

"It's free!" shrilled a diminutive girl beside him whose nose-end sported a rather discoloured three-inch nail.

"Free? echoed McGurk with horror, as if repeating a blasphemy.

"Free, mate," said the bearded man, who had already got halfway down his pint. "On account of your festivities, innit?"

"Who told you that?" McGurk was clutching on to his bar top as if to ward off unconsciousness.

"Couple of birds we met on the road," said the moustachioed youth.

"There must be some mistake," said McGurk feebly. "What did they look like, these, er, birds?"

"One was a right little cracker—tall, with glasses, looked like a

174

schoolteacher. The other was older, bit on the tubby side, with reddish hair and a bicycle. Free, they said. All day. Some sort of celebrations."

The eyes of Muriel Korbishley and Lord Bogger met briefly. Both indulged in a faint smile.

27

Unless he ever comes to write his memoirs, which is unlikely as the man, like many of his tabloid ilk, is only semi-literate, we shall almost certainly never learn from Mr Stan Bergholz what went on in that dingy guest-house in Keswick. As for the Rev Ximenez, she regarded the interview as a version of the confessional. Her lips, therefore, are sealed.

However, on the following morning, as a rather footsore cleric and her shabby minder (who seemed to be entirely unaffected by the hike he was now to reverse) set off over the fells back to Boggerthwaite. There, up on a clear stretch of road well away from New Age Travellers and his mother-in-law, Pc Costive was on the telephone to a superintendent at police headquarters.

"You have problems, son? said the super, not unkindly. "So have we. There's a multiple pile-up on the M6, a big anti-fox-hunt demo above Keswick, and a mob threatening to close down Sellafield. Added to that Carlisle traffic has seized up due to an extra-wide load breaking down on the Civic Centre Roundabout. You've got problems? You get on with them, son."

"But sir, we've got the Boggerthwaite Bleezins, we've got pig-racing in the streets...." The poor constable was beginning to sound as if the strain was getting a little too much for him.

"You've what, son?" The super's voice was harsh now, and entirely without sympathy.

"And brafflin' dancing, and, and, er—have you seen the paper this morning? Our vicar's coming back. The sex-change one. There'll be all hell let loose."

"Costive, get lost." And the phone went dead.

The newspaper story the officer had referred to had been exclusive to the Brute, his mother-in-law's favourite (indeed only) reading. She had pointed it out to him on his return from his first sighting of the travellers in order to change back into uniform. It is one thing to face a potentially hostile mob, he reckoned, dressed in some sort of authority, however brief; quite another to be wearing waders and a torn sportsman's jacket. "What terribly strange people you have in this village," said Mrs Jekyll. "Do you think it's something in the water?"

Her son-in-law was in no mood to discuss the dietary habits of those under his protection. He quite rudely snatched the paper from Mrs Jekyll's hand and read. The piece, as was usual with The Brute, was a little masterpiece of condensation. Short and to the point so that the readers' concentration should not be taxed. "Sex Change Vicar Ready for Second Coming" said the headline over a photograph of the Rev Ximenez pouting quite provocatively at the camera.

> The Vicar of Boggerthwaite, Cumbria, the Rev. Michelle Ximenez, who until a fortnight ago was known as Miguel, claimed last night that she had been chosen as the prophet of the Second Coming. She says she will defy Church attempts to remove her.
>
> It is a great responsibility,' she said. 'But I feel that as a woman I am well up to the task.' She did not know details of what would happen, but was waiting for them to be revealed.
>
> All I know just now is that there's going to be one heck of a shemozzle,' said the attractive, raven-haired, 36-year-old vicarette. 'Not the end of the world as we know it, but a very hectic time for everyone.'
>
> Ms Ximenez, who has been in charge of the little Lake District parish for six years, said that she would explain to her congregation how heavenly voices told her to change her sex 'to prepare the way' because God is really a woman. She will speak at a special

service today, in spite of instructions from the Church to resign.

'It is the Feast of St Ethelbogger, and I feel sure she will be by my side. After all, John the Baptist didn't exactly have an easy time of it.'

No-one at Diocesan headquarters was available to comment.

28

Mesdames Fatima, Scheherazade and Esmat Mahmoud, the first, second and third wives of the Squire of Mirkin Grange and presumptive Marquis of Stoatholme, were, as far as anyone could tell, indifferent to their husband's little hobby of philandering. They were well fed, well clothed, had standing as well as comfort, and had not been at all put out when they had found themselves some six months earlier required to share their matrimonial status with a young blonde girl from Hackney called Mandy, who had appeared one day after a visit by their husband to a trade fair in London. That is, she called herself Mandy; the three earlier wives called her 'the tart', but bore her no ill will or jealousy.

Mandy did not share their tolerant nature. When earlier that morning she had glimpsed her husband entering one of their bedrooms (a spare one as it happened, but fully equipped for use and occupancy) with a young and rather attractive looking woman in a tight polka-dotted dress and bare feet who did not seem to mind that Mr Mahmoud was guiding her with a hand firmly grasping one of her buttocks, Mandy was far from pleased.

Her first reaction sprang from her upbringing in Hackney. She wanted to kill or maim the stranger, having first gouged out her eyes and torn out her hair. Her recognition of the present situation told her to go more slowly, to think, and to act when that thought had ripened a little. Never during the few seconds that let her observe the door of the bedroom close firmly, did she feel there was any point in calling for the support of her three fellow wives. They would only have laughed. With this problem she was on her own. So she went downstairs and phoned her Mum, not in Hackney any more but at a bijou address at Chigwell, which is nicer.

"Lo, Mum? it's me."

"Who the 'ell's 'me'? You've got a name, 'aven't yer?"

"Me. Mandy. I've got bother, Mum."

"When didn't you 'ave bovver? Wot's the matter now?"

"You told me what a dirty sod he was...."

"Oh, "*im*"

"Well, you were right, Mum. I've just caught him going into one of the bedrooms with a woman."

"Wot sort of woman?

"A proper cow by the look of her. Nice-looking in a cowish sort of way."

"Perhaps she's seeing about the plumbing, Mandy."

"He'll be seeing to her plumbing, more like."

"Now Mandy, don't be coarse."

"Well....Mum, what am I going to *do*?"

"You are going to be very careful, girl. There's more than just your hurt pride involved, don't forget. You do anything rash and he'll not only dump you back where you came from, but I'll suffer and all. And I'm getting quite attached to my new life-style."

"Mu-um...."

"Did I tell you I'm off to India on Tuesday?"

"India?"

"I think it's India. It's an island, anyway. All palm trees and gin. Bahamas or something."

"That's the West Indies."

"India anyway. I don't know. But I do know I'm not losing

178

things like that if I can 'elp it. I slaved to bring you up, Amanda."

"Well that's good, isn't it? That's where they sent slaves, to the West Indies. So you won't be the first. Mum....what am I going to *do*?"

But Mandy already knew what she was going to do. It had come to her when her Mum was talking of slavery. She had had a touch of that herself, had Mandy, and she had no desire to go back to it. On the other hand....

29

Senator William Hudspith Wordsworth had a good nap that afternoon. The civic reception had rather tailed off, there being little that could be heard above the New Age assortment which had taken over the Dehydrated Rambler. The senator was rather glad of this, as the monstrous hangover he had acquired throughout the previous night was threatening to return with redoubled fury, no doubt prompted by the downing of two—no, it was three— pints of Owd Bogger. One of these noxious draughts can sometimes act as an efficacious dog's-hair with certain practised consumers, but three.... The only thing that can be said for three is that they make a good general anaesthetic.

So, Senator Wordsworth went to sleep. There was much debate about where he should go: Mrs Loudwater, as Chair of the council, was the natural choice as host, but she said, loudly and clearly, that she was not going to have a man in that state in her house. Mr Bean, as Clerk to the Council, made at that moment of her most vehement refusal, a discreet exit, trailing clouds of pipe smoke and muttering about council business. Lord Bogger said that while he would like nothing better than to have the company of a man with the undoubted experience of an Australian senator, and a descendant of the Bard of Grasmere to boot, present circumstances at Bogger Hall rather precluded direct hospitality. Mr

Magersfontein had disappeared, and only Matty Ouskin, who occupied a back bedroom at the cottage of la D'Arcy and la Korbishley, seemed willing to give shelter. But by this time, in spite of all the hubbub, Senator Wordsworth had wedged himself into a corner between the darts board and the juke box, and had fallen into a profound sleep from which even the heavy metal music which the Travellers kept playing next to his ear failed to awaken him.

The Travellers themselves seemed to have become reconciled to the idea that they were after all going to be required to pay for their drinks, and Mr McGurk, though still twitchy, was reconciled to coining in more money than he had seen at one time since he took the pub. When Pc Costive appeared, in the full majesty of his uniform, he found the place bursting at the seams, but comparatively peaceful. One young man with spiked hair and a studded black leather waistcoat even offered to buy him a pint, which, all this being in the course of duty, he felt obliged to refuse.

The Travellers, eventually managing to get served, had spilled out again, some of them, and had taken possession of a large part of the village green. It was a beautiful Spring morning, and they squatted or lay around on the grass, their toddlers toddling, their trannies blaring, their dogs barking and copulating. A group of youngsters were strumming guitars and blowing tin whistles and producing no tune immediately recognisable. There was a veil of thin smoke hanging over the scene, like a miasma arising from dewy grass on a hot morning. This mist, however, smelt very different. The young policeman sniffed, wrinkled his nose, and decided discretion was in order at this stage of the proceedings. As he picked his way through the mass of unkempt but quite happy humanity, he all but tripped over the semi-recumbent form of Old Billy Nattrass. He was attended by a very pretty young girl with red hair down to her waist which seemed to serve instead of more conventional clothing. She had plaited a daisy-chain, and was arranging it round the old misanthrope's neck. Old Billy, normally a pipe-smoker, was puffing away at a hand-rolled cigarette at least twice as fat as the commercial variety, and for the first time that Pc Costive had ever seen, wore a peaceful smile on his old horse's face. On recognising his uniformed enemy, Old Billy said: "The Ghosts of Hideon" and closed one eye.

....

Senator Wordsworth slept on. Someone had stuck a daffodil behind each of his ears, but this had had no effect on his slumbers. After the civic lunch, which had failed under the circumstances to materialise at all, he was supposed to be enjoying a conducted tour of the delights of the Bogger Valley. He was to have been accompanied by Mrs Loudwater and Lord Bogger, and Mr Bean was to have driven. Mr Bean duly looked back in at two o'clock, but the senator slept on. He had now developed a snore of quite stentorian proportions, which could be heard above the juke box and the chatter of the travellers. Mr Bean bought himself a pint, and discussed ley-lines with two girls. The senator snored on.

At three there was to have been a football match between Stoatholme Athletic (known locally as Stoatholme Paralytic) and a scratch team from the scourings of those banned from regular football in the surrounding towns and villages. They were to be known as the Lakeland All Stars, but the Bogger Valley betting was on the home side. At half-time there was no score, and Senator Wordsworth slept on.

At four o'clock a voice announcing itself as belonging to Mr Arpad Mahmoud's private secretary came over Mrs Loudwater's telephone. It was checking, it said, that everything was still in order for that evening's dinner-party at Mirkin Grange. Did Senator Wordsworth have any special dietary requirements, for example? Mrs Loudwater fought back a strong desire to say that as far as she could make out a controlled drip-feed of spirituous liquors, supplemented by a barrel or two of beer should do the trick admirably. She restrained herself, and assured Mr Mahmoud's man in honeyed tones that were far from genuine that everyone was looking forward to the soiree. Meanwhile, in his little niche at the Rambler, the senator slumbered on.

At four-thirty, with Mr McGurk serving the last of his November Owl Pie, someone brought the news—it was Jake Otter—that the Paralytics had won their football match by five fractures to three. Senator Wordsworth opened one eye, gave a tremendous exhalation of snoring breath, farted loudly, then went back to sleep again.

At around six o'clock, having had an unexpected free afternoon, the reception committee gathered again at the Rambler. It was still doing good business, the Spring sunshine had held, and travellers were still sunning themselves on the grass and making one hell of a racket for such a passive occupation. At least three musical groups were attempting performance in spite of each other, and Old Billy Nattrass, swathed in chains of daisies, had rolled up his trouser-legs and was doing a kind of war-dance round the hippie girl with the long hair, which had now fallen apart quite revealingly. The usual Friday evening white settlers from the South had been arriving for a while and most of them went into the pub—*their* pub—as if the crowd of ley-line worshippers were not there at all. Their principle seemed to be: if you don't like it, ignore it, and it will cease to exist. Senator Wordsworth was still asleep.

The reception committee stood in a half-circle around their guest and exchanged glances of bewilderment. Dr Harry Rhoid, as he felt befitted a local general practitioner, stepped forward at one stage, lifted the sleeping man's eyelids, let them drop back again, then produced a small mirror and held it to the senator's mouth, a quite unnecessary action considering that the man was still exhaling like a very healthy volcano. Seeing the results of the doctor's efforts, Mrs Loudwater was heard to remark: "Pity."

After another round of puzzled glances and head-scratchings, Mr Bean, ever practical, bent over the senator, jabbed his finger none too gently just behind the sleeping man's ear, and pressed hard. Senator Wordsworth opened his eyes and looked dreamily about him. "Just a trick us old bush-hands used to use," said Mr Bean modestly.

Senator Wordsworth rubbed his eyes, scratched his groin, smiled and said:

> "My heart leaps up when I behold,
> The Valley of the Bogger.
> Long may its rills and clemmits bold....

Christ, I've got a mouth like a vulture's arsehole."

"I think we can do without language like that," said Mrs Loudwater sourly.

"Gisser beer, mate," pleaded the senator.

"I really don't think...." began the Chair. Then: "Oh very well, get him a drink somebody."

The senator struggled to his feet, lumbered over to Mrs Loudwater, put his arm round her shoulder as one would with a long lost friend, and beamed at her. "You are a truly lovely lady," he said. "I'll bet you're the most astonishing little...." Perhaps it was as well for the lovely lady's modesty that the rest was drowned by another eruption from the juke box beside her.

But Mrs Loudwater was above all a practical woman. She had no time for blushes. Instead she disengaged herself from the visitor's embrace and watched while he downed in rather a short time a pint glass of Owd Bogger which Mr Bean had fetched from the bar and whose price he was now noting down in his council expenses notebook. Mrs Loudwater gazed at the senator. "He can't possibly go like that," she said. "He looks as if he's swum all the way from Boggerburra or wherever it is."

And truly the senator presented an unsavoury sight. His hair was ruffled, he was quite spectacularly unshaven, his tie had gone missing and his suit looked like something found outside an Oxfam shop in the rain.

"He's got no luggage," whispered the clerk. Then louder, to the senator, as if addressing the spokesman of some very backward tribe: "That's right, isn't it? No luggage. You-have-no-luggage."

"Luggage?" repeated Senator Wordsworth dozily. "I've got no bloody luggage. It's in London." Then a pause. "Somewhere."

"We'll have to get him some clothes," said Mrs Loudwater. She looked around her. Mr Bean noted with some relief that he was of an entirely different shape to the antipodean visitor, and breathed a quiet prayer of thanks that this was so. Lord Bogger: no—altogether too lean and tall, and anyway not a man who looked as if he had much of a spare wardrobe. Dr Rhoid? No, far too squat and round. Mr Magersfontein? Tall enough, but too skinny, and anyway his quilted waistcoat and corduroys, which were all that anyone had ever seen him wear, would be out of the question. Ms Korbishley no, of course. Eyes swivelled round to Mr McGurk, mopping his brow behind the bar, and wondering where on earth he was going to get enough replacement beer to see him through the Boggerthwaite Bleezins next day.

"Mr McGurk," said Mrs Loudwater, giving words to what everyone was thinking. "Would you be so kind as to make Senator Wordsworth a loan of a suit of clothes? You're just the right size."

Mr McGurk's eyes opened wide, as a large rabbit's might when confronted with a stoat. "Clothes?" he echoed, as if he had vaguely heard of such things but had forgotten quite what they were.

"Clothes," repeated Mrs Loudwater firmly. "Mr Mahmoud has not stipulated tails or even dinner jackets. So I think one of your better lounge suits should do the trick. That and the, er, usual nether garments." She peered down at the senator's feet. "I think his shoes may possibly pass muster if he gives them a brush."

"A suit, dear lady," spluttered the publican. "I haven't got a spare suit, and even...."

"And even I might remind you that you were elected to the

184

Bleezins Committee, and as a member of that you were pledged to make the whole thing work. So far it has not worked."

"But..."

"But nothing," snapped Mrs Loudwater. "I might remind you that you may well be in some sort of breach of contract with us. We were to have held our civic reception here in this very bar. Indeed we had it started. And then you allowed these...." Mrs Loudwater looked at the throng of drinkers around her as if seeing them for the first time. "This riff-raff to take over the place."

"I *am* in business, Gladys." Mr McGurk spread out his arms and hands, palms upward in a rueful, mock-Levantine sort of shrug.

"Never mind the Gladys. I am Mrs Loudwater, or Madam Chair if you prefer. As to business, you've made more money today than you've done since you arrived here. At our expense, I might say. So the least you can do is lend this unfortunate man a suit."

"A sort of penance, old cock," said Mr Bean, who considered himself pretty hot on theology. "*Mea culpa*, and all that."

McGurk was weakening. "I've no-one to look after the bar," he moaned.

"Then find someone, ninny," commanded Mrs Loudwater. "Here, I'll do it. I am not unfamiliar with the retail trade after all." And she lifted the flap of the bar top and installed herself behind the pumps, from where she glowered fiercely at the mix of weekend regulars and New Age low life.

Mr McGurk sadly eyed the Australian VIP and invited him into the inner recesses of the pub. "See if we can't find you something," he muttered.

"I'd far rather the lovely lady helped me change," said the much-recovered senator. "I could show you a bit of Aussie wild-life," he added, leering at Mrs Loudwater.

"Get upstairs," commanded the chairperson. "Get yourself changed, and hold your tongue."

And Senator Wordsworth did as he was told.

....

Promptly at five minutes to seven two large Mercedes saloons purred smoothly up to the front door of the Dehydrated Rambler. They steered regally between the battered old pick-ups and travel-stained trailers of those New-Agers who were still in the pub, like stately galleons through a harbour packed with squalid sampans and rotting junks. A young man smartly turned out in olive-green uniform, with peaked cap and dark glasses, alighted from the second car and entered the pub. He removed his cap on locating Mrs Loudwater, but not his spectacles. Transport, he told her with just the merest touch of an alien accent, awaited her. The Chair graciously acknowledged this information in her best Queen Mother voice, Merseyside version.

Senator Wordsworth was by now washed, brushed up, shaved, combed and arrayed in the raiment of Mr McGurk. Not the suit for weekly Holy Mass, but the one usually reserved for weddings, funerals and visits to his bank manager. It was dark blue and fitted the senator as if made exclusively for him. Mr McGurk had reserved a room for him for occupation after the soiree, having been prompted by the Chairperson, who was certainly not going to have any overgrown Australian lout staying with her for the night, as might well have been the case had he been any sort of gentleman. "Keep us some grog, mate," said the senator, and departed with the others.

They were a small party, so there was plenty of room for them in the two cars. As well as Mrs Loudwater and the awful senator, there were Mr Bean, Lord Bogger, Dr Rhoid and his wife Emma, a lady with the facial expression of one in a state of chronic irritation. There was Mr Magersfontein the agriculturist, and Matty

Ouskin the poet, who had to be invited, in spite of his own reluctance and the state of his clothes (a somewhat perforated sweater, frayed jeans and dirty trainers) because he had completed the lost Wordsworthian fragment and written the official Byng Anthem for the Bleezins. Ms Georgina D'Arcy had also been invited, but was nowhere to be found.

It was a beautiful evening. The sun was off the Bogger Valley itself, having sunk below the ridge of Great Mirkin Fell, but still bathed the slopes of Boggerbarrow on the opposite side, highlighting the patches of old bracken reddy-brown like splashes of camouflage paint on the predominant green of the turf. "What do you think of it, then?" Lord Bogger asked Senator Wordsworth.

"It's a crap pint, mate," said the Australian cheerfully. "Too bloody warm. But I'll get used to it, I reckon."

"I meant the place—the scenery."

"Oh yeah—the rills and clemmits. Which are the rills and which are the clemmits, sport?"

"I'm not absolutely sure, to tell you the truth," confessed Lord Bogger. "Rills are streams, I believe. We call them becks up here. But clemmits—I'm afraid no-one seems to know."

"Maybe it's something to do with women," suggested Senator Wordsworth. "My old ancestor was pretty keen on the sheilas by all accounts. Perhaps it's...." And he whispered one word in Lord Bogger's ear, amazing the peer by this show of delicacy.

From time to time along the road to Mirkin Grange they passed little groups of oddly dressed people, mostly quite young. Some were a little erratic in their gait, a little wobbly; others were singing, all looked quite happy. When the two Mercedes swept majestically past the rabbit-topped stone gateway of the Grange and into its drive there were more of them. They were sitting and standing around an amazing collection of ancient vehicles and caravans.

Tents had been pitched too—tepees as well as the more conventional kinds, and one or two groups had quite large fires blazing away merrily on the beautifully-kept turf. "Where you taking me?" asked the senator. "The bloody circus?"

Mr Mahmoud met the party at the top of his front steps. He was smiling broadly and wearing a cream-coloured summer suit of the kind favoured by the better-class pimps of Port Said. "My house," he murmured, "is your house."

"Whose are the gardens then, mate?" inquired Senator Wordsworth. "You given'em over to the nation?"

Mr Mahmoud changed his beam of welcome to an indulgent grin. "They are children of Nature. They are seekers after Truth, as we all are. They too are my guests. Come."

Mrs Loudwater fought back a strong desire to tell this over-rich international crook (though she had never thought of him as such until this moment) that he had some funny ideas about hospitality. Instead she took his proffered arm and allowed him to escort her into the hall.

"I am pleased to have these young people here, you see," he said. "It is a very English thing, is it not? To hold festivals in the grounds of stately homes. I have heard so, I think. We have ley-lines here—did you know that?"

Mrs Loudwater, who hadn't the smallest idea what he was talking about, said that she believed she had read something of the sort.

Waiting just inside the hall, near the foot of the staircase, was the female side of the Mahmoud menage. Mesdames Fatima, Scheherazade, Esmat and Mandy, stood in line, the first three dressed very sensibly, expensively and Englishly, in tweed costumes, pearls, thick country stockings and flat brogue shoes. Mandy had on a tight-fitting black dress so high in the skirt and so low in the neckline that its maker must have effected a considerable saving in material. Mr Mahmoud introduced Senator Wordsworth

188

to his harem and cracked his usual joke about "the wife", to which the visitor called his host a bloody hero and pointedly failed to take his eyes away from Mandy's decolletage.

There was a fifth female hovering in the doorway of the library. Something must have snapped the senator into a sudden realisation of her presence, for his gaze suddenly leapt from Mandy's so-called neckline with the avidity of a dog leaving a juicy bone for a plate of creamed chicken. She was quite the most beautiful girl the senator had seen, certainly since leaving his native land. "Copulating cane-toads," hissed 'Hud' Wordsworth. "Jist look at that, mate!"

30

Meanwhile in the London offices of the Daily Brute (or rather in its popular annexe, the Rabid Jackal wine-bar), tough, cynical news-editor Desmond Cardington-Sprott stared into a glass of mineral water like a clairvoyant seeking guidance from a crystal ball. It was no ordinary mineral water, this: specially imported 'from Greenland's Icy Mountains', it was far from cheap, and this glass was by no means the news-hawk's first this evening. "Blast him!" ejaculated Mr Cardington-Sprott.

"Absolutely, Des," agreed his titian-haired, heavy-bosomed assistant, Minette Mendoza, uncrossing and re-crossing her long, silk-sheathed legs and shifting balance on her bar stool for the hundredth time that session.

"I mean—what's the bugger up to?" rasped her boss.

"Exactly," nodded Minette, drumming her slender, beautifully-manicured fingers on the bar top.

A telephone rang behind the bar. An expensively coiffured barman with magenta silk waistcoat, full white shirt sleeves and sneering expression spoke softly into it. He too had been especially imported, but in reality from somewhere nearer Hoxton than the

Arctic Circle. He said nothing, merely held the instrument out towards Ms Mendoza, and slightly arched his eyebrows.

"Speak," commanded the news editor's personal assistant. And when whoever it was on the other end did as was bid, her eyes opened wide, and she grimaced in the direction of her boss. "Mr Bergholz," she said breathily into the mouthpiece. "Wherever are you?"

The answer brought a frown, but a frown so fetching that anyone seeing it would have felt protective rather than menaced (and would of course have been a terribly bad judge of women such as la Mendoza). "I'll see if I can get hold of him," said Minette. "But be careful—he's in a pig of a mood." She winked along the bar to the next stool. "Why? Well because he doesn't know what the hell's going on with you, of course. Think carefully, Mr Bergholz—and think jobwise if you know what I mean. Hold on—I'll try and find him." It was the longest speech Ms Mendoza had made since censuring her maid that morning over a matter of coffee temperature. She put the telephone receiver into her lap and smiled at her boss while she waited for half a minute before handing over the instrument.

"News desk," barked Desmond Cardington-Sprott. Then his anxious features relaxed and he spoke as gently as a lawyer scenting an expensive brief. "Stanley—good to hear you....Where are you?....Still up in the wilds, eh? .....Yes....Now Stanley—Stan— glad you rang: I didn't quite understand the pay-off to your last story....Yep, got it about an hour ago...What? Of course I can read....Now Stan, listen...."

The news editor of the Brute had tucked the telephone under his chin, a feat he still spent many of his less pressing moments trying to perfect. If there had been a cigarette handy he would have lit it, stuck it in his mouth, and tried to speak through it as well. Instead he rummaged in his pocket and pulled out a galley proof of Mr Bergholz's latest news offering. In smoothing it open the telephone slipped from beneath his chin and knocked over his glass. Ms Mendoza promptly and silently pushed it across the bar for a re-fill.

"It's this bit at the end," said the news editor. "Hallo, arc you still there, Stan?....Right. 'Ms Ximenez plans to start off her World Crusade at Wembley. "She will be bigger than Billy Graham," said her tour manager Stanley Bergholz (32).' Stan—what the hell?....what?....well, you're never 32, Stan, for a start....If it's meant to be a joke, Stan....Stan....You work for the Brute, man, you can't go running around Creation with transexual religious nuts....What? Stan....Bergholz, you're fired!" But the line had gone quite audibly and finally dead before the last sentence had been uttered.

Mr Cardington-Sprott put the receiver back on the telephone and stared at it for a long while. "He can't do this to me, the bastard," he said at length, and knocked off his arctic mineral water in one fierce and final swig.

31

The soiree at Mirkin Grange had reached the stage where the hungry were beginning to wonder how long it would be before food was announced, and the thirsty whether they could decently grab another glass of something before being summoned to table. Senator Wordsworth would normally have belonged to the latter grouping; indeed had already curled his fingers round the stems of several refilled glasses. But his heart wasn't in it. His heart was ticking away with an excitement engineered by the appearance of that beautiful young girl in the polka-dot dress. Mr Mahmoud had not yet introduced her to the company, and she stood a little apart, talking quietly to one of the serving women.

The host may not have noticed the senator's interest (he had of course; you don't get where Mr Mahmoud has got without noticing such things), but his fourth wife Mandy certainly had. She was at first more than a little miffed, for until the intrusion of the spotty-dressed bitch the senator's lascivious attention had been all hers, and fitted in very nicely with her own plans for the evening. But when her admirer's gaze switched from her pert little breasts right across the room to the hippy cow, it was as if the sun had left them to pop behind a cloud. They felt quite chilly, and if she had had a shawl around her shoulders she would have drawn it now across her neckline. "You were telling me about Australia," she said in the tone of voice a schoolteacher uses when trying to recapture the interest of a pupil distracted by the sound of a fracas in the playground outside.

"Oz? Oh yeah," said the senator, his eyes returning to her for a moment, then flicking to and fro across the room like twin tennis balls. "You'd like Oz."

"And why would I like it?" Mandy's tone was such that invited just a little sexual levity in reply. She had always been a hard-working girl, had Mandy.

"Fine girl like you...." Senator Wordsworth's ochre eyes settled back on her bosom again. "It's a land of fresh air and freedom, opportunity and...." Momentarily at least the statesman had lost his lines.

"I've always fancied surfing," purred Mandy, peering up at the senator as if consulting the top line of a railway timetable. "Do you have surfing where you come from?"

"Surfing? Not actually surfing, no, 'cos Boggerburra's about 400 miles from the nearest bit of sea. Or 400 kilometres, I can never remember. But we've got pony-trekking and bunjie-jumping and go-kart racing on Saturdays. Plenty to do...."

"I've always fancied lying on the beach topless...." Mandy stopped momentarily as if alarmed by the senator's sharp intake of breath. But seeing that he was not quite in the throes of an apoplectic fit, continued. "Well, bottomless as well if you're

192

allowed to do that sort of thing. I've always thought it silly to have all these white patches over your body, just because someone says you've got to wear a bit of cloth on this place or that."

"Oh definitely," gasped the senator, plunging desperately into his sherry. "I thoroughly agree."

"I don't have white patches myself," Mandy went on with a sweet little giggle. "But I have to use a sun-lamp just to even things out."

"I....I don't think I believe you," chuckled the senator with a desperate attempt at roguishness. Perspiration was beginning to collect on his brow.

"Seeing's believing," cooed Mandy.

"And what do you think of our scenery, senator?" It was the voice of Arpad Mahmoud, who silently as a cat had reached Wordsworth's elbow, and was now filling the small space between it and his fourth wife, Mandy.

"Scenery?" gulped the senator. "Oh yeah— t'riffic."

"Your grandfather was a great fan of our countryside," Mr Mahmoud went on. "As I am of your grandfather. What was it?

> 'I travelled among unknown men,
> In lands beyond the sea;
> Nor, England! did I know till then
> What love I bore to thee.'

It fits my case precisely."

"He was my great, great grandfather, actually," corrected the poet's descendant.

Mr Mahmoud stood his correction with a little bow, as if it had no great relevance. "The rills of our Bogger Valley," he intoned. "Its clemmits too, for that matter."

"Indeed," said the senator, recovering confidence. "And its hills—its sweet, softly rounded hills. I'm a great one for softly-rounded hills."

Mr Mahmoud had noted the direction of Senator Wordsworth's

gaze. "Some of our hills may look soft and sweet, senator, but they can be quite dangerous. Especially to those who do not treat them with respect. I think dinner is about ready."

32

The Goat and Compasses Inn at Stoatholme consists mainly, as we have seen, of one long bar which divides into two sections—the left end for the Sackvilles and the right for the Wormwalds. Until the next Christmas. Apart from the small midway section, which is used by the occasional summer tourist who happens in by mistake, and then rarely for very long, there is another space also licensed for the consumption of intoxicating beverages. It is called the Snug, and is tucked away next to the Gents down the present Sackville end.

On the evening prior to the celebration of the Boggerthwaite Bleezins, while Mr Mahmoud was lavishly entertaining his guests, the Snug at the Goat was occupied as it is occupied only on very rare occasions. It had been out of use for so long in fact, that landlord GBH McNally had had to renew its light-bulb and use a little force to open a window which had jammed shut with disuse and dead flies. It was now occupied by Ms Georgina D'Arcy, wearing her head-teacher's gear of sensible cardigan and three-quarter length skirt with wide hem, which combines respectability with the ability to move fast in an emergency. Her friend Muriel Korbishley was wearing her usual set of dark-blue salopettes encrusted here and there with clayish patches, as one might expect with a busy sculptress, and her green wellington boots. Each had a pint of some beer-seeming substance in front of her. Ms D'Arcy consulted a large, old-fashioned pocket-watch which she had with an easy familiarity extracted from the top pocket of her friend's dungarees, and which was secured to its button hole with a length of red binder-twine. "The buggers are late," she said.

"You ladies all right in here?" It was genial host Gordon McNally

194

himself, head round the door-jamb, all concern.

"I'm going to get a little cross if they don't turn up soon," said Ms D'Arcy.

Mr McNally grinned. "Sure, the Man who made time made plenty of it. Just enjoy your drink."

"That's part of the trouble, Gordon," said Ms Korbishley. "It's not so much the actual time, it's how much longer we can go on drinking this crap. It's like that stuff they rub on rugby players' thighs."

"You should be so lucky, dear," mock-lisped the landlord. "I could make you a cup of coffee if you'd rather."

"Do you know, I think that might be just the thing," put in Geordie D'Arcy. "We've got tricky work on tonight and we ought to keep our heads clear."

"Do you actually know these chaps?" To Muriel any person, irrespective of age or gender, was a 'chap'. GBH McNally was the publican chap, and the two gentlemen her friend had arranged to meet were the two Sunny Lea chaps. They had been due at eight o'clock and it was now nearly twenty past.

Geordie was abstracted, and kept craning her neck to see through a window which refused to be seen through. "I'm sorry, pet," she said. "Mind on other things. No is the answer. I've seen them, but I can't say I really know them. The old Sackville is a villain, and the old Wormwald is even more so if anything."

There was a steady hubbub from the main bar which occasionally peaked up into a burst of louder noise. Every time this happened Geordie stiffened and listened, like a hare in the grass.

"Old man Sackville was a bookmaker. Perhaps I should say *the* bookmaker round here. Apparently there were one or two others tried to start up, but they developed mysterious disabilities after a short while,. The business still stays in the family, with the old feller's awful son, Mark Sackville—known as Mental Mark. I teach his kids—Wayne, Debbie, Craig, Elvis and Nickla."

"Nichola?"

"No, Nickla. That's how it's spelt. I'm not kidding."

"And the old Wormwald chap—what's he?"

"The old Wormwald chap's Cecil—they pronounce is Seesill. He owns the big garage just outside Thugthwaite. Buys, sells, repairs, receives. His mechanics are reckoned the best converters of knocked-off cars in the North of England. They can turn a hot BMW into two minis and a scooter in twenty minutes flat."

"Really?" Muriel's eyes were round. She didn't know much about motors.

"No, not really, dear, but poor old Robin Costive's been after them for years. Ah, here's the coffee. You really are sweet, Gordon. I'd give you a kiss if I thought you'd enjoy it."

"Thanks honey, it's the thought that counts," said the landlord. "You should see what's going on out there. The funniest thing you ever saw. They've both turned up, but they don't know how to get through to here. One can't be seen to go before the other."

"Really!" Geordie snapped crossly. "No wonder their offspring are such a thick-headed bunch of no-hopers. No—I mustn't say that. Look—tell 'em it's their problem, but if they don't get in here straight away I'm going out there to fetch them."

Mr McNally disappeared, to return just two minutes later with two men, one to his left, the other to his right, whom he managed to propel through the door of the snug at more or less the same time. Ms D'Arcy rose, and did the greetings and introductions.

Muriel was full of surprise. After her friend's description of her two 'chaps' she had expected stereotypical villains. Quite what she wasn't sure, but something nearer Al Capone than St Francis of Assisi. In fact the head of the Sackville tribe, the old bookie Renfrew Sackville, looked like a benevolent banker invented by Dickens—chubby cheeks, pure white hair, guileless smile and a tendency to *trot*. A plump old pussy-cat? Wrong.

His companion of the moment, Cecil Wormwald, known to all around as 'Old Banger', to distinguish him from his eldest son and heir 'Young Banger', had the demeanour of a grave old shepherd from the hills. He was tall, rangy, slightly stooping over his walking stick. But fit. His face was lined, great strength of character showing in every fissure. Here, you might think, was a solitary whose mind was on nature and the eternal. Wrong again. Old Cecil thought of women, cars and cash, in the reverse order and a lot.

"Gentlemen," said Geordie grandly. "Thank you for turning up. What can I get you to drink?"

"Nay—can't let a lass buy...." began Mr Sackville.

"We'll get 'em...." said Mr Wormwald simultaneously.

Ms D'Arcy looked annoyed. "We'll have a little less of the sexism for a start. What do you want?"

The old men dropped their eyes. Muriel was quite curious to discover what chaps like these—men very much of a world she only guessed at—would chose instead of Mr McNally's putrid ale, whose taste no amount of hot, sweet coffee, it seemed, would ever remove from her mouth.

The two antagonists looked at each other, both daring the other to speak first.

Geordie D'Arcy put on the sort of face she used on these men's grandchildren and their numerous cousins, when they thought that playing silly buggers was preferable to lessons. "Look," she said with heavy patience. "We don't want to be here all night, do we? If you like you can each write your answer on a piece of paper and give it to my friend Muriel, who will pass the information on to me. In strictest confidence, I can assure you."

Did she imagine it, or did the flicker of a smile pass between the two old enemies? "I'd like a cup of coffee, same as you," they both said, almost exactly together.

"Milk and sugar?"

"No sugar, milk please," said old Sackville.

"Milk but no sugar," said old Wormwald. "Please."

While they were waiting for Mr McNally, Geordie D'Arcy leaned across the table and addressed a spot halfway between her two guests. "Right," she said. She'd called the register, thought Muriel, now lessons were to start. "We will get absolutely nowhere if we carry on like your descendants in the bar. I'm going to call a truce. It can last as long as you both like afterwards, but it's going to last here until we finish. This is what I tell the kids at school, and it works with them. I promise neither I nor my friend will breathe a word as to who spoke first or said what. It doesn't matter. Can we do that—can we have a cease-fire?"

Both men slowly looked at each other, and just as slowly nodded. God, she's wonderful, thought Muriel.

"The thing is this—you know they're having a shindig up at Boggerthwaite tomorrow? All the kids here have been working at it for a couple of weeks now."

"Aye, I'd heard summat about it," conceded Cecil Wormwald

"Our Nickla's been on about it," added Renfrew Sackville.

"The Bleezins," said Mr Wormwald, darting a swift glance at his old enemy.

"Hadmiral Byng and that," contribute Mr Sackville.

Geordie D'Arcy looked encouraged. "You mean you've heard of it before? It's not just something somebody made up?"

"Heard of it? Why, when I was a bairn...." Mr Wormwald began.

198

"The Bleezins goes reet back, lass," said Mr Sackville. "As a lad...."

"Yes, do go on. One at a time, though. We'll toss for who goes first if you like. My friend Muriel here'll have a coin."

"It's all right," said the two old men almost together, Tweedledum and Tweedledee. If they had bowed to each other the teacher could not have been more surprised.

"Shall I?" Mr Wormwald asked his old adversary.

"Aye—go on then." Mr Sackville nodded benevolently, a dreamy smile on his lips, as if dredging up old memories of his own.

"We lived up at Boggerthit then," said Cecil. "My father worked at Dabster and Tysons, you see."

"You might say everyone worked at Dabster and Tysons," added Renfrew. "It was the only work there was, bar farming."

"Mekkin' flinches and suchlike...."

"Aye, strigglin'. Your Dad was a striggler, wasn't he, Cecil?"

"A master striggler, Rennie. Like yours. Aye." Geordie D'Arcy wasn't to know, but this was the first time the two old villains had used each other's first names since VJ Night, when they had had a wonderful inter-family punch-up to celebrate the cessation of world-scale hostilities.

"And the Bleezins?" Ms D'Arcy prompted.

"Every April, the Bleezins were," said old Wormwald.

"Like a works holiday," said Sackville. "You know, like they have wakes weeks in Lancashire and that..."

"Only ours was never a whole week. Just the day," said Mr Wormwald. "Too tight to give proper holidays, was Dabster and Tysons."

"If you wanted time off you took it without pay," said Mr Sackville. "The good old days, I don't think."

"And what did they do at the Bleezins?"

"Why—the same as you're getting up to now, lass."

"Aye—we always had this replica, like, of Hadmiral Byng. What d'you call it—like Guy Fawkes, eh?"

"Effigy?" suggested Geordie.

"Aye—heffigy," said the two together.

"But why Admiral Byng?"

The two old men looked at each other, laughed. "No idea, pet. Traditional."

"Like Guy Fawkes," said Mr Sackville.

"But it weren't jist Hadmiral Byng," put in Mr Wormwald. "Was it, Ren? There was Holiver Cromwell, I remember...."

"Aye, Holiver Cromwell. There was William the Conqueror, 'cos he never did go down well in these parts...."

"Perkin Warbeck," said Mr Wormwald, as if remembering the name of a classmate long ago. "And Philip of Spain."

"Who was that other one, Ceecil? Mary Tudor, wasn't it?"

"That's right. I remember I got the job of stuffin' Mary Tudor—beggin' your pardon, Miss...."

"Do go on," said Geordie D'Arcy.

"Put these two bags of straw down her front. Girt big 'uns. Right out here, she was." And he cupped old hands two feet away from his chest. "There was the Sheriff of Nottingham too—we burned the lot."

"Aye, grand days," smiled Renfrew Sackville. "There was always a good scrap afterwards."

"As I say, that's when we was all up at Boggerthit. Long before they built Sunny Lea."

"Whatever happened?" inquired the teacher.

"Well, it started with the Devastation, didn't it, Ceecil?"

"Aye. March the 22nd, 1922, the Bogger Valley Devastation. Half the village slid into the river."

"Hundermined, see?"

"All them old rows of cottages—Inkerman, Sebastapol...."

"Halma, Scutari—all where the Timeshare is now, like."

"Old Lord Bogger as then was wouldn't pay any compensation."

"So everyone ups and teks off. Some to Canada—most of the Hanstruthers went to Canada, as I remember...."

"Aye, and Haustralia. A lot of them Nattrasses went to Haustralia."

"But my old Dad, he wasn't goin' to no Haustralia."

"Nor were mine. Canada neither. Kicked up a hell of a fuss."

"Didn't give 'em no peace. So in the end they had to rehouse us."

"And that's how Sunny Lea started."

"After that there were no Bleezins any more."

"Kind of fell into disuse."

Geordie D'Arcy listened, head cupped in her hands, intent. "One thing I don't understand, and no-one ever seems to know—how was it your two families fell out?"

The two old men looked at each other, apparently for some sort of inspiration. Then they shook their heads slowly.

"You don't *know*?" Geordie frowned, then grinned. "You mean you've been feuding since way back and nobody knows what about?"

"Aye," said Renfrew Sackville benevolently. "You might say it's traditional."

"Like the Bleezins," said Cecil Wormwald.

"So there was no happening—no action—to spark it all off?" Ms D'Arcy was shaking her head in wonder. "No-one put some lass up the stick and wouldn't marry her?"

Old Sackville looked almost horrified. "None of us'd ever marry one of them anyway."

"Let alone put one in the family way to start with," added his rival.

"What I *think* happened," pondered Mr Sackville, "was back to the Devastation. We weren't particular enemies before then...."

"The Wormwalds would fight anybody."

"So would the Sackvilles."

"And when all the others cleared out—the Hanstruthers and the Nattrasses and the Titmusses...."

"And the Fletchers. D'you remember little Millie Fletcher, Ceecil?"

"I do indeed...." Mr Wormwald smiled and went quiet, thoughts far away.

"Well, when all that lot went there was only really the two families left. Natural rivals, you might say."

"Aye—you had to have somebody to have a go at."

"No television in them days. None of these videos. We had to make our own hentertainment, eh?"

"You mentioned the Nattrasses," said Geordie. "It was Old Billy

Nattrass who first mentioned the Bleezins—gave the council the idea of starting them again."

The two old men looked at each other with a shared indignation. "Billy Nattrass? What'd he know about it?"

"Well, he's been a little vague, I must say," said Geordie.

"Vague? He's off his rocker, that one."

"Needs puttin' in a home, I'd say."

"That's as may be," said Geordie. "But don't you see—you've let Boggerthwaite take over your own tradition. Pinch it."

"But we *are* Boggerthit," the two chorused together.

"The *proper* Boggerthit," said Cecil Wormwald.

"They're jist bloody offcomers up there," said Renfrew Sackville. "Bloody hippies."

"And them yuppies."

"And yon bloody Irish poof at the pub, if you'll pardon me."

"And that Liverpool cow in the shop."

"What about Lord Bogger?" Geordie D'Arcy poked in suddenly.

"That Lord Bogger's a real gent," said Mr Wormwald. "Bought our Blocker a pint t'other night by all accounts."

"And our Throttler. Aye, in here, bought him a drink," said Throttler's Great-uncle Renfrew proudly. "Aye—a real toff."

Ms D'Arcy finished her coffee, looked at each of the old tribal chieftains in turn. "Then I think I've got an idea," she said.

33

By Boggerthwaite standards Mr Mahmoud's dinner-party might have been counted a masterpiece of hospitality. The food was superb—none of your squatting on a rug round a dish of sheeps' eyes and sherbet. This was more English than the English: hare soup, a sliver of smoked trout from the Bogger Beck, roast beef and Yorkshire pudding (with parsnips and brussels sprouts), followed by spotted Dick and lashings of custard. The wines? Well, with the soup an alluring little Gevrey-Chambertin; with the fish a delicate but highly-expensive Chablis; the main course was accompanied by a Limestone Ridge Shiraz in honour of the Australian guest (who wouldn't have known it from Cola), and the pud with a choice Gewurtztraminer (*vendange tardi* of course). Conversation was a little on the slow side to start with, and remained slow throughout, but the host did his best and the servants were attentive almost to a fault. Yet Mrs Loudwater was to say afterwards that never in all her years as a busy and dedicated chairperson, never in all the times she had been entertained in the service of the public, had she been so uncomfortable, so haunted by a feeling of unease, of impending disaster. Matty Ouskin, who has read about such things, said it reminded him of Belshazzar's Feast.

But if the chief guest, Senator William Hudspith Wordsworth, felt anything of the sort he showed no sign of it. Shrewdly, Mr Mahmoud had placed him between his oldest wife Fatima, whose English was still at a rudimentary stage, and Mrs Loudwater, who wanted as little to do with her Antipodean visitor as possible. Young Mandy had been tucked in at Mr Mahmoud's left hand, her charms well out of sight of the senator, who found himself faced across the table by the highly non-erotic rank of Mrs Emma Rhoid the doctor's wife, Matty Ouskin, and Mr Bean the clerk. The lovely Linda was on Mr Mahmoud's right, but largely hidden from the lascivious senator by a very bright table candelabrum.

There were toasts. Mr Mahmoud proposed a witty one to the guests, in which he likened Senator Wordsworth to a swallow, whose migratory sense must always bring him back to his roots in Old England. Mrs Loudwater replied, Jeremy Blink-Howell took rapid notes but failed, when he later came to transcribe them, to make more than a couple of grammatical sentences of them. Matty Ouskin gave his Ode to a Visitor from the Antipodes, which not everyone present had heard the first time. And then finally, after the Stilton, the senator was called upon.

He was, it has to be said, in a far better state than he had been earlier that day. He could stand for one thing, he could focus for another, and although that focus groped back and forward between the tantalising Mandy and the exquisite Linda, it did help to create the illusion that the senator was in some sort of control of himself. Senator Wordsworth would give a toast to the ladies.

His speech was a little masterpiece of racialism, sexism and downright boorishness, which we shall not quote here. No-one applauded, glasses remained unlifted until Mandy broke the ice by clapping enthusiastically and blowing big kisses in the senator's direction. Mr Mahmoud joined in good-naturedly, but not before flashing his youngest wife a glance which was far from good-natured, and the rest followed. Afterwards came the passing of the port (a thirty-year-old Graham, naturally), at which the ladies who had just been toasted were required to withdraw. Mr Mahmoud held open the door for them, and might have been seen giving a few quiet words to Mandy, who replied with no words but a tossing of her blonde mane. When Senator Wordsworth protested at the absence of the ladies Mr Mahmoud gave him a steely smile and informed him that it was one of our old English customs which had perhaps not yet managed to cross the Equator. Senator Wordsworth said this was bullshit and proceeded to tell a very rambling Antipodean story about three ladies from Melbourne. The atmosphere was described afterwards by Mr Bean the Clerk as '*un petit peu orageux*' by which he probably mean stormy. But then he will never use one English word when three foreign ones will do.

Meanwhile in the drawing room, a large expanse furnished throughout in light brown and pale blue, and which led into a conservatory full of palms and exotic ferns, coffee was served to the womenfolk. Here the atmosphere was rather less charged. Mrs Loudwater and Dr Rhoid's wife Emma talked about knitting-machines with Mesdames Mahmoud. It was uphill going at first, but produced the first laughter of the evening when Mrs Loudwater related how her late husband Roy had often referred to her as 'his little knitting machine'. That was in the days before she became active in politics of course.

Amanda Mahmoud had no part in this homely discussion. She had sidled away quietly up to Linda, and suggested that perhaps she might be interested in tropical plants and might care to have a look round the conservatory. Linda agreed: she had rather little option. Mandy turned out to be quite the knowledgeable little hostess. "These here," she said, with a wave of long scarlet-nailed fingers, "These here are cabbage palms. From New Zealand, you know. North Island, of course. Omapere Bay, actually, right up on the top left-hand side. Have you been to New Zealand, dear?"

Linda shook her head. She had once been to Tenerife with a publican: that was about all.

"I suppose you hope that *he*...." Mandy couldn't bring herself to say 'my husband' or 'Arpad'. "....will take you around a bit. Well, he might, but I don't think I'd like that."

Linda smiled her wide-eyed, butter-wouldn't-melt-in-mouth smile. "We'll have to see, won't we, dear?" she said. "So what are these big ferny things over here?"

"They're New Zealand too," smiled Mandy. "They're called toetoe plumes. The Maoris are very attached to them, I believe. I don't quite understand what game you're up to, girl, but I think we might do a deal."

"Fascinating," said Linda, happy-looking as a little girl in a toy-shop. "I really do love plants and Nature and that. What had you got in mind?"

Mandy wandered slowly further into the conservatory "I didn't know anything about botany when I first met....him. I'm not sure that he does yet. He acquired all this stuff when he bought the house. These are climbing vanilla plants. From the West Indies somewhere, I believe. Did you know that the word vanilla comes from the Latin 'vagina'? I thought you might have known that."

"Fascinating," said Linda. "What's the deal, then?"

But Mandy was in no great hurry. "All that over there is Indian hemp. You'll know it by other names, I think. He grows a bit for domestic use. We've met before, haven't we?"

"Could be," Linda smiled still. "You interested in ley-lines and that?"

"You used to work the top end of Berwick-street didn't you? Lot of ley-lines round there. Spelt differently, that's all."

"My, you do get around, don't you?" said Linda. "I packed all that caper in when I met Haitch. You haven't met Haitch, have you? He's gorgeous. Got me hooked on psychic archaeology. He's an Intuitive. He has a very well developed intuition. "

"Really? That's a new word for it," said Mandy moving on. "Now these are jacarandas from Australia. What I want you to do is to get that Australian jerk off my back. I thought it was a good idea at first to play him along and make....*him* jealous. But I don't think it's having any effect. I fancy keeping what I've got here, but I think it's you he's got his beady little eyes on at the moment. If you play the Aussie it'll get *him* so mad I'll have got my own back."

"What do I get out of it?" asked Linda, pinching the leaf of a fleshy-leaved exotic and sniffing her fingers. "Mmm—gorgeous."

"What would you want?"

207

Linda gave a little laugh, full of sisterly generosity. "Nothing, love. I've got what I wanted—a pitch for a little rave-up for a few nights—for the travellers, like. It'll be a change: your Arpad bloke's getting a bit heavy. I can look after myself, but Haitch might get a bit upset and I don't want to queer the pitch. I can handle the Oz all right. Another couple of nights and the Brethren'll want to move on anyway"

"You're a honey," cried Mandy. "What can I get you, though—a new motor?"

Linda looked almost shocked. "No fear, love. Haitch wouldn't like that at all. What we've got may look rough, but it goes like a bomb. All part of the image. No—you just keep your bloke sweet for a couple more days. I'll just fade into the background, and what happens to the Aussie—well, who cares?"

"Well," said Mandy gratefully. "If there's ever anything, you let me know. You haven't really met that Oz yet, though, have you? I'll try and introduce you, you lucky girl. And thanks again."

Now the original idea of ladies' withdrawal after a dinner party was to allow the gentlemen to let off steam with their unspeakable stories, to get well and truly smashed and then to be shepherded homewards or bedwards by the servants without the ladies being too embarrassed. Nobody had ever told Mr Mahmoud this. He felt that the party should continue on a mixed basis until he got fed up with it. He was bored in totally male company, had fulfilled the etiquette as he saw it, wanted to show off his women, and he still had some business to discuss with Mrs Loudwater about the events of the morrow. So, as Mandy was showing her new friend a prime example of a Ethiopian myrtle or some such, the gentlemen percolated through into the drawing-room.

They were led in by the host, but before further announcements could be made Senator Wordsworth came whooping through crying: "That's right—let's get at the crumpet!" Mr Mahmoud frowned.

Looking wildly about him, the senator made for the conservatory as Mandy and Linda moved in to join the company. He bounded up to them with the look of a large dog who has sighted twin bowls of food. He was by no stretch of the imagination at all sober. "Mandy!" he bellowed at the top of his voice. "There you are, you sexy little wenchette. Who's your gorgeous mate here?"

"Senator Wordsworth!" Mr Mahmoud's voice was not particularly loud, but it cut through all other sound.

Senator Wordsworth chose to ignore it. "Encher gonna interduce us?" he said to Mandy, his eyes feasting on the lovely Linda, who had all of a sudden gone all demure and vulnerable. Mandy was at a slight loss: she did not know Linda's name.

"Amanda!" Mr Mahmoud's voice, cold and commanding, cut through the hiatus.

Linda played up very well. "I'm Linda," she smiled, and could see over the senator's shoulder that Mr Mahmoud was furious.

"Linda?" echoed the senator. "Bloody hell—I bet you're the most astonishing...."

"Senator Wordsworth!" Mr Mahmoud was a man used to being obeyed. His voice was much louder now.

Still Linda played up. "I have been told I'm quite good at it," she said, stoking up the senator's fires with those wide, innocent-looking eyes. "At least, I've never had any grumbles."

"I'm Bill Wordsworth. William Hudspith Wordsworth, known as Hud. I'm from Australia."

"I'd never have guessed," smiled Linda. She had proffered a soft little hand to be shaken, and seemed in no hurry to retrieve it from the senator's paw. Mandy had meanwhile retreated, back to her husband's side.

"Do something for Heavens sake," Mrs Loudwater hissed to no-one in particular. No-one in particular did anything.

"Let's go in that greenhouse thing there," the senator urged Linda loudly. She, by her young body-language, seemed to be needing little persuasion. "I'll show you a bit of Aussie flora," said the senator.

"Senator Wordsworth—you are abusing my hospitality," said Mr Mahmoud in his loudest voice yet.

"Bullshit," said the senator, propelling Linda before him. Then, over his shoulder: "What hospitality, anyway?"

There was a general tut-tutting from the other guests, and Mrs Loudwater said: "Disgraceful!" Mr Mahmoud stepped forward and spoke to Linda. "I think you would be better away from this man," he said.

But Linda pouted. "Aw c'mon—he's sweet," she said. "He's my little fluffy koala bear." And she ran her spare hand down the senator's cheek.

"And I'm gonna let her have a blow at my didgeridoo," said Senator Wordsworth, raising doubts in more than one mind as to whether he was really Australian after all.

Mr Mahmoud appeared to be quite cool—icy in fact. Only those who knew him well (and there were few) would have detected a clenching and unclenching of his fingers and a tightening of the muscles of his cheek. But then, Mr Mahmoud was trying his best to be British. "Senator, this is absolutely not cricket," he said. "I think you had better leave. I shall arrange transport. You, Linda, will stay here."

But Linda laughed. "You can't order me about, mate," she said. "Can he, Bruce? I'm going to call you Bruce: all Aussies are called Bruce." And she put her soft bare arms around the ghastly senator's neck and nuzzled her nose against his. Women will sometimes do the most extraordinary things these days in the cause of sisterhood.

Mr Mahmoud actually clapped his hands. "Bring two pairs of gloves," he commanded. He didn't look at whoever the order was addressed to, didn't name anybody. Just commanded. Then, slowly and carefully he took off his dark glasses, put them into the breast pocket of his jacket, then just as carefully peeled off that garment and handed it, again without looking, to whoever happened to be nearest to obey his wishes. This happened to be Mandy, and she took the garment without a word, faithful little wife returned to the fold.

Senator Wordsworth's bleary eyes nearly popped. Then he started to laugh, which was the silliest thing in a succession of silly things he had done all evening. Then he detached the soft arms of Linda from about his neck and faced Mr Mahmoud, fists up, still laughing. "Fancy yerself, do yer, mate?" he said.

"We will do this thing properly, if you please," said Mr Mahmoud. "This is England. We will have the gloves. Queensberry Rules."

"Queensberry Rules OK," guffawed the senator. "Well, they're not OK for me." And he took a long right-hand swing at his host. He missed, but the momentum of his attempt threw him off balance and carried him over to Lord Bogger, who held him upright. It can surely have been only a manifestation of a fevered imagination that caused both Mrs Loudwater and her council clerk to imagine that they heard their peer mutter, very sotto voce: "Get in there, Hud!" Nobility would just not say a thing like that. Not proper nobility.

"If you would just stand back, ladies and gentlemen," Mr Mahmoud was saying. One of his oriental-looking male servants had brought him two pairs of brand-new boxing gloves and was handing his employer a pair.

"See to my guest first," said Mr Mahmoud.

But the senator pushed the gloves away quite rudely. "Bugger the Queensberry Rules. Bugger the Poms!" he said. If such things had been possible, Mr Mahmoud might have turned white. Instead he calmly put on his gloves, then he squared up, balanced neatly on the balls of his feet.

The senator blundered in again, and swung his same right. It might this time have connected if Mr Mahmoud had not blocked it with the back of his glove and danced sportingly back without attempting to land a return blow. "Careful darling," Mandy said quite audibly, but any satisfaction her husband might have taken from her display of fidelity was spoiled somewhat by Linda's behaviour.

"Kill 'im, Bruce!" yelled Linda. "Go on—you can do it!" Was she overplaying her new role? She couldn't really tell any more.

Senator Wordsworth advanced again. Once more he took a right-handed swing at his opponent. This time, again having blocked the attempt quite easily, Mr Mahmoud dabbed out a couple of very swift right jabs, one, two, which both connected with the senator's nose. Not very hard blows, but enough to bring tears to the eyes and rage to the head. Wordsworth tried to hurl himself upon his adversary now, but Mr Mahmoud danced sideways and let him sprawl on the floor without another blow being struck. "Had enough?" he inquired.

For answer, the descendant of the Great Bard of Grasmere clambered to his feet, snatched up a coffee pot from a handy side-table, and hurled it at Mr Mahmoud's head. The entrepreneur dodged. the pot shattered one of the conservatory windows, and Mrs Loudwater fainted. Whether hers was a genuine faint or not will never be known. Mr Bean holds that she is far too tough an old bird for swooning, and that she was just fed up with being out of the limelight for so long. He quite enjoyed slapping her round the chops to revive her. When she had recovered a little she was led to a handy armchair by Gloria Sackville, on duty again this evening, and revived with a little drop of what she fancied.

Meanwhile, no doubt to save further expense on window-glass and crockery, Mr Mahmoud danced towards his opponent, gave him a vicious straight left to the abdomen, and as the senator folded forward with a wheeze like a deflating tyre, cracked him under the chin with a hard right cross. Senator Wordsworth did a number of things; he buckled at the knees, jerked back his head and shoulders, span a half-circle round to his right, and was sick. Then he went down. Mr Rory McGurk was not going to be pleased at the state of his best suit.

Action over, the guests were to be seen standing around like minor characters in the last act of Hamlet. The lovely Linda, having seen her opportunity, had made a discreet exit, no doubt back to the tattooed arms of Big Haitch. Mr Mahmoud took off his gloves, put on his jacket again, and motioned to two of his henchmen. "Have him removed," he said. "No doubt his friends will see him back to wherever he should be" And marshalling his womenfolk around him, Mr Mahmoud made for the door.

Mrs Loudwater, clucking, made an attempt to forestall him.

"I am most terribly sorry...." she was saying. "Quite disgraceful...."

"I shall bid you all goodnight," said Mr Mahmoud stiffly.

"But we'll see you at the Bleezins in the morning, won't we?" said Mrs Loudwater, "Eleven-thirty sharp. You're judging the kiddies' costumes. Don't forget now."

Mr Mahmoud paused. "Madam," he said "After this evening's exhibition I want nothing more to do with your celebrations or your committee. And I shall have to reconsider my entire future attitude to the welfare of the village. Goodnight."

No-one saw it, but Lord Bogger exchanged a smile of some satisfaction with Mrs Gloria Sackville, demure in the white pinafore and black dress.

Exeunt, bearing a recumbent senator from Boggaburra, New South Wales.

34

The morning of the Saturday of the revived Boggerthwaite Bleezins dawned as fair as the day before. The sun was quite warm by nine o'clock, there was hardly a cloud in the sky, but a light thickening of the atmosphere over towards Keswick and a complete absence of wind told aborigines like Mrs Sylvia Anstruther and Old Billy Nattrass that the day might well turn out rather differently from its predecessor. A clairvoyant, taking in the human scene, would no doubt have had doubts as to the day's finishing as had originally been intended.

Old Billy was busy quite early. His head was a little fuzzy, but duty must never be allowed to be blocked by such a trifle as a hangover. Mr Nattrass had to ring the bell of St Ethelbogger's Church. This was unusual on a Saturday, unless there was a wedding, but he had had his instructions clearly enough over the phone the previous evening. Mattins at ten, a special service to commemorate the Feast of the local saint, prelude to the Bleezins themselves. Old Billy hadn't realised it was St Ethelbogger's Day, neither had he read the papers lately, being preoccupied with long-haired young women, daisy chains and much dancing, smoking and drinking. He shook his head as a dog will on emerging from water, and put on his best suit.

Old Billy liked to refer to himself as the verger of St Ethelbogger's. This was not an official appointment: the parish was nowhere near able to pay a regular man. But somewhere deep in this dried-up old soul the misanthrope must have had some vestige of Faith, or at least a healthy fear of hell fire, for he undertook the duties, such as they were, and they were not onerous, for nothing, and that was not like Old Billy. Actually he would have preferred being one of the churchwardens. There was more of a social aura surrounding a warden, but the positions had been filled long since. The vicar's warden was Dr Harry Rhoid and the peoples' was little Tot Titmuss the postman. Old Billy met up with Dr Rhoid now as he walked to church: both lived out on the Stoatholme side of Boggerthwaite, and the good doctor kindly waited for the verger at the bottom of the lane leading up to High Scutterings Farm. "What a glorious morning, William," were his first words. He was a simple little man who liked to think good of everyone, and even of the weather, which seeing that he had lived in the Lake District for forty-odd years, tells you quite a lot about his character.

"It's going to be quite a turnout," the little doctor went on. "Look—there are coaches already."

And he was right. They had reached the turn in the road where you can see around and down into the centre of Boggerthwaite. Two large coaches were already drawn up by the village green, there were twenty or thirty cars either already parked or jostling for resting-space, and people were milling about in far larger numbers than Old Billy remembered ever seeing since Coronation Day—the one before the war when real people still lived in the village.

"I'm so pleased," enthused Dr Rhoid, "that old tradition is coming back. This is how it must have been in the old days, you know. A church feast day was just that—people feasted. They went to church and then, when they came out, there was fun and games in the churchyard and round the village green."

"Aye," said Old Billy, looking at this watch. There was something very wrong with so many people out so early.

"This of course is how your Bleezings started. St Ethelbogger's Day—special service in honour of the saint, then high-jinks afterwards. I think this is going to be a wonderful revival. " The low jinks at Mr Mahmoud's on the previous evening seemed to have left no bad taste in the doctor's mouth.

Like most rural churches in these days of sinful materialism, St

Ethelbogger's drew only a handful of people most Sundays—Mrs Anstruther, Mrs Bryony Costive and Darren, and one or two of the weekend visitors and Timeshare punters. But this morning the place was besieged. The village green was full of visitors of all shapes, sizes and nationality, including a solemn file of po-faced young Japanese with video cameras round the lych-gate and poking around the gravestones in the yard. As Billy and the doctor arrived a large coach bearing a banner proclaiming "UK-OZ EXPATS" drew up, disgorging a mob of beefy looking men wearing dark blue blazers and singing Waltzing Matilda. Or bits of it.

"Isn't it wonderful?" gushed Dr Rhoid. "Someone must have been praying very hard."

Old Billy grunted again. he had spotted among a group packed up against the church porch a good half-dozen of the pressmen who had descended on the village the previous week, including one who had bought him several whiskies. "Where's the vicar?" they were all yelling now at him as he tried to clear a way to the door.,

Billy had watched television for years in the pub; it was cheaper than having one at home. "I have no comment to make," he said in the manner of all the politicians he had seen. He shoved the big old key in the door lock. Turning, it made a noise like an ancient tractor being hand-cranked. At the press that followed the door's opening, Dr Rhoid showed surprising presence for such a dumpy little man. "Stand back," he commanded. "This is the House of God."

"When's the Second Coming happening, then?" someone shouted from the back. Dr Rhoid frowned. He had not read the papers either. As the crowd pressed into the body of the church he made an half-hearted attempt to hand out hymn-books but gave up after a couple of minutes. Old Billy was far more practical: he pushed every available collecting box into the path of the crush. He had no fear of their being pinched or plundered, for none had contained any coin for months. Then he cleared a space at the back of the church, unwound rope from a cleat on the wall, and started to toll the single bell. Traditional this, but otherwise pointless. St Ethelbogger's was already full.

"Christ!" exclaimed Dr Rhoid, forgetting himself. "How's Mrs Anstruther to get in—she's supposed to be playing the organ. They'll need something to amuse them: service isn't for another half an hour."

Mrs Anstruther would have to manage the best way she could, grunted Old Billy, but without adding the epithets he would normally have chosen for his old enemy, and shouldered his way down the packed aisle to the vestry. He unlocked the door and led Dr. Rhoid inside.

Now neither Billy nor the warden had given a lot of thought to the practicalities of this special service. If they had they might have wondered, both of them, how a vicar who had not been seen by most of the congregation for many weeks, and about whom the most scurrilous things had been suggested in the Press, would arrive for the service. Dr Rhoid was about to start wondering this, and eventually to share the question with the verger, when both became aware that they were not alone in the vestry. Indeed, a light was burning in its little ante-room a previous incumbent had used to accommodate his five dogs and one bicycle during Divine Service, and further investigation revealed the Rev Ximenez and a strange man sitting at a small table picking bits off an old chicken carcass and pouring tea from a thermos flask. "Dr Rhoid, Mr Nattrass," greeted the vicar. "How good of you to come." And: "Allelujah, brothers," hailed the unknown man.

The vicar did the introductions. "This," she indicated, "is Brother Bergholz. He is managing our Crusade."

Verger and warden looked at each other in puzzlement. Then Brother Bergholz prepared to speak. He had changed somewhat since we last met him. Now he had lost his seedy hack's togs and

217

grubby raincoat, and was arrayed in a long, greeny-black cassock set off at the neck with a glimpse of dog-collar. A heavy pectoral cross hung round his neck and such hair as he had was sleeked down to his scalp. "Peace be with you, my brothers," he said. Then, in more business-like tones; "Just to put you guys in the picture: Sister Ximenez here has had it revealed that she is to herald the Second Coming. Only it's going to be a whole different ball-game from the First. This time the Saviour is to be a woman. It's obvious when you think about it."

"Quite so," gulped Dr Rhoid, to whom it was very far from so. Old Billy said nothing.

Brother Bergholz went on: "Now just as Brother John the Baptist prepared the campaign last time, it has been ordained this time that Sister Ximenez shall make the paths straight. My humble part in all this is to prepare the way for the Preparer of the Way, in a manner of speaking. In other words, I'm acting as Michelle's agent—publicity, bookings, all the corporate side of it. We shall follow the opening of our campaign here with rallies at all the major venues in the country. Already we've got Middlesborough Football Ground and a holiday camp at Skegness. It will be a hard and strenuous journey that we face, but we must take up our burden as the Chosen, the Elite. Any questions?"

"How did you get in?" Old Billy Nattrass was always practical.

Ms Ximenez smiled serenly. "I have a key to the outside door of the vestry. We came in last night and...."

"We've been watching and praying," said Brother Bergholz.

Old Billy had forgotten about the back vestry door. Normally he would have entered this way himself and unlocked the main church door from the inside. But the pressure of events had disturbed his routine. He looked at the back door now in time to see it open, and the pale, strained face of Constable Robin Costive peer round the jamb.

"Yes officer," inquired the vicar. "What is it?"

"I was hoping *you* could shed some light on that," said the constable. "There's all hell let loose out here. Likely to be a breach of the peace if it isn't one already, and I would be inclined to take the view that you are likely to be held responsible."

"Ent you got no fishin' to do?" Old Billy piped up.

Before the harassed constable could think of a reply, which if he had had his way would have involved the use of truncheon, handcuffs and cat-o'-nine-tails, he was quite roughly jostled from behind and two burly young men in clerical garb stood in his place on the threshold. They looked like pantomime brokers men with dog-collars. "Allelujah, brother," Brother Bergholz greeted them.

"We must insist that this travesty is not allowed to proceed," Said the first newcomer.

"We have an injunction from the Bishop," said the second.

Ms Ximenez still smiled sweetly and calmly. "Then you can go back to your bishop and tell him that nothing will stop me from following Divine Revelation—nor angels, nor principalities nor powers. Sorry and all that."

"Then we must forbid you the use of the church," said the first diocesan official.

"Yes, it's our building," said the second.

"And it's my Living," said a third voice, and Lord Bogger appeared in the doorway. "St Ethelbogger's is in my gift, gentlemen. I am Lord Bogger of Bogger Hall, and I say who preaches here and who doesn't. Reverend Ximenez—it's all yours."

The first broker's-man-clergyman turned to face Lord Bogger, bristling with a fine dogmatic anger. "You realise of course that this person is preaching heresy, and that you are condoning blasphemy."

"Well, it seems to pull the punters in more than your version," said Lord Bogger. "They're queueing outside."

Ms Ximenez got to her feet. "Look, I shall try to keep everybody happy. Gentlemen, keep your building. I shall do as they did in the days when the Church was too poor to be corrupt—I shall preach in the open air." And she made towards the door. As she did so a sound like a whole zoo in sexual torment screeched and thundered from the body of the church. The windows shook, and bits of plaster fell from the ceiling. "Mrs Anstruther seems to have made it after all," said Dr Rhoid.

"Allelujah, it's a sign," put in Brother Bergholz.

35

Mr Rory McGurk was a late sleeper at the best of times. Country publicans who wish to make any money have perforce to keep late hours to satisfy the desire of their clientele not to go home to their wives until they absolutely have to. This makes them the tired, irritable and liverish men so many of them are. Mr McGurk was a prime example. At official closing time on St Ethelbogger's Eve the pub had still been full of New Age seekers after truth and intoxication who were making their own amusement with ribald comments about the diehard regular weekenders—those, that is, who had not chosen to see how things were and got themselves back to their cottages and caravans. Just as McGurk was managing to persuade some of the more unruly ones to pack up and call it a day, in came Senator William Wordsworth, escorted by the loyal Matty Ouskin. The senator had recovered his legs and his voice and was loudly suggesting that everyone ought to have a drink on him.

Mr McGurk counter-suggested that by the state of his clothes— *his* clothes, by the way—it looked as if several people had already had quite a number of drinks on him, literally. Senator Wordsworth threatened to knock Mr McGurk down, and then subsided into his favourite seat by the juke-box and went soundly back to sleep.

It was there that a very bleary-eyed McGurk found him the next morning, looking like a latter-day Silenus presiding over the ruin of the night before. There were glasses everywhere, plates brimming with the less digestible parts of November Owl Pie, crisp-packets and cigarette-ends. There was, miraculously perhaps, only one broken window and this had been patched with a sheet of cardboard. As he picked his way through all the detritus Mr McGurk could hear much evidence of washing-up going on in the kitchen beyond the servery. Clouds of steam wafted through the hatchway, and the high-pitched strains of some lachrymose work-ditty from the Philippines. One part of Mr McGurk wanted to open the front door, run, and keep on running; another, smaller but stronger, kept saying: "Think of the takings, boy." The smaller voice won quite easily.

It was while considering what to do about the window repair that our landlord became aware of unwonted activity about the village green. It was half-past nine in the morning, yet the place already resembled the car-parking area of a popular horse racing course. Cars and coaches were everywhere, and to his horror Mr McGurk could see the brewery dray, which he had ordered in the previous day as an emergency measure, was stuck a good hundred yards from the pub and was rapidly being blocked in by further parking vehicles. The driver and his mate—both large, ale-nurtured young Cumbrian hearties—were beside him now, asking what the effin' eff was going on, how he effin expected them to effin' deliver beer, and what the eff was he going to do about it? With the promise of much baksheesh and the help of three or four New Age layabouts who had been kipping all night outside the pub and were complaining of thirst, Mr McGurk organised a grand barrel-rolling through the mud between dray and cellar-hatch. The beer, thankfully, was not proper beer and would take any amount of bumping. There was more of it than the pub usually sold in a good month. The drayman and his mate stood and watched.

"Are you open?" strangers increasingly began to enquire. "It says Morning Coffee but there's no-one there."

Mr McGurk knew it said Morning Coffee: he had had the sign painted to his own specifications years before when he was younger, keener, and still expectant of an early fortune. He also knew full well that there was no-one there to serve coffee, even if there had been any coffee to serve, which he rather doubted. Donna, the girl from Sunny Lea, who helped with the cleaning, served coffee on the rare occasion that a lost visitor called for it, but she appeared not to have turned up for work today. "Unexpected pressure," burbled Mr McGurk, wiping his forehead. "Doing what we can." Japanese tourists solemnly videoed him trying to cope with the rush. In a week or two's time they would be just as solemnly showing the results to friends back in Kyoto and explaining the vagaries of British modes of recreation.

Momentum increased, old Jake Otter came up bleating that the pigs had arrived, causing a moment of misunderstanding which raised in the publican's mind visions of a police raid and the loss of his licence. But the old phoney explained that this was a wagon full of pigs for racing down the street during the festivities. "The record's nine minutes, thirty-one seconds, set up in 1932 by a landrace boar named Roger. Where am I going to tell 'em to put 'em?"

Mr McGurk managed not to make the first and obvious reply that came to mind, for he had other worries. A party of thirty or so hefty, balding men in blazers with kangaroo badges, looking like a middle-aged team of rugby veterans in search of a match, ranged around the pub chanting: "Izzie an Ozzie, is he, was he?" or some such, and demanding beer. They were met at the door of the Rambler by Senator William Hudspith Wordsworth dressed in a chef's outfit, tall hat included, which he seemed to have exchanged for the soiled suit borrowed from the landlord the previous evening. There were roars of affectionate recognition, like "Allo Hud, yer boozy old bastard!", the senator mounted an empty beer-crate and conducted the horde of his fellow-countrymen in the loud and seemingly endless repetition of the word "Beer!" To add to the cacophony and confusion the single bell of St Ethelbogger's began to toll as if in melancholy remembrance of some well-loved local swain, and Pc Robin de Vere Costive arrived with a stern expression and told Mr McGurk that he would have to do something about the parking round his pub as it was creating an obstruction contrary to section something, sub-section inaudible of the Road Traffic Act. "And I want it done by the time I come back," said the officer, heading like all righteous men for the church.

Some five minutes later, having been physically threatened by two of the Australian gentlemen, bruised quite badly on the toes by the dropping of the final keg of beer from the dray, and been videoed eight more times by Japanese tourists, who may have been coming round for a second go for all he could tell, Mr McGurk saw issuing from St Ethelbogger's lychgate a quite remarkable procession. It appeared to be headed by Dr Rhoid with his churchwarden's staff of office, followed by the vicar and another clergy-looking person in black cassock, and by a jostling throng of lay persons. The procession made its way through the tangled mass of parked cars, past the pub, and off on to the footpath to Great Mirkin Fell and the Buzzard Stone. But if Mr McGurk was amazed he showed no signs. He was past all that.

36

There are no fewer than three regular footpaths leading from the Bogger Valley up to the top of Great Mirkin Fell via the Buzzard Stone, where they meet. One leads from near the centre of Boggerthwaite village, which is the one the Rev Ximenez and her flock were taking; another, rather longer but gentler, winds up from Stoatholme; while a third, steeper than the others and in some places involving simple rock-scrambles, climbs up from near Mirkin Grange.

It was on this third path that, quite early that morning, for the sun rises around six o'clock at this time of the year, a party of strangely garbed and mostly young people started their ascent. There were men in white robes with climbing boots and thick socks showing beneath the hems; others with shaven heads and yellow robes banging little tambourines, and a slightly separate party of people without common uniform headed by a number of guitarists (or people attempting guitars, which can be an entirely different thing), and a bearded giant with a saxophone who stopped every fifty yards or so to collect enough wind to blow the thing. The lovely Linda was among this bunch, still barefoot but clad now in a very fetching tight mini-skirt and a rather skimpy sweater. Haitch was with her, escorted by the two hounds which had seen off Mr Mahmoud's rotweilers a couple of days earlier. They gambolled around Haitch's legs when they were not making short forays after sheep, and were generally having the time of their lives.

When they all got to the Buzzard Stone the chaps in the long white robes stood around in a tight circle and chanted something that sounded rather like a slow version of Jailhouse Rock in what could have been Welsh. The others took it in turns getting in a position to line up the rising sun above the Buzzard Stone, and several were heard afterwards to say what an uplifting experience that had been, though most would have admitted under a truth drug that it had looked a bit like any spring sun rising over any lump of rock. Having partaken of the spiritual uplift, drawn vibrations from the stone, communed with Mother Nature or become one with the Greater Cosmos, most of them sat down on the grass and smoked pot. It was not at all cold on that hill top for a change, yet some people seemed insistent upon keeping others warm, usually but not exclusively members of the opposite gender. The bloke with the saxophone played something that may indeed have been The House of the Rising Sun, was sternly rebuked by one of the men in white nightshirts for having entirely missed the mystical significance of it all. The saxophonist said "Bollocks" and switched to Colonel Bogey. Big Haitch scratched himself luxuriously, while Linda lay beside him on the grass, eyes closed to the sun's increasing heat, smiling, and saying "Wow!" from time to time. The dogs barked happily and the lads with the shaven scalps shuffled round and round the Buzzard Stone tapping their tambourines and giving off a low, fluctuating humming sound like a wonky generator.

Boggerthwaite village cannot be seen from the Mirkin Grange side of the shelf that holds the Buzzard Stone, so it was something of a surprise to the hippy host assembled when quite suddenly over the rise appeared Dr Rhoid bearing like a standard a gold cross on top of a pole. At least, it was gold-coloured, but like much that glisters it was in fact made of brass. Good enough brass, though, and it looked right. Behind Dr Rhoid came the Rev Michelle Ximenez, dressed quite fetchingly in white surplice and black cassock, her black lace mantilla draped over head and shoulders. Her face was beaming, as it had never done when hung with the black beard of a previous existence. Close behind her, like a dog at heel, walked Brother Bergholz, late of the Daily Brute. He seemed to be muttering to himself, whether in prayer or protest against the gradient was not clear. Behind this clerical party straggled, swarmed, limped and staggered a motley collection of folk. Some looked like clergymen, others like gentlemen and ladies of the Press. There were at least two television crews carrying huge video cameras and puffing loudly, with sound recordists and camera assistants lugging tape recorders and tripods big as surveyors'. There was a party of ramblers, all geared up as if to try the Himalaya—fleecy cagoules, knee breeches, woolly balaclavas, rucksacks and maps hung round their necks in plastic cases. They had come from somewhere on Tyneside for the day to hike the Mirkin Ridge, and had somehow got caught up with the church procession. Members of St Ethelbogger's congregation were there too—Mrs Bryony Costive with her Bernese Mountain Dog Rudi and her mother Mrs Jekyll holding young Darren's hand and wondering if he was warm enough. Mrs Sylvia Anstruther strode up like a good'un, sorry to have left the organ behind in church, but determined to support her vicar, whatever sex it was. Various denizens of the weekend cottages, caravans and the Timeshare Stockade, gabbling in the accents of Black Country, Merseyside and Greater London, had come to see the fun, and Pc Costive, walkie-talkie in hand, brought up the rear, still trying vainly to summon help from Police Headquarters. Look here, son, the Chief Inspector had said, we've a bridge collapsed near Whitehaven, a multiple pile-up on the M6, an anti-fox-hunting rally at Windermere, a mass sit-down at Sellafield, and a couple of serial killers at Carlisle, and you think you've got problems. What— New Age Travellers? Now that's different. Just do a holding operation, son; we'll get a squad down just as soon as we can. Believe that, Pc Costive said to a passing Jake Otter, and you'll believe anything. "You what?" said Jake Otter.

At the top of the rise the procession halted. Dr Rhoid planted his crucifix like an explorer claiming territory, Ms Ximenez turned and faced her flock, and Brother Bergholz cried "Allelujah, brethren" to the bewildered looking knot of Druid folk. "The Kingdom is at hand. Or rather Queendom, allelujah!"

"Get stuffed," said the Chief Druid, who was a big chap with tattoos on the backs of his hands. "This is our spot. Go and find your own."

"Peace and love, brother," said Bergholz. "Now shove off— you've had your turn." Surprisingly perhaps the Druids fell back muttering, but such, it seemed, was the power of the new True Faith.

"Dearly beloved brethren," intoned the Rev Ximenez in a loud, clear voice, which seemed, so some people said afterwards, to ring with the bright sunshine of the morning. "We are gathered here today among God's holy hills to celebrate the feast of our own St Ethelbogger.

"She too was a woman of the open air, a poor shepherd whose

flock could afford no church of bricks and mortar, stone and timber. She preached here at this rock, and converted the folk for miles around, so that this valley, this blessed valley, took its name from her, the place of St Ethelbogger. She banished the dark forces of paganism from this hill and drove off the devils of ignorance and superstition."

Ms Ximenez then swept the gathering with her eye. "There are, however, many ways to God, many paths to Heaven, and I say to all our friends here—join our Crusade, renounce your mistaken beliefs, and prepare for the new Messiah."

"Allelujah!" chanted Brother Bergholz.

"Are you saying that you are the new Messiah?" It was one of the diocesan brokers' men, who had followed on after locking up the church. He was an angry-looking man. Insomnia? Piles? Ms Ximenez wondered: there was usually something physically wrong with his sort.

"I am saying nothing of the kind, brother," she said. "There cometh One mightier than I after me, the latchet of Whose shoes I am not worthy to stoop down and unloose. You'll be familiar with the quote?"

"The blasphemy!" roared the angry clergyman, working himself up into a fine old state. "I'll tell you who you are—you are the Whore of Babylon, Mother of Harlots and abominations of the Earth."

Now, as we have seen, Stan Bergholz was not a big man. But neither was he a shrinking violet. He was up to that angry cleric like a bouncer on a noisy drunk in a night club. He bristled. His face was thrust up within an inch of the clergyman's and his chin was jutting. "Would you care to repeat that, sir?" he challenged, the 'sir' being heavily loaded. "So that the representatives of the media can take good note, and the Law too, in the fulness of time."

227

The angry clergyman obliged. "Mother of Harlots and Abominations!" he roared, still in a fine old state.

"Thankyou," said Brother Bergholz. "You will be hearing from our solicitors in due course." And he returned to Ms Ximenez' side.

But his show of resistance did not daunt the clerical traditionalists for long. As Michelle Ximenez started to explain the nature of her revelations, a group of about a dozen stalwart vicars filtered through the crowd and formed a phalanx, a scrum perhaps, for some of them looked like rugby players—gone a little to seed maybe, but with that very physical air about them, muscular Christians to a man. Any time now, Dr Rhoid, who knew about such things, remarked to Tot Titmuss, they'll start removing their trousers and singing "If I were the Marrying Kind."

They did not. Instead they shouted: "Scarlet woman, Harlot, Whore of Babylon!" and then broke into rhythmic chant: "Out, out, out demons, out!".

In vain did Ms Ximenez raise her voice, to no avail did she call on St Ethelbogger for intercession. She was being drowned out, and she noticed that some of the New Age people, notably the men in the white druidical nightgowns, were beginning to join in an increasingly triumphant chanting.

But perhaps the patron saint of the Bogger Valley was working quietly in the background after all, for just as the day seemed lost, over the brow of the hill, like the Sixth Cavalry in the corniest of westerns, marched—not a monstrous regiment of women exactly (some of them were quiet comely, and one or two decidedly attractive), but a host of very determined looking females. There were lady vicars, deaconesses of a variety of persuasions, nuns, and a formidable band of civilians grouped around a banner announcing "Lesbians for Christ" in large red letters. Others carried individual placards, nailed to battens. "Say No to Male Bigotry" was one of the milder messages; a little more extreme was a plea for the castration of bishops.

The militant ladies took in the state of affairs at a glance and moved with menace towards the chanting clergymen. The chant faltered, broke, tailed off, then ceased altogether. One or two of the men seemed to know that while large banners are unwieldy and tend to get tangled in a fray, individual placards make very handy and quite damaging weapons. They did what any group of rugby hearties would have done—they put their heads down, grasped one another where they could, formed a scrimmage, and went for the opposition.

37

Stoatholme First School was a little hive of activity that fine Saturday morning. Ms 'Geordie' D'Arcy had been there since the break of day, putting finishing touches to this and last minute adjustments to that. The pupils whose normal arrival at weekday school was at best reluctant and snail-like arrived early and noisily. They were dressed in a great variety of costumes, all having something to do with the history of the Bogger Valley (or so their teacher had assured them). There were little cavemen and cavewomen in furs or purloined clippy-mats; there were Roman soldiers (although most historians will tell you that it is extremely doubtful whether the legions penetrated as far in as Boggerthwaite); there were Vikings (who almost certainly did), Normans and Norwomen, who may have done, Cavaliers, Roundheads, Hanoverians and kilted Highlanders, and, for no reason but for the general air of festivity, three little Red Indians, a Zulu warrior, and a Nazi storm-trooper.

The effigy of Admiral Byng had been built up by the children over the previous two weeks. They had done the old sea-dog proud. He was a good seven foot tall with a huge cocked hat on top of a fiercely black-bearded papier-mache head. His jacket was pink because it had been made from an overcoat in that colour donated

229

by one of the Wormwald ladies who had once worn it at a wedding and wanted rid of such reminders of the occasion. The admiral had epaulettes of gold, much braiding of a similar colour, and sashes of dark blue. His breeches, once left behind in a skip by a rambler who had got himself soaked through on the fells, had originally been of a dark dun colour, but it's wonderful what a pot of white paint will do. This was the paint left over from the daubing of the school during winter, and it had been doing nothing particular since but going hard. Admiral Byng's innards were stuffed with straw which had been liberally splashed with petrol siphoned from a visiting probation officer's car, and a number of plastic bottles filled with oil purloined from the back kitchen of the Dehydrated Rambler.

And this last touch seemed to be about the only contribution made by Boggerthwaite village itself. The original idea of the council's Bleezins Committee had been to choose four Byngers from the great and good of local society—Messrs Magersfontein, Otter and Nattrass as well as Dr Rhoid had been mentioned. None had seemed keen on the idea of getting mixed up with a bevy of schoolkids from Sunny Lea, so the idea had been quietly dropped. Into the breach, though, at almost the eleventh hour, had stepped Mr Renfrew Sackville and Mr Cecil Wormwald. Their respective sons (Mental) Mark Sackville and Walter Wormwald (also known as Headbanger) made up the number. They were dressed in nautical uniforms left over in a hurry from a performance of the Pirates of Penzance by a semi-professional theatrical group which performed round schools in the area and had mistakenly thought Stoatholme to be just another primary school like the rest.

Cecil Wormwald had provided the open truck on which the Admiral was to be paraded, and which was also to serve variously as his flagship and the island of Minorca. Not to be outdone the Sackvilles had borrowed or stolen (never begged) a tractor and large trailer which was to represent the French fleet. The cease-fire and truce which the tribal leaders had agreed with Ms D'Arcy had spread generally to both children and adults. Everyone turned out to see the fun and chatted to one another quite amicably. Nobody locked their back-doors while they were out, and it was to stay a matter of wonder for months that not one house was entered burglariously or in any way feloniously during the whole of the day's proceedings.

The general air of a village *en fete* was added to by the arrival, shortly after nine o'clock, of an Army recruiting team complete with a couple of small marquees and a tank, albeit a little antiquated and surplus to foreseen requirements in foreign parts. In these days of comparative peace with no-one to get the public scared about, and money being short, even for affording high-ranking officers, the army was cutting down on sending old-sweat sergeants out with shillings to beguile susceptible youth. But there were still means and ways. The ways lay less around decrepit colliery villages these days and more in places like the Lake District, which promised a pleasant day out for those recruiters (they call them Careers Officers now) who liked a quiet life. A young man out of work in a backwoods area might not actually be able to join up as easily as his predecessors when the country needed cannon fodder, but there were pictures to look at of bright lads his age ski-ing and sailing and playing in some foreign surf that is forever England with servicewomen who it is rumoured will forever think of England while play is going on. And there is the tank. It is not actually supposed to move, that vehicle, but lads can sit in it and pretend they are zapping some foreign devil who has threatened our oil supplies. It can move, of course, but it is not supposed to until it's time to shift to another farm show or gymkhana in a nice little village with a good pub and some spare totty.

The Stoatholme children, for once, did not seem particularly beguiled: they were more interested in the prospective fiery fate of Admiral Byng, whoever he was. One or two lads were a little intrigued, though, wondering perhaps whether if the truce between Sackvilles and Wormwalds was to continue, they might have to

231

look further afield for antagonists, and there were one or two of the girls who seemed more attracted by the fresh faces of the soldiers than by the village lads they mixed with every day.

As to the Bleezins themselves, the original idea had been that at eleven o'clock sharp the procession would move off up the Boggerthwaite road preceded by the Thugthwaite Silver Prize Band to the village green outside the Dehydrated Rambler. An impressive list of dignitaries, celebrities and anyone really who might help to boost Boggerthwaite's image had been invited, and they would watch while the children of Stoatholme School re-enacted the assault of the port of Mahon, Minorca. After this the unfortunate Admiral Byng was to be borne on the shoulders of the Byngers to the Buzzard Stone and there set alight. Then there would be high jinks in the village below, including the traditional racing of pigs. That was the original idea. What happened was different— quite different indeed.

The Clerk, Mr Bean, had worked hard at the invitations, and his work had been remarkably fruitful. With one or two exceptions all the VIPs turned up—the local MP, an Under-Secretary of State for the Environment, two persons from English Heritage, the Euro MP, someone from the Australian High Commission, a good half of the local district council, prospective sponsors from a number of well-known outdoor sports equipment manufacturers, from the makers of the sort of foodstuffs believed to be popular with adventurous outdoor types, and from a company which made mountain bikes. There were travel agents, public relations consultants, and the chairman of the brewery responsible for the production of Owd Bogger had come all the way from Burton on Trent where this apparently local liquor was in fact specially brewed for Cumbrian pubs. And there was a jumpy-looking blonde actress, star of one of our most popular soaps, who had come to open the festivities officially. How, nobody was quite sure, but they would think of something. The Press had been invited of course, but were already busy witnessing the unscheduled performance on the flanks of Great Mirkin Fell above.

All these dignitaries had arrived in good time in a variety of cars which rivalled each other for sleekness and luxury. The only trouble was that for all their expensive gadgetry, none of them had the means to park in a space already occupied by other vehicles like brewer's drays, weekenders' jeeps, tourist coaches, pressmen's taxis and the garishly unroadworthy-looking wagons of those seekers after Truth and Beauty, the New Age Travellers. All these vehicles had taken up every inch of space within half a mile of Boggerthwaite Village Green, and were going to have enough trouble extricating themselves when the carnival was over, never mind making room for official Mercedes and Rollers, which were therefore forced, most of them, to carry on through the village and out towards Stoatholme.

Mrs Gladys Loudwater, Mr Bean, Mr Magersfontein and Jake Otter stood awkwardly on a small platform outside the Rambler and helplessly watched the official looking cars arrive and just as quickly melt into the melee and depart again. "Do something," Mrs Loudwater kept saying. "Can't you do something?" She appeared to be addressing Mr Bean, but he seemed miles away, probably enjoying in his mind activities which had nothing whatever to do with Boggerthwaite's big day.

Pc Costive was nowhere to be seen, neither was Lord Bogger, and Mr McGurk was still desperately trying to get his pub ready to open. Senator Wordsworth was much in evidence, though, capering about in his chef's outfit and conducting the coachload of his fellow countrymen in songs whose words grew more and more raucous and less and less tasteful as the carnival starting time approached. Mrs Loudwater closed her eyes to ward off an attack of nausea. She did open them again, but only temporarily, and the last thing she saw before sliding out of consciousness and into the arms of Mr Magersfontein (for Mr Bean had looked the other way) was a

233

rush, a charge, like something out of a John Ford epic, as down the fell and into what was left of the village, poured a stream of red-faced clergymen hotly and victoriously pursued by a body of women belabouring them with placards.

38

Young Garth Wormwald was having the time of his life. He stood on the prow of his battle-gallon, sails straining above him, and watched out of his good eye as the French fleet sailed out to meet him. The drivers of the two vehicles which represented the ships were enjoying themselves too. They had followed the Thugthwaite Silver Prize Band all the way round the labyrinth of the Sunny Lea Estate followed by all the kids in their fancy dress, and now they had pulled on to that stretch of open ground normally used for displays of courtship and aggression by the many local dogs and known as the Rec. A large heap resembling a funeral pyre dominated its centre, consisting of all the junk normally left littered around the Rec which had been speedily gathered together with a collective zeal hitherto unknown in the little community. Boggerthwaite village had not even been mentioned.

"Fire!" bellowed Garth Wormwald, and the gunners on the deck behind him put matches to rockets stuck in specially made cannons and watched while they streaked away towards the other vehicle which was heading towards them at a fast and erratic pace. The rockets were good and noisy, for they were no Guy Fawkes Day junk sold to kids in shops: these were of the type used by coastguards and air-sea rescue teams. One thing about Sunny Lea: somebody somewhere in it could always get his hands on practically anything.

"Fire!" screamed Wayne Sackville, skipper of the French ship, and a similar rocket salvo streaked out to score a direct hit on its English counterpart's fo'c'sle, otherwise known as the driver's cabin. It gave Mental Mark quite a fright when it went off, and caused him to swerve so violently that three British seamen were hurled over the gunwales into the sea. A roar of appreciation went up from the crowd as the three lads picked themselves up and clambered back aboard. The British tried to retaliate. "Stand by to ram!" shouted Garth Wormwald, and the driver did just that: he took a long, sweeping circle at high speed, then bore down on the French vessel. "Hang on tight, skipper!" he yelled back to Garth, his face alive with the maniacal expression that had earned him his soubriquet. But the French vessel braked sharply just as impact seemed inevitable and Mental Mark overshot the Rec, went straight through the wooden fence at the bottom of someone's garden, and ploughed on through the remains of a cabbage patch until coming to rest amid the ruins of a garden shed.

"Arrest that admiral!" It was Geordie D'Arcy striding across the Rec and blowing a whistle. Immediately a mob of British tars swarmed over to the stricken van and dragged Garth Wormwald from a wreckage of rigging and sails. He fought like a good'un, did Garth, but was eventually overpowered and frog-marched to the French ship, which was now a British court—it said so on a big banner held up to its side: "BRITISH COURT MARTIAL".

After a few moments' solemn palaver Ms D'Arcy appealed to the crowd: "Admiral Byng has been found guilty of cowardice in the face of the enemy. What's to be done with him?"

"Shoot him!" chorused the young mob, bloodthirsty delight on all their faces. For all they knew Garth Wormwald might really get shot, things were happening so authentically.

"Aye, shoot the little bastard!" It was the voice of the owner of 49a Mozart-avenue, Sunny Lea, whose cabbages and garden shed had just been demolished.

Garth Wormwald stood firmly to attention as his captors fixed the blindfold around his eyes, and met his end as befits a British sailor and gentleman. As the volley of shots rang out he pitched backwards clutching his stomach and landed in one of the many heaps of dog-turd which are a feature of Sunny Lea Rec.

"What d'you think of the show so far?" Lord Bogger asked Mrs Gloria Sackville.

"They're having the time of their little lives," replied Gloria . "It was a great idea." And she gave his waist a considerable squeeze.

Now the outside world seemed to be moving in on Stoatholme. This arrival was on no-one's timetable, but it was happening—the official and semi-official cars which should have parked up at Boggerthwaite were parking here instead, their occupants climbing out and in some cases even applauding.

....

Meanwhile up in the chaos of parked vehicles which was about all that could be seen to distinguish Boggerthwaite village, Mr Rory McGurk, a man almost on the brink of a nervous breakdown, drew back the bolts on the front door of his pub and threw them open to the sun and his customers.

The first obliged, entering in warm rays which lit up the polished bar and the mirrors and bottles behind it. The second did not. There was no-one on the doorstep. Cars there were in plenty, and battered old wagons and coaches with their drivers asleep or reading their Saturday tabloids. A disconsolate group comprising a partially recovered Mrs Loudwater, Mr Bean, Mr Magersfontein and Mr Otter stood as survivors will stand after an unexpected city air-raid, peering about them, shaking their heads and looking generally in need of treatment for deep shock. Shakily Mr McGurk tiptoed out of his bar and joined them. As if in answer to his unasked question Mrs Loudwater spoke. "They've gone," she said in a voice choked with feeling and overtones of the Mersey. "The ungrateful bastards have all gone." And she glared down the road towards Stoatholme.

Following her gaze Mr McGurk could see the tail end of the exodus making its way up the hill—New Age Travellers, Australian expats, church-looking individuals, even Old Billy Nattrass, deep in conversation with Dr Harry Rhoid. They were stopping and talking to someone through the window of a car. Then the car moved off again and they waved. The car came on towards the pub, and the remains of the little civic committee could see clearly the face of their vicar, beaming like the sun, and being driven by one they did not recognise. Ms Ximenez mouthed: "God bless", and raised a hand in benediction. As she did so a slight figure, dressed not inappropriately for the occasion in a city suit with collar and tie, made towards the vehicle, flapping hands. The window wound down again. The slight figure introduced itself. "I'm Jeremy Blink-Howell," it said. "Of the Daily Brute."

"Allelujah, brother," said his predecessor in another life. "Now piss off." And put down his foot.

....

The four replacement Byngers—two Sackvilles and two Wormwalds, as was deemed proper in Stoatholme—stepped forward, and hoisted the effigy of Admiral John Byng into the air. It was balanced on a light wooden framework of pallets, to which were attached four handles, in the manner of an old-time sedan chair. Perhaps it was fitting, with all the tradition the valley had of manufacturing the grips at Dabster and Tyson's Mill, that these were of the finest rams' horn, cunningly turned by hand. In spite of everything old skills die hard in such places as the Bogger Valley.

Anyway, the effigy was hoisted up on to the flat-cart behind the tractor donated by the Sackvilles, and, again preceded by the Thugthwaite Silver Prize Bank, which had been wetting its collective whistle quite unofficially behind the Goat and Compasses, it still wanting some few minutes to legal opening time, moved off in procession. After one lap of the Rec to the strains of Old Comrades and Colonel Bogey, the Byngers stepped forward once more, effortlessly hefted old Byng into the air and balanced him on top of the pyre in the centre. Then Matty Ouskin, shyly at first, but then, encouraged by smiles and beckoning from

Ms D'Arcy, rather more boldly stepped forward, cleared his throat, threw back his head and orated:

> Earth hath not anything to show
> More craven than old Admiral Byng.
> The way of all cowards must he go,
> With a yo-ho-ho, hey dinga ding dyng.

And as a rattle of applause raked round the Rec. "Hobbler" Braithwaite, who by virtue of having once jogged in the Great North Run on Tyneside was the nearest the valley had to an athlete (it is not clear where he came in that race, but he did finish), trotted on to the field dressed in white T-shirt and very brief shorts and carrying a torch of the sort used to open the Olympic Games. Leaving a long pall of spark-spattering black smoke behind him, Hobbler stopped at the pyre and waved his torch around his head in salutation to the crowd. The torch promptly went out.

Ms D'Arcy, who being head teacher in a place like Stoatholme was always ready for life's little mishaps, relit the torch with her friend Muriel's lighter, and Hobbler applied the new flame to the tinder just below Admiral Byng's feet. There was a short hiatus, then a whoosh of flame, and Ms D'Arcy declared the Bleezins well and truly open.

"Not the Boggerthit Bleezins, you'll notice," she said. "But the Bogger *Valley* Bleezins, a tradition as old as these hills." (Hobbler Braithwaite was not the only one who at this peered round at the horizon as if discovering the fells for the first time.) "This is *your* day, and you're going to enjoy it. I might just mention, in case it had escaped your notice, that Mr McNally's establishment is now open, and will be dispensing refreshments for the rest of the day."

There was a loud cheer at this and Admiral Byng's boozy red face seemed to beam out of the fire before his effigy exploded with a loud bang and scattered fiery fragments in all directions.

....

Now a VIP is really only like the rest of us. Scratch him, he bleeds; deprive him of food, drink, love and affection and he is liable to fall into despondency. VIPs are fine if they are given a carpet, preferably red, to be greeted upon. They are happy if they arc herded together with others of their own standing and invited to mix in a special enclosure away from the *hoi polloi*, rather as prize-winning ewes and tups are segregated at agricultural shows. They like the flashing of photographers' bulbs, the curious, crab-like, backwards walk of television camera crews. They also like champagne and thin slices of smoked salmon, although these days white wine and canapes will do almost as well. They like being called upon to make speeches, they thrive on applause, and they are contented and fulfilled VIPs if they are allowed to get away to their chauffeured cars within a reasonably short time of arriving. What they cannot cope with is being ignored.

And so it came to pass that the Boggerthwaite Bleezins VIPs were in a generally discontented mood. Having been unable to be received, as planned, on the village green, their drivers had moved them on until they found themselves, most of them, at the edge of a field by the particularly insalubrious council estate that is Sunny Lea. Here they got out of their cars, milled around a bit, recognised and greeted one another where appropriate, preened themselves a bit, took frequent glances at their watches, and whenever two or more were gathered together on the muddy grass and bits of broken tarmac on the periphery of the Recreation Ground, they grumbled.

Terrible organisation, they agreed; never been so insulted in all their lives; heads were going to be made to roll. "What's her bloody name?" keened the MP to the woman from the Council for the Preservation of Rural England. "Loudwater or something, isn't it? I'll bloody Loudwater her."

The general public seemed to be quite unimpressed by the presence in their midst of men and women dressed in city style and draped in one or two instances in chains of office, but then there were plenty of other strangely-turned out people that day witnessing the Byng-burning and moving on to Mr McNally's establishment. There were Australian drunks, long-haired hippies, Hare Krishna devotees, Lesbians for Christ, Wormwalds, Sackvilles, Druids, clergypersons, and lots of dogs. So it came as a bit of a surprise, a shock even, to the knot of VIPs to be borne down upon by a rangy-looking old gent wearing a dark blue blazer with some sort of badge on its breast pocket, and carrying a long shepherd's crook which he waved at them rather menacingly. "Ye'll have to shift!" he shouted. "You're right in the way!"

"I don't think you can be aware," said an under-secretary of something pretty important, "who you're talking to."

The under-secretary was quite correct. Mr Otter neither knew nor cared. And he said so. "You're right in't bloody road," he bellowed, and made wild semaphore motions with his crook.

"I've never been treated like this in my life," protested the Chair of some committee of the District Council. She spoke too soon. It was not her day. Suddenly a roar went up from the motley crowd, and a phalanx of solid, rotund creatures, like a pack of four-legged experts on Rugby League, came snorting and grunting with wild delight, straight at the persons of great importance. The racing pigs appeared from the state of them to have run via the middle of the stagnant pool opposite the Goat and Compasses, a feature which serves Stoatholme as village duckpond and receptacle for any rubbish the council fail, for reasons of their own hygienic safety, to remove in the normal manner. They were pink no longer, those pigs, if indeed they had ever been so.

But they were happy pigs, and enthusiastic. Obeying some instinct for direction unknown to anyone but Jake Otter, they ploughed on at a rate of knots quite surprising in such bulky creatures. The lady district councillor was apparently targeted by the leader of the race, and borne some dozen yards on its broad and smelly back before being deposited at the flying feet of some dignitary from the Arts Council, who promptly measured his length in a particularly unsavoury patch of Stoatholme recreational amenity. The other pigs swerved to avoid him, but not much, and two public relations types, the MEP, the chairman of the brewery, and some industrialist who under more favourable circumstances might have been expected to cough up a fairly healthy sum to sponsor future Bleezins, were all sent more or less flying as the pig race went joyfully on its way. It was lustily pursued by the dog population of Stoatholme, which is considerable. Hanging on to the neck of the back-marker with one hand, and waving a chef's hat with the other, was that flower of Antipodean public life, Senator William Hudspith Wordsworth. "Get up there, yer fat bastard!" he yelled as he went through.

....

Mrs Loudwater was not around: she was in the bar of the Dehydrated Rambler with Mr Bean, her Clerk, and Mr Magersfontein. Mr McGurk was serving large gins and tonic by way of consolation. There were no other customers. Outside the hostelry a sign read: "Open all day. Today's Special, Boggerthwaite Byngburgers, £4.99."

....

If Mr McGurk's trade might be described as disappointingly slow to non-existent, at the sign of the Goat and Compasses, a mile away, something close to Bedlam raged. A happy Bedlam. Mr GBH McNally had taken on extra staff, bought in the best part of a dray-load of beer (which, being of the fizzy variety, could be dispensed straight away), procured dozens of cartons of plastic glasses, and invited in a firm of mobile caterers from the town who were friends of a friend and now extremely busy selling hotdogs, pork sandwiches, meat pies, hamburgers and sausage rolls.

No-one seemed to mind that the beer was fizzy or the glasses of plastic. They were all happy. They were happy without the usual Stoatholme stimulus of family feuding. Sackvilles drank with

Wormwalds, and paid their turn, and Wormwalds did the same with Sackvilles. The New Age contingent mingled: Old Billy Nattrass had found his young female admirer of the previous day and was doing something no-one had ever seen him do before—getting his hand down his pocket to buy her a drink. The militant female contingent had stacked their placards outside the pub like battle trophies and were for the most part engaged in happy banter with the dog-collared gents who had not so long since fought them in the Battle of the Buzzard Stone. Mrs Sylvia Anstruther drank something bubbly with Matty Ouskin and Geordie D'Arcy looked on as if overseeing a greatly enlarged class. Even the weekend contingent from the Boggerthwaite cottages, caravans and Timeshare Stockade were joining in, singing in a variety of foreign accents.

Paul and Sadie from Luton were there (well, just outside Luton, actually), as were Stew and Stevie-baby, and Julian, Michelle and Liz from Manchester. The only dissenting faction seemed to be the young couple who the previous weekend were so keen to buy a ruin from Old Billy Nattrass. The blonde lass was giggling in fine style, Simon Stonechat was sipping his tonic water with rather more than his usual avidity, but he might have been heard in loud conversation with his mobile telephone to announce that perhaps, after all, on second thoughts, all things considered, Boggerthwaite was not quite what he had been led to believe.

Meanwhile in another part of the Goat, Lord Bogger, squeezed into a little cupboard under the stairs, which contained, as well as two bicycles and a selection of mops and brooms and brushes, a payphone for the use of those who had anybody to call up (usually the casualty department of the cottage hospital), was dialling with one finger while trying with one of the other hand to exclude from his ear the sounds of raucous jollity from the rest of the pub. When he had made his connection, found the person he wanted, and exchanged a few quiet words, a smile of some satisfaction crossed

his face. "Yes," he said. "I really do think you should—that's if
you still want to go through with the deal."

....

"I shall sue, of course." Mr McGurk was still in spite of inactivity,
in a fine old lather. "I shall most definitely sue."

"And who are you going to sue?" Mrs Loudwater said with more
than a little sneer in her voice.

Mr McGurk did not seem to have considered the question fully.
"Don't worry," he stuttered. "I shall just sue." Then, as if the idea
had just descended; "I shall sue your council for a start."

Mrs Loudwater exchanged glances with Mr Bean, in which there
was a kind of bitter merriment. "Do you know how much the Parish
Council has in the kitty, Mr McGurk?"

"I shall sue the police authority for certain," said the publican.
"I shall have that idle bloody Costive court-martialled or whatever
it is they do. He's done nothing—absolutely nothing. Couldn't
even handle traffic. Look at that lot out there—parked all over the
place. You'd need a tank to shift that lot...."

As if in answer to his idea, a noise like the start of Armageddon
came from the pub car park. The remains of the Bleezins Committee
watched in fascination as first an ancient pick-up belonging to some
absent New Age Traveller lurched forward a few yards, rose in the
air, and then keeled over with a crash. A coach which had previously
blocked the hotel doorway for want of anywhere else to move slid
sideways against all the rules of how motor-coaches should
proceed, squashing two cars next to it and finishing up on its side.

In the gap between ruined pick-up and damaged coach emerged
a long metal tube waving like the proboscis of some prehistoric
creature long thought extinct. An armoured body followed, great
whirring tracks ground into metal, then with a huge lurch a British
Army tank, nearly new but not quite, buried itself into the wall of
the Dehydrated Rambler's Carvery and came to a halt in a pile of

rubble beside the pool table. A few seconds later two very young faces peered through the cloud of dust, grinning with a great fulfilment before vanishing. One was unmistakeably that of a young Wormwald, the other of a juvenile Sackville. But just which of those proud clans no-one would ever be able to say.

Mr Mahmoud's arrival at Stoatholme village was only slightly less spectacular. He emerged smiling broadly from his own personal Land Rover, shook hands with a waiting Lord Bogger, kissed Ms Georgina D'Arcy, and accepted from the hands of Mr G.B.H McNally himself a glass of something which sparkled and winked in the afternoon sunlight.

"It is my great pleasure," said Mr Mahmoud to the crowd which now gathered around him, "to witness this happy manifestation of one of our oldest British traditions — the Bleezins of the Bogger Valley." (cries of hear, hear!)

"It is also my pleasure to be brief, and to tell you that to honour this day...." and here he turned with a smile to Lord Bogger, "to celebrate my own deep connections with the village of Stoatholme, I have decided to contribute a little something to make sure that this tradition never dies, and that for at least one day in the year there will be a real old English merrymaking.

"I shall endow a brand-new sports centre, lay a first-class cricket pitch on the Recreation Ground; there will be a completely modern new library at Ms D'Arcy's school, so that the children can learn the history of their proud birthplace and of our country. And....and the rest of today's drink is on me."

There was a roar as big as the sort that follows Cup Final goals. Geordie D'Arcy gave Lord Bogger a hug and then another to Mr Mahmoud and a third to her friend Muriel in case she was feeling left out. Lord Bogger called for three cheers and then gave Mrs Gloria Sackville a big hug as well.

....

244

There is a small tarn a good three miles from Boggerthwaite in a little fold under Great Mirkin Fell which used to be renowned among locals for its brown trout, of which one JB Winter of Penrith at one time caught a record specimen weighing five pounds, nine-and-a-half ounces.

Pc Robin de Vere Costive had once landed a two-and-a-half pounder there himself, and hoped one day to do even better. This could even be the day, he thought to himself, and executed a promising cast as he watched through the reeds a line of police vehicles making its way a long the valley, no doubt to help him in pursuit of dangerous New Age Travellers. But where would they all park? As the constable considered the question the sky darkened, and Boggerthwaite's rain put in its usual appearance.
